HISTORY AND CRIME

SAGE FOCUS EDITIONS

HISTORY and CRIME
Implications for Criminal Justice Policy

Edited by
JAMES A. INCIARDI
CHARLES E. FAUPEL

Preface by **RICHARD M. RAU**

SAGE PUBLICATIONS   Beverly Hills   London

6-3-82

The essays presented here are the product of a Special National Workshop held pursuant to Contract No. J-LEAA-004-79 awarded to University Research Corporation by the National Institute of Justice, United States Department of Justice, under the Omnibus Crime Control and Safe Streets Act of 1968, as amended. The points of view or opinions expressed do not necessarily represent official policy or positions of the National Institute of Justice.

HV
6021
·H57

For information address:

SAGE Publications, Inc.
275 South Beverly Drive
Beverly Hills, California 90212

SAGE Publications Ltd
28 Banner Street
London EC1Y 8QE, England

Printed in the United States of America

Library of Congress Cataloging in Publication Data
Main entry under title:

History and crime.

(Sage focus editions ; 27)
Includes bibliographies.
1. Crime and criminals—History—Addresses, essays, lectures. 2. Criminal justice, Administration of—History—Addresses, essays, lectures.   I. Inciardi, James A.   II. Faupel, Charles E.   III. Series.
HV6021.H57   364'.9   80-19532
ISBN 0-8039-1410-5
ISBN 0-8039-1411-3 (pbk.)

FIRST PRINTING

CONTENTS

PREFACE

History is important for many reasons. The most obvious is that it allows learning to be perpetuated and experience retained. The same benefits accrue from historical research. Using analytical tools adopted from social science research—comparative analysis, time series analysis, and combinations of these and other techniques—historical analyses of events offer insights relevant to today's problems.

Although popular today, the application of historical research to the study of crime and justice accelerated only recently. In 1968, the creation of the National Institute of Law Enforcement and Criminal Justice provided a mechanism for coordinating the then-fragmented field of criminal justice research and spurring the involvement of a range of disciplines in the study of crime and justice. Social historical research helped shape some policies of the new research Institute. Roger Lane's *Policing the City* and David Rothman's *Discovery of the Asylum,* for example, influenced the direction of research in urban policing and rehabilitation. Some early studies supported by the institute included aspects of history, resulting in the development of short histories of robbery and restitution.

By the mid-1970s, the institute began to take a more active role in historical research, prompted by the interest of Mr. Blair G. Ewing, then-Acting Director of the institute, and the publication of *Rogues, Rebels and Reformers* by Ted Robert Gurr. In 1978, the institute launched an extensive application of historical methods in its study of responses to crime by federal, state, and local governments in 10 American cities over the past 30 to 50 years. This project will use a major historical research tool, time series, and should generate a substantial amount of useful information.

Along with this emphasis on incorporating more historical approaches in the research of the institute, Mr. Ewing set in motion a more immediate response, which would place all these tools on display at one time. In January 1979, Mr. Ewing asked one of the editors of this book, Professor James A. Inciardi, to undertake the task of assembling an international

7

group of outstanding historical researchers in the field of crime and justice for a national workshop and publishing their invited papers. The workshop drew together 16 outstanding researchers in history and criminal justice. They met in Chantilly, Virginia, on October 11 and 12, 1979, to discuss their work and to respond to questions from a lively audience composed of institute professional staff and other interested researchers.

It was appropriate that the keynoter for the workshop was the man whose research had influenced its conception. Professor Ted Robert Gurr accepted this task with dedication. His presentation, "Development and Decay: Their Impact on Public Order in Western History," set the tone and direction for the remainder of the workshop.

The views the audience expressed to me both during and after the workshop were all positive; this was an inspiring experience and one of the most successful workshops held by the institute. It should be noted that the values of the historical perspective on criminal justice research were appreciated by the large audience, most of whom were very experienced in social science or system analysis research applied to the present or immediate past.

One of the most frustrating things for any researcher is to have to relearn something. One valuable contribution of this workshop was knowledge about ideas or concepts that need not be relearned. For example, an interesting comparison was made between the high murder rate during the 1920s, presumably caused by bootlegging and the increased use of alcohol, and the high murder rate during the late 1960s and early 1970s, presumably related to the rise in the use of drugs. It appears that the use of these two types of addictive drugs had similar consequences from which much can be learned.

The major participants in this endeavor were Mr. Blair Ewing, who conceived the idea for the workshop and, hence, this publication; Dr. Carolyn Burstein, who initially managed the development of the workshop with the support of Mr. Harry M. Bratt, who replaced Mr. Ewing as Acting Director of the institute; and Professor James A. Inciardi, who put the whole package together. The credit for the accomplishments of this effort must be shared equally. Mr. Ewing will be remembered for his farsightedness, Dr. Burstein for her persistence, and Professor Inciardi for his completeness. I was privileged to have participated with them in this venture.

Richard M. Rau
National Institute of Justice
Bethesda, Maryland

ACKNOWLEDGMENTS

"Acknowledgments," in our own view, is a way of reinforcing the understanding that this volume is not solely the work of the editors and contributors, but rather a collaborative effort involving many individuals from a variety of locations. As such, we deeply appreciate the efforts and support of those who made possible the history and crime workshop and contributed to the success of this volume. Among the past and current staff of the National Institute of Justice, we wish to thank Blair G. Ewing, Carolyn Burstein, Richard M. Rau, Walter R. Burkhart, Harry M. Bratt, Lawrence A. Bennett, Paul Estaver, Paul Cascarano, and Louis A. Mayo, Jr. From the University Research Corporation and the National Criminal Justice Executive Training Program, we extend our appreciation to Sheldon S. Steinberg, Gary D. Reiner, and William J. Araujo. We must also thank Henry Cohen, Leopold Pospisil, Eugene Watts, and Michael Wadsworth whose presentations were crucial to the success of the workshop although they are being published elsewhere and are not included in this volume. Finally, we wish to express appreciation to Joanne Walter of the University of Delaware for her continued patience in working daily with the editors during the preparation of the final manuscript.

James A. Inciardi
Charles E. Faupel
Newark, Deleware

INTRODUCTION

JAMES A. INCIARDI
CHARLES E. FAUPEL

What is history and of what use might it be for the study and understanding of contemporary social phenomena? Can we derive from history any illumination of our present condition or some guidance for judgment and policy? Or does history make no sense? Is it simply the "bucket of ashes" that poet and folklorist Carl Sandburg once suggested; the "set of lies" mutually agreed upon that Napoleon maintained; or perhaps the combination of guesses and prejudices that the Durants once postulated? Such questions have long since plagued both the scholar and those faced with the products of written history. To Voltaire, history was "little else than a picture of human crimes and misfortunes," and to others it was simply false and the substance of legend.

But most historians would argue strongly to the contrary, holding that history can be many things and represents the foundation of intellectual life. History, as such, can mean the study of the past and the totality of human experience. Or more properly as the late Allan Nevins offered, history might be defined as "any integrated narrative, description or analysis of past events or facts written in a spirit of critical inquiry for the whole truth."[1]

Within the context of Nevins's brief comment, the nature of history becomes many things. It is a *story*, a *record*, an *explanation*, and a *recognition* of the presence of continuity in human affairs. As a story and record, history is an account of men and women in their relationships with society with some sense of chronological sequence, reconstructed on the basis of certain evidence. As an explanation, the story and record of history attempts to place the events of the past into some meaningful and orderly perspective; not only does history tell us *what* happened and *when* it happened but also *how* and *why* it happened. And as a recognition of continuity, history is also *change* and has a consciousness of the connections between previous and subsequent events.

Having offered some preliminary comments on the substance of history, the questions still remain as to the uses and implications of history. Opinions on this issue range a continuum to both extremes, from industrialist Henry Ford who dogmatically stated that "history is bunk" to philosopher George Santayana who argued that "those who cannot remember the past are condemned to repeat it." Moving to a more moderate position along this continuum, history can indeed serve some useful pruposes although it will never be an infallible teacher.

Historian Lester D. Stephens has warned us that although one can draw *lessons, analogies,* and *predictions* from history, such products of the historical enterprise are rarely clear-cut and must be carefully scrutinized.[2] The lessons of history can emerge as generalizations about the past which may have some tentative applications for the present or future. Historical analogy, on the other hand, suggests that certain consequences might issue from events which are comparable to other events in the past. Stephens notes, however, that lessons and analogies can easily be fallacious as a result of the quality of historical evidence, the limitations of the historian's own abilities, and the general lack of inevitability of history to ever fully repeat itself. And for these very reasons, he continues, even further constraints can be placed on the realm of historical prediction:

> The limitations of historical lessons and analogies necessarily reduce the possibility of forecasting future historical events. To predict the future on the basis of what happened in the past is somewhat like shooting an arrow at a distant target in a large field at twilight. Thus about the best the historian can do is locate the general direction of the target and aim in that direction. The target will at best be barely perceptible, and a number of factors may intervene so that the target moves or the arrow is thrown off course by a sudden gust of wind. Fortuitous circumstances are ever-present in the life of man, and man's reaction to events is never so constant that we can state with lawlike precision that he will behave in the same way at all times.[3]

Yet even given these cautions and limitations and although the lessons of history may not be fully clear, this does not suggest that history is of no value. History, quite appropriately, can indicate the possibility that certain consequences can issue from events which are comparable to other events of the past; and history, as something more than a simple compilation of facts, can generate an understanding of the processes of social change and demonstrate how a multitude of factors have served to shape the present.[4]

For decades, researchers in the fields of crime and justice have focused on a variety of historical data in an attempt to better understand how and why any number of social institutions as well as legal and criminal endeavors came into being and persisted, with the hope of determining how these may have shaped many of our contemporary criminal justice practices. In addition, such efforts also sought to better comprehend the phenomena of crime and the etiology and patterns of criminal behavior in an effort to more properly structure mechanisms for their management and control. Such studies included Thorsten Sellin's examination of the effects of slavery on the development of corrections,[5] George Rusche and Otto Kerchheimer's thesis on punishment and social structure,[6] James F. Richardson's historical analysis on the New York City police,[7] and Joseph L. Albini's research on the American Mafia,[8] to name only a few.

Among the many historical studies of crime and criminal justice, sociologist James A. Inciardi's analysis of professional theft can be used here to illustrate how a historical analysis can have implications for contemporary criminal justice policy.[9] The first intensive examination of professional theft emerged in Edwin H. Sutherland's classic work *The Professional Thief* more than four decades ago.[10] Sutherland had described the professional thief as a member of a unique and closely knit underworld fraternity that focused on nonviolent forms of criminal behavior, pursued with a high degree of skill in order to maximize financial gain and minimize the risks of apprehension. The more typical forms of criminality undertaken by the thieves Sutherland was describing included pickpockets, shoplifters, safe and house burglars, forgers and counterfeiters, sneak thieves, extortionists, and confidence swindlers.

What separated the professional thief from other criminals who engaged in the same types of offense behavior were the social organization and occupational structure which circumscribed their criminal enterprise. The professional thief made a regular business of stealing; it was his occupation and means of livelihood and, as such, he devoted his entire working time and energy to stealing. The professional thief also operated with proficiency. Like members of the legitimate professions, he had an organized body of knowledge and skills that he utilized in the planning and execution of his activities, and he was a graduate of a developmental process that included the acquisition of specialized attitudes, knowledge, skills, and experience. Moreover, in identifying himself with the world of crime, he was a member of an exclusive fraternity that extended friendship, understanding, sympathy, congeniality, security, recognition, and respect. And, too, as a resident of this remote corner of the underworld, he had access to specialized patterns of communication, a complex system of argot, and a network of contacts within the legal profession and criminal justice system which enabled him to steal for long periods of time without going to prison.

Following the work of Sutherland, Inciardi's historical research documented that professional theft emerged as an outgrowth of the disintegration of the feudal order in Europe during the years 1350-1550 and that it remained relatively unchanged for centuries.[11] The types of crime, techniques, skills, attitudes, patterns of recruitment and training, interactional setting, style of life, and to some extent the argot of twentieth century professional thieves were characteristically like those contemporary to previous periods. And this system of criminal behavior seemed to persist in its unchanged and unmolested state in spite of social and technological changes, combined with the repressive efforts of the criminal justice system, due to a highly functional structure of low visibility built around its subculture.

Professional thieves, for example, maintained a low profile in the nexus of victim-offender relationships due to the nature of the crimes and victims that were targeted. Confidence games and extortion presented little risk since the victims themselves were violators of the law and were acting in collusion with the thieves. Shoplifting offered only a limited danger since businessmen were reluctant to accuse those persons of theft who often appeared to be legitimate customers. In other instances, such as pickpocketing, the thief's manipulative abilities often allowed him to arrange payments of restitution in lieu of complaint and prosecution. Immunity was furthered by the complex of contacts which enabled a thief to fix many of those criminal cases which did come to the attention of the criminal justice system.

Immunity perpetuated contact among the members of this segment of the underworld. The lack of molestation permitted the development of a subculture and social organization aimed at maintaining the thief's low profile and visibility. An intricate network of relationships and linguistic constructions developed for the purpose of barring amateur and violent criminals from the ostensible profession. Codes of ethics developed for the purpose of keeping members of the profession in line. The communication network distributed information regarding case fixing and fixers, fences, and untrustworthy members of the profession which served as a further defense system. The size and complexity of the large urban centers where professional thieves were most common also offered them unique advantages—anonymity, a highly mobile wealth upon which they could prey, and the crime and vice areas within which thieves could segregate themselves. In these sections of a city, the social network of thieves, fixers, and receivers of stolen goods maintained itself and remained isolated from legitimate society.

For some 400 years professional thieves maintained this posture. Efforts at their control were typically focused on the behavioral aspects of the criminals; serious attempts to curtail their activities were either sidestepped or thwarted by means of the functional underworld systems of protection, isolation, group support, and fixing. Technological change presented only minimal obstacles to the continuance of professional theft—while it phased out some types of crime it ushered in others.

Historical study has indicated that although this criminal behavior system sustained itself for many centuries, it began to decline shortly after World War I and all but perished by the 1970s. The events that eroded the security and longevity of the criminal profession were haphazard, unintegrated, and evolved over a century-long period. In brief, the evolutionary development of private police systems and police technology and communications, the bureaucratization of the criminal justice system, the growth of air travel and other rapid transportation systems, the enactment of federal laws aimed at interstate flight, and the shrinkage of vice areas all served to erode the foundations of the professional criminal underworld. While none of these activities was directed specifically against the professional thief, they did increase his visibility. Over time, he was more often identified, apprehended, prosecuted, convicted, and sentenced. The end result was to make the enterprise unprofitable, severely curtailing the number of new recruits to the profession.

In this instance, the lesson of history was that professional thieves had been able to persist for many centuries only because they operated within a loosely organized structure which had evolved for the purpose of maintaining immunity from apprehension and control. When the criminal justice system did attempt to intervene, it focused its efforts on the individual thief or on groups of thieves, but never on the functional structure that protected them. Historical study has demonstrated that when changes in science, technology, law, the organization of justice institutions, and American social patterns inadvertently joined to erode the foundations of this functional structure, the professional underworld began to colleapse. And this lesson of history indeed has implications for crime control in contemporary society. A historical analysis of organized crime or other persistent forms of criminal behavior patterns might provide insight into the mechanisms that enabled these to develop and endure, suggesting alternatives for their management and control.

At the upper levels of federal criminal justice machinery, historical studies of crime and justice had received only limited attention, and only minimal funds had ever been allocated for historical research. In early 1979, however, Mr. Blair Ewing, then-Acting Director of the National Institute of Justice, U. S. Department of Justice, contacted the senior editor of this volume to explore the possibility of organizing a workshop that focused on historical approaches to crime and justice. It was his hope to demonstrate to individuals in the federal justice bureaucracies that historical studies of crime and criminal justice could provide alternative perspectives for understanding current problems, that historical research adheres to the canons of scientific inquiry, and that there were a variety of historical topics that ought to be placed on the federal research agenda. In short, the workshop was organized and took place on October 11-12, 1979, in Chantilly, Virginia. It was deemed a success both by those who participated and attended, and the discussions which were generated by the effort continue. The essays which appear in this volume represent an outgrowth of the majority of papers presented at the workshop, and the balance of the essays are scheduled for publication elsewhere. The complete schedule of participants who participated in the workshop is listed below.

Harry M. Bratt, Acting Director, National Institute of Justice, U.S. Department of Justice

James A. Inciardi, University of Delaware

Richard M. Rau, National Institute of Justice, U.S. Department of Justice

Ted Robert Gurr, Northwestern University

Eric Monkkonen, University of California, Los Angeles

Henry Cohen, Loyola University

David J. Rothman, Columbia University

Nicolas Fischer Hahn, Northeastern University

Leopold Pospisil, Yale University

Eugene Watts, The Ohio State University

James F. Richardson, University of Akron

Carl B. Klockars, University of Delaware

Mark H. Haller, Temple University

David Miers, University College, Cardiff, Wales
Mary Gibson, Grinnell College
Margaret A. Zahn, Temple University
Roger Lane, Haverford College
Thomas J. Duesterberg, Stanford University
Michael Wadsworth, University of Bristol, England
Theodore N. Ferdinand, Northern Illinois University.

ORGANIZATION OF THE BOOK

The papers presented at the workshop represent a broad spectrum of substantive concerns and demonstrate the utility of a historical approach toward the elucidation of the nature of crime and the criminal justice process. In addition, three of the papers included here—those of Professors Duesterberg, Miers, and Gibson—provide challenging cross-cultural perspectives which add yet another dimension to our understanding of crime and the criminal justice process through history.

The four sections of the book represent the range of phenomena which can benefit from the academic eye of the historian. The first section deals with general theoretical and methodological issues.

The articles included here make a significant contribution toward establishing some broad parameters for conducting historically oriented research in crime and criminal justice and toward providing a historical context for an interpretation and understanding of the issues. The leading essay, "Development and Decay: Their Impact on Public Order in Western History," by Ted Robert Gurr discusses current patterns of crime and institutions of criminal justice as manifestations of four long-term processes of modernization: industrialization, the growth of cities, the expansion of the power of the state, and the humanization of interpersonal relations. By dislocating many people, particularly those in the hinterlands and bringing them together for purposes of production, the resultant economic despair early in the industrialization process, and increased opportunity for crime, profoundly affected the nature and extent of crime. This further resulted in policies aimed at regulating the new working classes. With the maturation of the industrial process, economic conditions improved for the laboring class, with a corresponding shift in policy concerns toward violations of so-called public order.

Urbanization, while not entirely separable historically from industrialization, had its own affect on crime and criminal justice. By virtue of the
fact that scores of people were brought together in close proximity, crime
became more readily observable, which in turn motivated upper and
middle classes to demand more effective criminal justice policies, which
gave special attention to new and more sophisticated forms of criminality
unique to urban areas.

Third, Gurr maintains that increasing nationalization occurring in
Western societies broadened the base of authority of the state to include
control over heretofore unrecognizable forms of crime: drug use, child
abuse, and industrial pollution to name just a few. Parallel to this development in policy, police forces have been centralized at a national level (the
United States being an exception), which has resulted in the contradictory
situation of a fragmentation of many specialized agencies *within* the
centralized system.

Finally, the greater concern with humanitarian values has led to an
increased concern over a broad spectrum of issues which would not
otherwise have been labelled as criminal, including deprivation of the poor
and underprivileged, which during the 1960s fueled a barrage of political
protests.

Gurr concludes his essay by suggesting that these four processes are not
inevitable, and there may be possibilities for innovative changes provided
that they are feasible given current views of crime and punishment and
given the current alignment of political and institutional forces.

The other article in this section, by Monkkonen, surveys some of the
quantitative work that has been done on crime and the criminal justice
system in the past. A timely methodological commentary, Monkkonen's
article, "The Quantitative Historical Study of Crime and Criminal Justice,"
argues that the problems encountered in doing quantitative historical
research do not stem from an inadequacy of statistical tools, but rather lie
in data collection itself and model design.

The studies Monkkonen selects for methodological analysis effectively
utilize statistical techniques ranging from simple percentaging to the more
sophisticated regression and path analysis. The difficulty, however, lies
within the data collection process itself. Several specific problematic areas
are delineated, which should prove to be of value to the researcher doing
quantitative historical research: (1) nineteenth and early twentieth century
data on offenses in the United States are limited to records of the criminal
justice system (e.g., conviction rates versus crimes known to the police);
(2) data are not centralized for ease of accessibility; (3) consistency across

individual data sources is problematic; and (4) because of differences in recording techniques through time, typologies for organizing and analyzing data may not be comparable.

Even more problematic than data sources, Monkkonen suggests, are the models employed to interpret the data. They are simply too grand (and hence too vague) to guide practical research efforts.

Monkkonen concludes by calling for an interdependence between the social historian and the policy-oriented social scientists. While differences in orientation exist between these disciplines, a mutual understanding of these differences should facilitate communication between the two, and scholarship should be richer for it.

The second section of the book takes a historical view of crime. While only two forms of criminal activity are addressed here (illegal enterprise and homicide), the three articles included here amply demonstrate the values of the social historian to an understanding of the phenomenon of crime.

Leading the section on "Historical Analyses of Crime" is Professor Mark H. Haller's essay, "Illegal Enterprise: Some Historical Perspectives and Public Policy." Here, Haller discusses the relationship between illegal enterprise and criminal law. Because the nature of much illegal enterprise is profoundly affected by technological, cultural, and political factors, the role of criminal law as a strategy in controlling these activities is often limited. To illustrate his point, Professor Haller traces the history of the parlor house, bookmaking, and loan-sharking operations in the United States, and the socio-political milieu which nurtured these activities.

Consideration of the broader socio-political factors has implications for effective control over these activities as Professor Haller insightfully demonstrates. Illegal gambling syndicates, for example, flourished in a grass roots political structure subject to the influence of gambling entrepreneurs. Law enforcement efforts proved relatively ineffective in such a structure. This contrasts sharply with efforts to mitigate the social effects of loan-sharking. Reformers recognized the moral and structural milieu which fostered the emergence of this activity and sought to destigmiatize consumer borrowing and encourage legitimate lending companies to extend credit to consumers and small businesses. Their successful efforts resulted in illegitimate lending companies being competitively forced to a marginal position in the market place. While law enforcement certainly plays a role in the effective control over illegal enterprise, Professor Haller's analysis highlights the need to consider the broader cultural, structural, and political processes in policy formation.

The second article included in this section, "Urban Homicide in the Nineteenth Century: Some Lessons for the Twentieth," by Professor Roger Lane investigates the trends in homicide rates through the nineteenth and early twentieth centuries. While inadequate recording and investigation procedures in the nineteenth century cloud the actual rate of homicide, the trend is quite clear: Homicide rates were declining through much of the nineteenth century and through the first half of the twentieth.

Lane accounts for these trends by applying a socialization model which served as an interpretive basis for Gold's "Suicide-Murder Ratio." The model argues, essentially, that individuals are socialized to either internalize expression of aggression (which results in suicide) or to give it external expression (homicide). While the model is itself social-psychological in orientation, Lane's work represents a unique attempt at linking such an individually oriented model to wider social and historical processes. The nineteenth and early twentieth centuries marked an increased expansion in industrialization, which itself was dependent upon a stable, highly disciplined work force. Self-restraint was the name of the game, and the socialization process which fostered internalization of aggression permeated not only the work place but the educational institution as well. The result of this structured internalized aggression was a rising suicide rate accompanied by a declining homicide rate. The period following .1950, however, marks a rising homicide rate in an era characterized by "postindustrial stagnation." Lane supports his hypothesis by demonstrating that the line dividing suicide victims from homicide offenders is not one of income or even race differences, but rather the type of occupation in which one was engaged. Homicide offenders occurred mostly within the ranks of those unemployed or engaged in nonroutinized occupations, whereas those committing suicide were to be found primarily among those whose work requires self-control and "a steady pace insured by constant supervision and equally constant awareness of the clock." The linkage that Lane draws between the nature of socialization and the industrialization process as these are manifest in homicide rates demonstrates the value of historical retrospect in the interpretation of crime.

Dovetailing closely with the essay by Lane is "Homicide in the Twentieth Century United States," by Margaret A. Zahn, one of the more prolific contemporary writers on homicide. In the present essay, Professor Zahn closely analyzes homicide rates in the twentieth century along various dimensions as reported by a number of researchers. More specifically, in addition to overall homicide rates, Professor Zahn examines the sexual and racial contribution of homicide, victim-offender relationships, and manner of death of homicides since the turn of the century. Briefly, homicide rates peaked in the late 1920s and early 1930s, gradually declined through the early 1960s, and have sharply increased since that time. Homicides have remained highly intrasexual and intraracial in nature, although intraracial homicides have increased somewhat in the last few years. With regard to victim-offender relationships, homicides between strangers are proportionately higher during periods of higher homicide rates (late 1920s and late 1960s to early 1970s), while homicide between acquaintances are predominant during periods of lower rates. Likewise, the use of firearms in homicide tends to be more frequent during high homicide periods. Coincidentally, homicide rates peaked at times when illegal markets were prevalent, which may account for the more anonymous nature of victim-offender relationships and higher use of firearms during these periods.

Of particular value to the historically oriented researcher is Dr. Zahn's insightful preliminary discussion of methodological difficulties in analyzing homicide trends through time. Due to data collection inadequacies, differing definitions of what constitutes homicides across investigating agencies, and a lack of consistency in the way data are recorded, comparisons are difficult and caution must be used in the interpretation of trends over time. Professor Zahn exercises such caution in her subsequent discussion of homicide trends in the twentieth century United States, thus providing us with a greater and more refined understanding of contemporary homicide patterns.

The third section of the book takes a historical view of criminal legislation and criminal policy. The lead article, "The Politics of Criminal Justice Reform: Nineteenth Century France," by Professor Thomas J. Duesterberg shows, in cross-cultural perspective, the ways in which broad-scale political considerations have tempered and shaped criminal justice practices. Duesterberg distinguishes three historic phases in French criminal justice policy which are linked to broader political reforms. The first phase symbolized by the Napoleonic Code marked a protest against the inhumane and repressive practice of the absolute monarchy, and in this context new methods of controlling crime were devised which relied upon the powers of retribution and deterrence. Soon after the fall of the Napoleonic empire, the Napoleonic system came under fire, due largely to abuses of it. In this second phase social liberals reasoned that crime could more effectively be controlled and human dignity better protected by making more discretionary the application of law, and reforming the penal system, with an emphasis on correction and rehabilitation rather than merely punishment. In 1871, after a prolonged period of political repression at the hands of Louis Napolean, the Third Republic was born. In order to establish and maintain the democratic regime, social reform was perceived as imperative. This reform effort prompted a host of changes in criminal justice policy, including penal reform, institution of laws protecting society against "dangerous" elements (alcoholics, criminally insane, and so on), and the introduction of parole and probation procedures, among others.

By delineating this relationship between broad political change and reform in the system of criminal justice in France, Professor Duesterberg effectively demonstrates, more generally, the political limitations inhibiting or promoting criminal justice policy.

"History and Policy in Juvenile Justice," by Professor Theodore N. Ferdinand traces juvenile justice in the United States from the early nineteenth century to the present in an attempt to demonstrate how historical events affect the policy and administration of juvenile justice. Professor Ferdinand concisely and articulately recaptures the ever-broadening scope of juvenile justice, from its relatively narrow jurisdiction in the early nineteenth century (basically to look after the interests of children in the absence of parents or guardians) to the pervasiveness of authority which the system claims today. Early in its development, the juvenile justice system saw fit to pass judgment on the *adequacy* of parenting; and with the founding of the juvenile court, the state broadened *parens patriae* to include delinquent children who had formerly been tried in adult criminal courts. Ferdinand concludes his eassay with an evaluation of *parens patriae* and argues for a narrowing of the authority of *parens patriae* to those juveniles whose problems are of a *personal* nature and which pose little problem to the community. A criminal court oriented specifically to juveniles, with all the due process protections of an adult court, is recommended for criminally delinquent juveniles. A primary lesson to be learned from history, in Ferdinand's view, is that sweeping changes cannot be made without a firm understanding of the forces which have given rise to an maintain current systems. The policy maker is hence advised to take such forces into consideration in order to be more fully aware of the strengths and limitations of his or her own domain, and thus more intelligently guide his or her own policy making.

"Eighteenth Century Gaming: Implications for Modern Casino Control," by Professor David Miers provides a cross-cultural as well as historical perspective on gaming legislation in Britain from the period of the

Restoration to the present. Professor Miers delineates two "models" of gaming legislation: the first is the "player protection model" which is oriented toward the protection of gaming participants from unaffordable losses (in the case of the lower classes). This model dominated gaming legislation in Britain until the Gaming Act of 1968, which, in addition to player protection concerns, introduced measures to restrict casino licensing so as to eliminate criminal infiltration into the gaming enterprise. These measures comprise the second model delineated by Miers, which he terms the "Casino Control Model."

While the present gaming policy in Britain reflects both the player protection model and the more recently introduced casino control model, gaming in the United States is regulated almost exclusively on the casino control model. Miers cites the revenue-generating objective of United States gaming as a principal factor contributing to the reliance on this model. Simply stated, the players protection model, with all of the restrictions it imposes on actual gaming operations, ultimately limits the amount of revenue that may be generated for the state. Because of these fiscal concerns and because, unlike the British experience, there is no historical premise for player protection in the United States, Professor Miers concludes that player protection concerns will not likely serve as relevant considerations in present-day modeling of casino legislation.

Professor Mary Gibson's essay, "The State and Prostitution: Prohibition, Regulation, or Decriminalization?", addresses the legal status of prostitution in historical and cross-cultural perspective. Professor Gibson historically analyzes prostitution in Italy and France as well as the United States as she conceptualizes three broad types of policies governing this enterprise. *Prohibition,* which characterized church-dominated Europe and indeed the United States even today, views prostitution as an intolerable evil which must be repressed. Because of the voluminous manpower required for policing prostitution under such a policy, prohibition has proved virtually ineffective. Furthermore, it is discriminatory against women in that, in practice, it is only the female half of this mutually consentient duo who is subject to sanction.

A second broad policy has been *regulation* which was introduced in nineteenth century France as an answer to the problems inherent in prohibition. Under this system, the prostitute was required to register with the local authorities, submit herself to periodic health checks, and report to a hospital if infected. Implicitly accepted under this policy was the inevitability of prostitution given the male sex drive, which must find expression. Prostitution was thus viewed as a safety valve. Again, however, regulation is an inherently discriminatory policy. The responsibility for spreading infectious disease is placed squarely on the woman, with no legal recognition of the obvious role that the client plays in the spread of venereal disease. Furthermore, under many localized policies, the freedom of the prostitute is restricted in other ways as well, including when she can go into town, how often she can see her children (if she has any), and so on. Not only is regulation discriminatory, Professor Gibson maintains, but it is ineffective as well. She cites evidence from Italy that the number of registered prostitutes *declined* in the face of an increasing population, indicating an increasing number of "clandestine" prostitutes, and those who registered were often delinquent in reporting for health checks.

The third policy, which the author proposes for serious consideration in the United States, is *decriminalization*. Only under such a policy can sexual equality be assured. While decriminalization does not view prostitution to be inevitable as does regulation, it recognizes the reality of its existence and places primary emphasis on protecting the constitutional and human rights of the prostitute. While this policy has found wide acceptance in Europe, the United States has unfortunately responded to the problems of regulation by retreating to the earlier prohibitionist stand.

Professor Gibson concludes her essay with three suggestions for consideration by experts and policy makers. First, not only should the *act* of prostitution be decriminalized but solicitation should be as well, since this is one of the necessary tools of the trade. Second, laws against renting to prostitutes should be repealed so as to decrease their reliance on pimps. Finally, dissemination of information concerning the causes and cure of venereal disease to the entire population seems imperative.

Despite the reader's position regarding the desirability of the decriminalization of prostitution, the value of this article lies in the conceptualization of historical policies governing prostitution, with a clear presentation of the issues and problems involved in each. As such, Professor Gibson's essay should prove of immense value to policy makers and researchers in the area.

The essays in the final section of the book focus on the administration of criminal justice legislation and policy. The section title, "Historical Analyses of Law Enforcement and Corrections," reflects the two levels of criminal justice administration addressed here. Professor James F. Richardson opens this section with his article, "Police in America: Functions and Control." This article utilizes a number of books published since 1960 on the history and current situation of police departments for purposes of making some tentative generalizations about the functions of American urban police, their modes of control, and how these have changed over time.

Richardson traces the evolution of the police in America from the early nineteenth century which was characterized by mutually autonomous groups of salaried night watchmen, elected constables, and mayoral-appointed marshals. Corruption and abuses of power in this system fostered the emergence of bureaucratic police departments designed principally to maintain public order.

By the 1930s an impersonal, nonpartisan police force was developed whose principle function was law enforcement rather than simply order maintenance. The police had, by this time, taken on the role as "crime fighters."

In recent decades, scholars have noted that noncriminal functions have taken up much of police time—functions such as arbitrary domestic disputes and enforcing traffic codes.

Richardson sums up by suggesting that caution should be exercised in making any generalizations concerning the functions of American police. While models of police functions provide us with popularly accepted roles for police, actual behavioral roles are influenced by numerous factors, not the least of which is the policeman's own world view.

"Jonathon Wild and the Modern Sting," authored by Professor Carl B. Klockars, is, so far as we know, the only piece of scholarship in the social sciences to explore the nature of sting operations. As a backdrop for his analysis, Professor Klockars examines the career of Jonathon Wild, an eighteenth century figure who (to say the least) had questionable scruples. The point of interest for Klockars, however, is the dual role played by Wild: that of "Thief Taker General" (a law enforcement role) and a fence. Wild's role as a fence, with the contact with the underworld that it entailed, placed him in an excellent position of power. His image of Thief Taker General was maintained by turning over to the police carefully selected criminals, all the while enjoying a profitable career as a fence, facilitated largely by the higher prices he paid for stolen goods.

Wild was, of course, first a fence and the role of Thief Taker General was devised secondarily to insure his fencing operations. This distinguishes Wild from the modern sting operations which are run by law enforcement officials posing as fences in order to capture law breakers. The parallel which Klockars draws between Wild and the modern sting, however, elucidates the nature of the dual role played by contemporary sting operations.

But what of the effectiveness of sting operations? As was the case with Wild, such modern methods of policing which incur tremendous economic and psychological costs demand exemplary success which, in Klockars' view, facilitate distortion and exaggeration of effectiveness to be presented for public view. Through an analysis of the data presented in *What Happened,* an official document of several sting operations, Klockars challenges the validity of the interpretations made therein and, in so doing, makes his position clear: Sting operations are limited in their effectiveness, particularly considering the costs incurred in operating them. Still, they probably do not radically depart from the heritage by Wild: Less important than effectively reducing the incidence of property crime is that the *appearance* of such effectiveness is maintained.

Professor Nicolas Fischer Hahn probes the history of women's prisons in a timely essay, "Matrons and Molls: The Study of Women's Prison-History." The essay consists principally of reviews of literature in both the field of criminal justice and women's studies. Until very recently there was a paucity of information on corrections for women in the traditional criminal justice literature. In recent years, however, studies have revealed that women's prisons have played a prominent role in the history of prisons and prison reform. Women's studies literature, too, has paid minimal attention specifically to women's prisons, although considerable attention has been focused on female deviance generally.

Possibly the greatest contribution made by Professor Hahn in this brief essay is her concluding discussion of potential resources which, to date, have been virtually unexplored by social researchers as sources of valuable information on the history of women's prisons. At a time when the role of women generally in society is taking on renewed interest, it becomes increasingly imperative that reliable sources of information be made available. Professor Hahn's contribution in this regard is certain to be invaluable to anyone involved in this important aspect of research on women.

"For the Good of All: The Progressive Tradition in Prison Reform" by Professor David J. Rothman is an appropriate conclusion to this section as it concisely summarizes the reform tradition in corrections and poignantly elaborates the problems inherent in this tradition. Professor Rothman suggests that the progressive tradition rests on three major premises. First, it is possible to both incapacitate and rehabilitate. Guarding men securely and working toward their rehabilitation are not seen to be in inherent conflict. Second, the criminal act is seen to be symptomatic of a more pervasive criminal character. Hence, reformers bandied the slogan, "Treat the criminal, not the crime." Third, on the basis of the above two premises, prison reformers found it necessary to draw up a novel design for prisons based on community and treatment models. The prison was to serve both as a place where prisoners would be prepared for a role in normal society (community model) and where they could receive treatment for their maladjustment (treatment model). Taken together, these two models "justified a sentencing system that was open-ended and indeterminate."

Professor Rothman takes issue with these premises and locates the critical issue in the questionable assumption that it is possible to incapacitate and to rehabilitate at the same time. Invariably, custodial duties took precedence over rehabilitative goals, and corporate punishment was commonplace. On the basis of overwhelming historical evidence against the compatibility of the two goals, the author suggests than anyone proposing to accomplish both goals must bear the burden of proof for the feasibility of such a program.

At the same time not being willing to tear down prison walls entirely, Professor Rothman suggests some modest, but possibly more realistic policy proposals. First, he suggests that sentence time should be issued in "spoonfuls" rather than "bucketfuls" which characterizes the American correctional system at the present time. Second, more marginal cases should be diverted from the prison system. Finally, the author suggests that up to the present time attempts at creative solution to the problem of crime have remained incidental to the criminal justice system. Such innovative thinking should become mainstream in the criminal justice process.

By way of summary, the essays contained in this book, far from constituting a comprehensive historical treatment of crime and the criminal justice system, do represent the way in which historical analysis can contribute to our understanding of the nature of crime and the criminal justice process in its various aspects: criminal behavior, criminal legislation and policy, and law enforcement and corrections. It is hoped that this collection of essays will stimulate further historical research in this area.

NOTES

1. Allan Nevins, *The Gateway to History* (Lexington, MA: D. C. Heath, 1946), rev. ed. (Garden City, NY: 1962), p. 39. Professor Nevins (1890-1971), among the

best known of American historians, began his career during the early part of this century as a journalist with the *New York Evening Post* and literary editor of the *Nation,* and later joining the faculty of Cornell University. In 1931 he was named De Witt Clinton professor of American History at Columbia University and remained in that chair until his retirement in 1958. During his long and active scholarly life he wrote and edited more than 60 volumes, including *The Heritage of America* and the Bancroft Prize winning *Ordeal of the Union.*

2. Lester D. Stephens, *Probing the Past* (Boston: Allyn and Bacon, 1974), pp. 112-127.

3. Ibid., p. 119.

4. James A. Inciardi, Alan A. Block, and Lyle A. Hallowell, *Historical Approaches to Crime: Research Strategies and Issues* (Beverly Hills, CA: Sage, 1977), p. 28.

5. Thorsten Sellin, *Slavery and the Penal System* (New York: Elsevier, 1976).

6. George Rusche and Otto Kirchheimer, *Punishment and Social Structure* (New York: Columbia University Press, 1939).

7. James F. Richardson, *The New York Police: Colonial Times to 1901* (New York: Oxford University Press, 1970).

8. Joseph L. Albini, *The American Mafia: Genesis of a Legend* (Englewood Cliffs, NJ: Prentice-Hall, 1971).

9. James A. Inciardi, *Careers in Crime* (Skokie, IL: Rand McNally, 1975).

10. Edwin H. Sutherland, *The Professional Thief* (Chicago: University of Chicago Press, 1937).

11. James A. Inciardi, op. cit.

THEORY
AND
METHODOLOGY

1

DEVELOPMENT AND DECAY: THEIR
IMPACT ON PUBLIC ORDER IN WESTERN HISTORY

TED ROBERT GURR

This essay offers a general historical perspective on how patterns of crime and systems of criminal justice in Western societies have been shaped by historical processes of modernization, and what implications the reversal of these processes might have for public order in the future. The concepts and theories suited to this kind of systematic historical inquiry come mainly from macro-sociology while the evidence is largely the fruit of historians' labor, especially economic and social historians. The main contribution from political analysis to the historical study of public order is an understanding of the functions and complexities of political systems. The definition of "order" is inherently a political process and so is the establishment and operation of the police, courts, and penal institutions which implement legal conceptions of order.

The central theme of this essay is that past and present patterns of crime and criminal justice are the product of powerful and fundamental socioeconomic and political processes. More specifically, the ways in which crime is defined and dealt with in Western societies have been shaped by four aspects of "modernization": (1) industrialization, (2) the growth of cities, (3) the expansion of the state's powers and resources, and (4) the humanization of interpersonal relations. Other aspects of modernization may be relevant as well, but I regard these four as the most fundamental influences on public order. The significance and general nature of these processes is not much in doubt: Over a period of two centuries they have fundamentally transformed the shape of Western civilization. What is less well-understood is how they have altered our conceptions of crime, the incidence of criminal behavior, and the character of the institutions we have established to maintain public order.

The impact of these processes on crime and criminal justice is not merely a matter of historical curiosity.[1] Our economies, cities, public sector, and values continue to change, and not necessarily in a linear or "progressive" fashion: What goes up may also come down. Growth, stasis, and decay all will work changes in public order, and the better we understand their past effects, the better our chances of anticipating what will happen in expanding and slumping economies and in growing new cities and decaying old ones. It is a matter of some dispute among scholars whether knowledge of the past can ever enable one to anticipate the future with any accuracy, since past and future situations have unique as well as common properties. But there is a second way in which macro-processes are relevant to contemporary policy and action. If my basic assumption is correct, that the shape of public order is *determined by* these processes, then the range of possibilities for effective policy changes may be narrower than we might think. We optimistically expect that "crime can be reduced" if we somehow find the right balance of deterrence, punishment, and rehabilitation or that criminal justice policies can be reformed once we have overcome "political pressures" and "bureaucratic inertia." In fact, we may be bumping up against irreducible limits set by the structure and dynamics of contemporary industrialized, urban society. One simple illustration is the high and rising rate of property crime in almost all contemporary Western societies. I think, for reasons that will become clearer below, that affluent and heterogeneous societies, whatever their policies of public order, are intrinsically susceptible to high rates of theft. If this is so, the tractable policy problem is not how to reduce theft, which is impossible beyond some more or less narrow limits, but rather how to manage it and minimize its social costs.

In the discussion which follows, I treat each of the four dimensions of modernization in turn and sketch some of their general effects on criminal behavior, the politics of public order, and the character of criminal justice systems. Some of these effects are quite obvious and can be documented by substantial evidence. Others are more speculative and are offered here as hypotheses which should be fruitful for systematic historical research.

The analysis centers on modernization's typical effects. In the last section of the essay I turn to the issues of variability and reversal: What kinds of occurrences, and what aspects of modernization itself, might combine to alter the prevailing patterns of public order?

INDUSTRIALIZATION

At the risk of great over-simplification, the Industrial Revolution had three profound socioeconomic consequences for the Western societies that began the process in the late eighteenth and the nineteenth centuries. First, it pulled an undifferentiated and dispersed mass of rural workers together into cities. Second, social heterogeneity increased enormously, thanks to the specialization and diversification of economic activity and the emergence of distinctive occupational groups among employers, workers, and new classes of professionals. Finally, it brought about an unprecedented increase in material wealth, accompanied at least at first by increased economic inequality, followed in some but not all "mature" industrialized societies by a lessening of inequality.

EFFECTS ON THE INCIDENCE OF CRIME

Let me suggest two basic premises about the etiology of crime in modernizing societies. First, want breeds theft. The more abruptly and unexpectedly people are afflicted by economic distress, the more likely they are to steal. Second, social dislocation breeds deviant behavior. The break-up of stable communities and migration of people from rural to urban areas erodes, or allows people to escape from, prevailing norms of conduct and patterns of social control. These premises help explain some general effects of industrialization on the character of crime in Western societies.

First, the early stages of industrialization changed the locus and extent of economic distress. In rural areas, as labor was drawn away from traditional occupations, there was some economic distress and a tendency toward increased property crime. The greater effects, however, occurred at the industrializing center. To the extent that more people were attracted to the cities than could be integrated into the workforce, the cities became cesspools of want and despair. High levels of theft, alcoholism, and interpersonal violence characterized many European cities at this stage—but not all of them, since some were able to provide economic opportunities for most migrants. Of course this is a broad and tentative generalization, but it is consistent with what has been reported about crime changes during the early stages of industrialization in Britain, Scandinavia, and Imperial Germany.[2]

A second, key generalization is that advanced industrialization is accompanied by changes in the character of property crime. It appears that once industrializing societies move past the threshold at which most people's material wants are satisfied, property crime becomes a function of increased opportunity. From this threshold onward, as material prosperity grows, so does theft. There is suggestive empirical evidence for the existence of such a threshold in the history of crime in the United States and a number of European societies. Before the Great Depression of the 1930s, there was a tendency for economic slumps to be accompanied by increased property crime. Since then, and especially since about 1950, rising prosperity and rising property crime have gone together in virtually every Western society. The timing of the shift is somewhat problematic, since studies of some countries suggest that it may have occurred early in the twentieth century. The exact causes also are problematic. But the fact of the shift is not much in doubt; there is too much evidence for it.[3] It should be an intriguing subject for further historical and comparative study to identify when and in what social circumstances want gave way to opportunity as the main factor in determining the incidence of property crime. Of equal interest is whether either tendency has been inhibited, in particular times and places, by unusual patterns of (in)equality and social control.

EFFECTS ON THE POLITICS OF PUBLIC ORDER

It is well-documented by historical studies that a major consequence of the early stages of industrialization was rising demand for the protection of private property. When only a few benefited from the wealth generated by early capitalism, and many poor were abroad in the land, uprooted by new economic forces, property was at risk—the more so since it so often took the form of portable goods and money, which was more readily stolen than the holdings of wealthy rural gentry. The upper middle classes were typically the most ardent advocates of tougher and more consistent laws, enforcement, and punishment for property offenses. There was a parallel concern, shared by the middle classes and the political elite, for regulating the new urban working classes, and especially the unassimilated, unskilled people at the very bottom of the class ladder. They were called *lumpenproletariat,* "dangerous classes," or "criminal class," but by whatever name they were seen as a chronic threat of crime and riot. (There were also economic reasons for regulating the activities and movements of these people, since they were a potential source of labor—hence statutes against vagrancy, which have a long European history.) Many of the historical characteristics of criminal codes, police services, and penal systems in Western societies derive from the desire of those who devised them to control a dangerous underclass. And those historical origins have left many contemporary residues despite more than a century of reforming efforts. Basic legal and institutional patterns, once set, can be varied but are very resistant to fundamental change.[4]

As industrial societies matured, moving into the stage of mass consumption, the earlier demands for protection of public order have moderated considerably. Material wealth is more abundant and more widely distributed, and insurance systems protect most people against most losses. Abundance means greater opportunity and less necessity for theft; it also means that the loss of property is not nearly as painful to most victims as it was a century ago. Independently of the changing balance of cost and opportunity for theft, most of the working classes have been assimilated into the social and political order and their behavior is more predictable in the perceptions of the middle and governing classes. The black underclass in the United States is the only significant group in contemporary Western societies which inspires the kinds of fear which the nineteenth-century bourgeoisie felt for the "dangerous classes."

The attainment of basic economic and social order shifted the attention of the prosperous classes to other manifestations of social disorder, a shift that was already under way in most Western societies by 1900. Middle class reformers and the authorities became increasingly concerned about "victimless" and nuisance activities. As a consequence, the force of the law and the efforts of the police were brought to bear on the problems of alcoholism, gambling, prostitution, drug use, loitering, vagrancy (again), and delinquency. Some of these (alcoholism and vagrancy) had long been regarded as social problems but were now brought systematically under official control. Others, including prostitution and gambling, were for the first time elevated to the status of deviance, while juvenile delinquency was virtually invented as a category of behavior that required public and police attention. Of course, this shift was not directly, or only, a consequence of industrialization. What is especially significant, I suggest, is that a "law of the instrument" was at work. The techniques of legal criminalization, uniformed policing, and incarceration had proved effective in controlling theft and the threat of riot, which were real and serious social problems early in the Industrial Revolution. Once the fact and fear of crime and disorder ebbed, the techniques now were applied to other social problems which earlier generations may have regarded as deviant, but which—vagrancy excepted—were seldom a public responsibility, much less a criminal matter.[5]

EFFECTS ON THE CRIMINAL JUSTICE SYSTEM

There was one significant, direct effect of industrialization on the development of criminal justice systems: It provided the resources, in the form of public revenues, that made it possible to establish new (and expensive) uniformed police forces, court systems, prisons, and reformatories. But this was a sufficient, not a necessary, condition for the foundation of modern criminal justice systems. The necessary conditions were the problems of disorder generated by the Industrial Revolution and the demands for public order by its beneficiaries against the threats posed by its victims.

THE GROWTH OF CITIES

In most Western societies, urban growth went hand in hand with industrialization, but urbanization as such had a number of distinctive effects on the problems and politics of public order, independently of industrialization. The growth of cities had at least these three major effects on the conditions of crime and public order:

(1) It involved selective migration to the cities, especially by young people with few ties and fewer resources—a group that in all places and ages is especially susceptible to crime.

(2) Migration from culturally diverse regions, and from other countries, brought about increased interaction among heterogeneous people. As a consequence, the traditional, mainly informal social controls which operated in rural communities lost much of their force.

(3) New mechanisms of social integration developed to replace disintegrating traditional ones, including occupational associations, new religious creeds and organizations (for example, Methodism in England), and in some settings the re-creation of community at the neighborhood level—the so-called "urban villages." Some of these new communities developed deviant, occasionally predatory subcultures which posed a threat and challenge to public order as conceived by dominant social groups.

EFFECTS ON CRIMINAL BEHAVIOR

The effects of urbanization on crime vary across time and among societies, so it is difficult to offer simple generalizations. One clear-cut uniformity is that almost everywhere, large cities have higher crime rates than towns or rural areas. For example, Lodhi and Tilly's quantitative historical study of France shows that urban *departements* consistently had higher crime rates than rural ones.[6] English criminal statistics, from their inception at the beginning of the nineteenth century, show that London and other cities had higher crime rates than rural areas. A study of contemporary American cities by Archer et al. demonstrates that the largest cities have the highest homicide rates and that large cities in most other contemporary societies also have consistently higher rates of crimes against persons than their societies as a whole.[7] Paradoxically, however, the same study shows no consistent increase in urban crime rates as cities grow—though the time series data are too short to include the historical period of greatest urban growth in Western societies. Confirming historical evidence is provided by my comparative study of London, Stockholm, and Sydney from the early nineteenth century to about 1970. The periods of most rapid growth in these cities, absolutely and proportionally, occurred between the 1850s and 1930s—an era during which rates of personal and property crimes were generally declining.[8]

A quantitative study which gets below the surface of broad generalizations is McHale and Johnson's longitudinal and cross-sectional analysis of urban growth, industrialization, and crime in Prussia from 1871 to 1913. In this study the cases are districts rather than cities. In the take-off stage of German urban and industrial development, from 1871 to 1885, the more prosperous and urbanizing districts had lower crime rates. After 1885, however, property crime went up in those same industrialized and urban districts and declined in the poorer, rural districts. The authors' explanation is that imbalance between the processes of urban and industrial change was responsible for the shift:

> In the mid-1880s, it was not the urban-industrial areas that were experiencing stress in Germany, but the rural areas of eastern Prussia. The cities seemed to be capable of managing growth. . . . After the turn of the century, we note that societal stress lessens in the eastern region because of depopulation and social change, and becomes more pronounced in the swollen urban-industrial centers.[9]

Evidently urbanization both as a process and phenomenon has had complex effects on crime in Western cities. The only reason for doubting that crime has been greater in cities is the suspicion that crime was and is better recorded and more carefully policed in cities than in rural areas. This is especially problematic in nineteenth-century societies, in which modern policing systems were first and most efficiently established in cities. From another point of view, the actual incidence of urban versus town and country crime is beside the point. Crime is more visible in cities, in the sense that more people are likely to know about a given offense. It also is more threatening in cities because victims are much less likely than in small communities to know or to be able to seek redress from offenders. So historically (as well as in contemporary American cities) there are compelling reasons for concluding that the *fear* of crime is concentrated in cities, which in itself is a socially and politically salient reality.

EFFECTS ON THE POLITICS OF PUBLIC ORDER

The concentrated fear of crime among the prosperous upper and middle classes in growing cities was a compelling motivation for their demands for more effective criminal justice policies. It was not enough to rely, as did the rural upper classes, on legal prescriptions of horrendous punishment for the handful of offenders who were unlucky enough to run afoul of local bailiffs and wardens. The urban bourgeoisie sought a more consistent and pervasive defense against the ever-present fear of crime. Moreover they were imbued with the rationalistic ethos and mechanistic faith in social engineering of the new capitalist era, which meant that they were disposed to favor rationally articulated legal codes, professional policing systems, efficient and incorruptible courts, and a penal system that applied punishments in proportion to the offense. (One can speculate that while some judicial reformers opposed corruption, that is, the sale of judicial favors, on principle, the general run of the middle classes opposed it because it introduced an expensive element of unpredictability into the judicial process.)

EFFECTS ON THE CRIMINAL JUSTICE SYSTEM

Many of the distinctive characteristics of the new and reformed features of criminal justice systems in nineteenth-century society reflect their urban origins: They were designed to meet problems which had come to a head in the growing cities of industrializing economies. The new criminal codes gave elaborate attention to offenses that were distinctive if not unique to urban areas, including the more artful forms of theft, receiving, fraud and embezzlement, illicit sales of alcohol, public drunkenness, and others. New policing systems similarly reflected urban realities. The older European models for policing cities relied on a parish-based watch-and-ward system, without central command or coordination; or alternatively a centralized, quasi-military system in which officers worked out of a central office or barracks. Either might suffice in a small city; large cities, on the other hand, required decentralization of police manpower, to keep close to the potential problems, and centralized command to ensure coordination of efforts against offenders (and rioters) who moved from one district to another. And of course crime and the fear of crime were sufficiently common in large cities that full-time professional police officers were required, not part-time volunteers or bored garrison troopers. The success of the new police in apprehending offenders created another problem, namely, what to do with them after they were apprehended. The jails and workhouses were inadequate to their numbers, and also inconsistent with the rational plans of reformers who believed that offenders ought to be segregated, punished, and trained in proportion to the severity of their offenses and their prospects for rehabilitation. Hence, new penal institutions and new professionals to look after them were required.

NATIONALIZATION

By nationalization I mean the growth of the power and resources of the state. It is not ordinarily defined as an aspect of modernization but it has, in fact, gone hand in glove with industrialization. There are four main dimensions of nationalization which have some bearing on the questions at issue here. First, there is a centralization of political authority at the national level. This was a characteristic of most continental states before the onset of the Industrial Revolution; elsewhere, decentralized systems survive, even though decentralization invites inefficiency of administration (as in the United States) and the risk of national disintegration (as in Canada and Belgium). The second facet of nationalization is the state's increased command of resources. Democratic governments have sharply increased their absolute and proportional share of national product in the last two centuries and especially since 1900. It is doubtful whether any nineteenth-century government absorbed more than one-tenth of the national product except in time of war; in the late twentieth century, Western governments routinely take in and spend between 20% and 50% of the national product.[10] A third dimension of nationalization is development of mechanisms of group participation and representation in government. I am referring not only or primarily to electoral systems but also to the multitude of channels by which various class, corporate, and associational groups exert influence on legislatures and administrators. Finally, as a consequent of all of the factors cited above, governments have vastly expanded their scope of action, by assuming responsibility for a host of general and specialized social and economic functions. Western governments have become general social service states which are expected to respond to virtually every kind of collective problem and issue which is brought to public attention.

The growth of the state's powers and resources has had little effect on the incidence of criminal behavior, but it has had a considerable impact on the politics of public order and the character of criminal justice systems.

EFFECTS ON THE POLITICS OF PUBLIC ORDER

The expansion of the state has been accompanied by a steady increase in political expectations and demands of governments for public order.

Some of these demands concern the scope or range of questions of order for which the state is expected to assume responsibility. I alluded above to the expansion of reformers' interest in the nineteenth and early twentieth centuries from protection of persons and property to the criminalization and control of victimless crimes and nuisance behavior. The aim of reformers throughout Western societies now is toward the decriminalization of much of what was criminalized a century ago, but not necessarily toward reducing the state's scope of responsibility. The typical expectation is that the state provide help and treatment rather than criminal sanctions for, say, addicts and alcoholics. At the same time, other groups advocate the criminalization of socially undesirable activities that thus far have escaped the state's purview, for example, industrial pollution of air and water, public smoking, or parents' spanking of children. The hope or expectation that the state's powers will be used to punish behavior that outrages the sensibilities of any significant social group has become a fixed feature of Western political and social thought.

While much attention has been directed at the boundaries of public responsibility for deviant behavior, even more has focused on how those responsibilities are carried out. The quality and character of policing has been the subject of public scrutiny and outcry as long as organized police forces have existed. Much the same is true of the criminal courts, though they usually have been less controversial than the police. Probably the most effective of all nineteenth-century efforts at reform in this domain was the John Howard Association, which was instrumental in persuading governments to undertake far-reaching penal reforms.

The sources of effective advocacy of change in criminal justice systems have changed markedly over time. As the bases of political participation expanded, there was a shift from elite-oriented policies of public order to mass-oriented ones. In the nineteenth century, as observed above, demands for a more active governmental role were made mainly by and on behalf of the privileged classes, but the effective source of such demands has moved down the class ladder so that now governments are arguably as responsive to, say, urban workers' concerns about safe city streets as they are to upper-middle-class suburbanites' concern about property crime. And the punitive policies of long stints at hard labor favored by nineteenth-century reformers gave way, under pressures from more enlightened reformers and working class politicians, to a more flexible reliance on fines, probation, rehabilitation, and parole. Certainly it is no longer possible for any Western government to define criminal behavior solely from the point of view of the elite, and it is not possible for conservatives to reinstate harsh punitive policies on a broad basis. Other influential groups are too much concerned that their own oxen might be gored by such policies: They might not personally fear long prison sentences, but they evidently fear the tax costs of building more prisons.

One final noteworthy change in the politics of public order is the diversification and fragmentation of the relevant interest groups. At any given time in the nineteenth century there were ordinarily only a handful of active, influential interest groups concerned with crime and justice. But in this century each country has seen a veritable explosion of activist groups. There are innumerable contemporary professional groups, reformers, and academic experts competing for the attention of legislators and administrators, most of whom have more precisely articulated views and demands—hence more influence—than any segment of the general public. The John Howard Association has innumerable contemporary counterparts, representing every conceivable constituency from prosecuting attorneys to defenders of battered children to advocates of homosexual rights to police chiefs.

EFFECTS ON THE CRIMINAL JUSTICE SYSTEM

Initially, the growth of the state and the reforming impetus in criminal justice converged in a number of Western societies to bring about rationalized systems of criminal justice that were national in scope and more or less well-articulated with one another. Consolidated criminal law codes replaced the pastiche of individual acts and ordinances that prevailed in most Western societies—though decentralized countries like the United States and Australia have lagged far behind most others in the development of uniform criminal codes. National systems of courts had long since existed in Western states, but were expanded, reorganized, and obliged to follow national standards in staffing and procedure—again with some laggard exceptions. Police services also have been nationalized in practice if not always in name, by bringing local forces up to national standards and often by subjecting them to national control. Some European countries have wholly nationalized police operating in local units or districts; others have developed (or retained historic) nationalized police for some functions but rely on specialized police under local control for other functions. The United States is very much the exception in resisting what is otherwise a pervasive trend toward national police systems.[11]

I suggest, though, that the historical tendencies identified above have created a contradictory situation. Criminal justice systems have come under more or less centralized national control, far more than was the case two centuries ago. But they have also grown so large that organizational control has become fragmented at the center, all the more so because so many interested groups have gained access to the legislative and administrative decision-making processes. The paradoxical consequence of the proliferation of criminal justice activities and advocacy is that there cannot now be a single centralizing or reforming impetus in the criminal justice policies of any but the smallest and most homogeneous Western societies. There may well be too many agencies carrying out too many functions at the behest of too many interest and client groups for us to talk about *the* criminal justice system in anything but a metaphorical sense.[12]

HUMANIZATION

The processes of economic modernization have been accompanied by an equally significant, though less well-studied, shift in prevailing values which I call "humanization." Three of these changes have been particularly telling for the problems and policies of public order. First, interpersonal aggression is subject to much stronger internal and external controls than once was the case. The contrast is sharpest with medieval European society, in which violence within the community was widely celebrated and practiced. Given's careful recent study of homicide in five rural countries in thirteenth-century England shows that their murder rates were about 15 times greater than those of contemporary London, for example.[13] For the family and among neighbors we have nonstatistical but persuasive evidence from diaries, novels, and social history that aggression is less tolerated: One does not have to go far back into the social history of most Western societies to find ample evidence that it was common and acceptable practice for heads of households to beat wives, children, and servants; for employers to physically abuse disobedient workers; and for officials to use corporal punishment on soldiers, deviants, and prisoners.

The long-term decline in interpersonal violence is probably a manifestation of a related change in the value and respect accorded to individuals, irrespective of their status. Obviously there is much dehumanization and callous disrespect for others in contemporary Western societies, but they are residues of what were once prevailing social attitudes and practices. A third change is more intellectual than normative and has to do with our perceptions of the causes of individual behavior, and deviance in particular. There has been a gradual, long-term erosion of the once-unchallenged assumption that deviants and criminals were morally flawed. The nineteenth-century reincarnation of this traditional view attributed criminal behavior to physiological flaws. The prevailing view now, of course, is that the social environment is largely responsible for most socially and personally harmful behavior.[14]

EFFECTS ON THE INCIDENCE OF CRIME

Fragments of statistical evidence from England spanning 700 years document a long-term decline in homicide in that society.[15] More recent comparative evidence is provided by studies of court and police records which show that murder and serious assault declined in a number of societies between the mid-nineteenth and mid-twentieth centuries. Lane's study of Boston indicates that arrest rates for murder fell from about 7.0 per 100,000 population around 1860 to less than 2.0 in 1950. Assault arrests declined by a 4-to-1 ratio over the same period.[16] My comparative work on London, Stockholm, and New South Wales shows similar century-long trends.[17] Such declines were not universal: Longitudinal data for assaults show increases in nineteenth-century France and Germany.[18] But this may well be explained by increased public and official attention to behavior that earlier was accepted as normal. The apparent reversal of the declining trend in violent crime since 1950 is discussed below.

Let me also suggest another, more debatable effect of humanitarian values on crime. One of the corollaries of the contemporary emphasis on individual needs and rights is a sharpened sense of personal injustice about material inequalities. The relative deprivation of the poor and the young (most youth *are* relatively poor in income and material possessions) can fuel political movements with socialist and egalitarian aims. It may also lead individuals to act on Prudhon's principle that "property is theft," redressing unjust inequalities by stealing what one wants and needs. Few thieves presumably have self-conscious social justifications for theft, but I am suggesting that internal inhibitions against theft are considerably weaker now than they were 50 or 100 years ago in most if not yet all Western societies.

EFFECTS ON THE POLITICS OF PUBLIC ORDER

Some of the most articulate advocates of humanization in criminal justice systems were the reformers, active throughout the nineteenth and early twentieth centuries in most societies, who sought the abolition of capital punishment and an end to the reliance on corporal punishment of prison inmates.

Their efforts, and the disposition of authorities to heed them, are evident in the steady decline in reliance on capital punishment during the nineteenth century and its virtual absence, except in South Africa and the United States, since the early twentieth century. The parallel efforts to introduce programs of rehabilitation and remission of sentences were less visible and coordinated but collectively have had far wider impact. Such policies are the products of the principles that offenders, like other people, deserve humane treatment and can be led rather than coerced away from crime.

Quite a different kind of political manifestation of humanitarian trends is an increased concern for protecting people from lesser forms of interpersonal violence. Aggressive acts which once were acceptable, or if not acceptable then a private matter outside the state's competence, have steadily been brought within the purview of the criminal justice system. Once again, reformers and professional interest groups have been instrumental in accomplishing these changes: increased attention to petty assault and disorderly conduct, more sensitivity to victims of sexual assault, criminalization of wife-beating and child abuse, and so on. Simultaneous with the effort to extend controls over aggressive behavior, other reformers have pushed for the decriminalization of moral offenses on grounds that it is the individual's right to engage in unconventional acts provided others are not hurt by them.

EFFECTS ON THE CRIMINAL JUSTICE SYSTEM

The effective advocacy of humanitarian reforms has had an enormous impact on criminal justice systems and practices during this century. Changes in the scope of the criminal law have been modest; some aggressive behaviors have been brought within its purview, some moral offenses have been removed from it. The day-to-day activities of the police have been more substantially changed by their obligation (not always accepted) to respect the rights and persons of suspects. The most fundamental changes are to be found in the criminal courts and the penal system. Courts are far more solicitous of defendants' rights and far less harsh and arbitrary in their decisions than was historically the case. The most fundamental change of all, judged in historical perspective, is the contemporary emphasis of courts and penal systems on rehabilitation and alternatives to imprisonment. In theory this is a complete turnabout from the practices introduced by the reformers who designed the prison systems of the nineteenth century. Of course the practice of rehabilitation has lagged far behind theory, and more so in the United States than Northern Europe, but the fact remains that the contemporary offender, even when found guilty, is likely to suffer only a small personal fraction of the retribution which fell on his nineteenth-century counterpart.[19]

ON THE VARIABILITY AND REVERSIBILITY OF MODERNIZATION'S EFFECTS

By emphasizing the typical effects of modernization, I do not mean to minimize the significance of variations among contemporary societies in problems and policies of public order. Nor is there any lack of possibilities for innovative change, provided they are consistent with prevailing views about crime and punishment and are feasible, given current alignments of political and institutional forces. The general point is that historical processes have determined and therefore set limits on what is and can be done in the present. Within these historically determined limits there is much actual and possible variation. Western societies have been influenced in somewhat different ways by processes of modernization—some are more prosperous, urbanized, centrally controlled than others—and have followed distinctive patterns of institutional development. As a result they differ in historical and contemporary patterns of crime and criminal justice systems.

More important than the unevenness of modernization is the fact that many other factors intervene between macro-historical processes and the contemporary shape of public order. The effects of modernization can be altered temporarily, and sometimes permanently, by exceptional political, social, and economic events. We know, for example, that war and revolution have sharp short-term impacts on the incidence of crime, typically leading to an increase in crimes against the person, and often to greater property crime as well.[20] If violent internal and external conflict are endemic to a society, such effects may be enduring. They may help explain, for example, why the base level of violent crime is higher in the United States than in most other Western societies. The peaceable modern histories of Switzerland and most of Scandinavia similarly may be part of the explanation for their relatively low levels of violent crime.[21]

The ills of industrial economies—depression, inflation, unemployment, and shortages—are another source of short-term variation in problems and policies of public order. They are likely to alter both the incidence of property crime and the kinds of treatment accorded it by authorities. Abrupt demographic change is still another common source of variation in problems of public order: Sudden changes in birthrate, often associated with war or depression, alter a society's age structure, with substantial future effects on the size of population at risk as offenders and victims.[22] These are examples, not an exhaustive list, of the kinds of episodic conditions which may stretch but ordinarily do not permanently alter the limits within which crime is defined, practiced, and policed in modern societies.

The most challenging questions have been left to last. First, what if processes of modernization reverse? Regions within countries can go into protracted decline, in fact can "deindustrialize." It has happened in some of the British Midlands and is happening now in parts of the northeastern United States. The cities which depend on industries which are declining decay as a consequence: Capital, jobs, the middle classes, and tax revenues emigrate to better places, with results that are typified in the United States by the decline of cities such as Newark, Philadelphia, Baltimore, Youngstown, and Cleveland. These cities are not dead—hundreds of thousands of people still live and work in them—but they are very different from the growing, optimistic cities in which modern criminal justice systems were forged. We have not much evidence yet about how urban decline, as a general process, affects the quality of public order and the workings of criminal justice systems. It is customary to think of decaying cities as cesspools of crime and deviance, but in fact contemporary rates of property crime are higher and growing more rapidly in cities such as Phoenix and San Jose than in the Newarks and Clevelands. In a mobile society enterprising thieves, like restless workers, move where the weather is good and the pickings are easy.[23] I suggest that we need a good deal of imaginative historical and contemporary research on the ways in which protracted economic decline and urban decay have affected crime and criminal justice in Western societies. We cannot (yet) study whole societies in which these conditions obtain, but there are examples enough of decaying towns and cities in the burnt-out heartlands of earlier phases of the Industrial Revolution.

Another aspect of "demodernization" is equally problematic and more difficult to pin down. Is there a selective or general erosion of humanitarian values in Western societies? If so, why and with what consequences? If our willingness to do violence to one another is a bellwether of dehumanization, as I think it is, then it is worrisome that serious crimes against the person have risen sharply in most Western societies during the last 20 years or so (some exceptions: Switzerland, Austria, Greece, and— culturally not part of the West—Japan). Elsewhere I have argued that the increase may be explained by the coincidence of three factors, not necessarily enduring ones: the explosion in the size of the youth population in the 1960s, the public legitimation of violence under the guise of both entertainment and politics, and the development of an alternative, hedonistic set of "postindustrial" values among many young people.[24] It might be worth looking for evidence of roughly comparable developments in historical settings, perhaps in the aftermath of the American Civil War or of World War I in continental Europe, to determine how such conditions work themselves out. The widespread increase in crime also has led to some erosion in support for humane policies of criminal justice, evidenced in the United States by a hesitant return to the death penalty (echoed by demands in some European countries for the same remedy) and by advocacy of better policing and more severe and certain sentencing of offenders. Though the *politics* of public order are changing under the impact of high crime rates, operating policies seem not to have changed much. Most Western societies have moved so far away from reliance on prison systems, for example, that courts must respond to a flood of new offenders by expanded use of noninstitutional alternatives. The somewhat paradoxical consequence of the general reluctance to invest more in prisons is that a larger proportion of offenders in a period of high crime avoid imprisonment than in the more orderly 1950s. Call it a hypothesis, one worth testing against hard evidence.

Finally, what if the processes of modernization have led to unresolvable contradictions in public order? As an example, consider the following evidence for a syndrome of paralysis in Western criminal justice systems. On the one hand there is a high and rising level of property crime in most of our societies, caused by the coincidence of increased motivation (aggressive individualism), opportunity (material prosperity), and low levels of deterrence (the nonpunitive character of most criminal justice policies).

For a somewhat different set of reasons, some of them episodic, crimes against the person also have increased, though they remain well below their historic levels in most places. On the other hand most Western criminal justice systems have characteristics that make it very difficult to do more than manage rising crime. Responsibility for criminal justice administration is divided among many agencies, each responsive to a variety of interested groups advocating quite different kinds of policies. There can be no powerful coordinated movement in any one direction because too many groups and interests are pulling in other directions. Moreover, one large range of alternatives, the resort to more consistent and severe sanctions, is foreclosed because it runs against prevailing humanitarian norms. This diagnosis seems to fit the contemporary American situation and also that of Britain; I am less certain about where else it applies. In any case it is not offered as a complete analysis, but as an example of how some kinds of historical processes, carried to their conclusions, may lead to painful dilemmas of public order for which there are no simple or obvious solutions.

CONCLUSION

In conclusion the reader is reminded that the macro-historical approach taken here is intended to identify the ways in which the processes of industrialization, urban growth, state expansion, and humanization have altered public order in Western societies during the last two centuries. The same processes that have shaped modern societies have set the main trends and patterns in the problems, policies, and institutions of public order. A lesser theme within this framework—"lesser" because I lacked space to develop it more fully—is the impact of fateful episodes of political, economic, and social change that have caused deviations from these trends in particular societies. The macro-approach is intended to complement and provide a general framework within which to interpret more narrowly focused historical inquiry, which treats such questions as the history and treatment of specific kinds of offense, the sources and effects of particular innovations in criminal justice policy, the development of police or prisons in a society, and so forth. These specific problems are the stuff of most historical analyses of crime and criminal justice, and most of the other contributions to this symposium.

NOTES

1. For a fuller discussion of the uses of history in the analysis of contemporary crime, see James A. Inciardi, Alan A. Block, and Lyle A. Hallowell, *Historical Approaches to Crime: Research Strategies and Issues* (Beverly Hills, CA: Sage, 1977), as well as the other contributions to this volume.

2. On Britain and Sweden see Ted Robert Gurr, Peter N. Grabosky, and Richard C. Hula, *The Politics of Crime and Conflict: A Comparative History of Four Cities* (Beverly Hills: Sage, 1977). On Imperial Germany see Vincent E. McHale and Eric A. Johnson, "Urbanization, Industrialization, and Crime in Imperial Germany: Parts 1 and 2," *Social Science History*, Vol. 1, (Fall 1976), 45-78, and (Winter 1977), 210-247.

3. Many trend and correlation studies show that from the eighteenth to the early twentieth centuries, property crime tended to increase during hard times. But for the 1920s onward, in both Britain and the United States the pattern is reversed: The greater the economic prosperity, the more property crime. For such findings about England see V.A.C. Gatrell and T. B. Hadden, "Criminal Statistics and their Interpretation," in *Nineteenth-Century Society*, edited by E. A. Wrigley (Cambridge, England: Cambridge University Press, 1972), 336-396. For Boston, see Theodore N. Ferdinand, "The Criminal Patterns of Boston Since 1849," *American Journal of Sociology*, Vol. 73 (July 1967), 688-698. A comparative study using national data for the United States, Canada, England and Wales, and Scotland is M. Harvey Brenner, "Effects of the Economy on Criminal Behavior and the Administration of Criminal Justice: A Multinational Study," paper presented to the Conference on Economic Crisis and Crime, United National Social Defence Research Institute, Rome, 1975. A study by Leroy C. Gould, "The Changing Structure of Property Crime in an Affluent Society," *Social Forces*, Vol. 48 (September 1969), 50-60, examines the relationship between the amount of property and the extent of theft in the United States and concludes that a negative-to-positive shift occurred in the mid-1940s.

4. Three studies which provide evidence on the themes of this paragraph are David H. Bayley, "The Police and Political Development in Europe," in *The Formation of National States in Western Europe*, edited by Charles Tilly (Princeton, NJ: Princeton University Press, 1975), 328-379; Gurr, Grabosky, and Hula, *op. cit.*, chap. VI.4; and Allan Silver, "The Demand for Order in Civil Society: A Review of Some Themes in the History of Urban Crime, Police, and Riot," in *The Police: Six Sociological Essays*, edited by David J. Bordua (New York: Wiley, 1967).

5. On the history of English vagrancy laws see William J. Chambliss, "A Sociological Analysis of the Law of Vagrancy," *Social Problems*, Vol. 12 (Summer 1964), 67-77. On the history of delinquency and attempts to control it, especially in the United States, see Anthony M. Platt, *The Child Savers: The Invention of Delinquency* (Chicago: University of Chicago Press, 1969). Evidence on the criminalization of deviant social conduct in Britain, Australia, and Sweden is given in Gurr, Grabosky, and Hula, *op. cit., passim* and summarized on pp. 688-692.

6. Abdul Q. Lodhi and Charles Tilly, "Urbanization, Crime, and Collective Violence in 19th-Century France," *American Journal of Sociology*, Vol. 79 (September 1973), 296-318.

7. Dane Archer et al., "Cities and Homicide: A New Look at an Old Paradox," *Comparative Studies in Sociology*, Vol. 1 (1978), 73-95.

8. Gurr, Grabosky, and Hula, *op. cit.*, chap. VI.1.

9. McHale and Johnson, *op. cit.*, 244.

10. Representative empirical studies of the growth in the public sector and its historical and contemporary determinants are B. Guy Peters and David Klingman, "Patterns of Expenditure Development in Sweden, Norway and Denmark," *British Journal of Political Science,* Vol. 7 (July 1977), 387-412, and David R. Cameron, "The Expansion of the Public Economy: A Comparative Analysis," *American Political Science Review,* Vol. 72 (December 1978), 1243-1261.

11. A general study of the institutional and political implications of the growth of the state is Gianfranco Poggi, *The Development of the Modern State: A Sociological Introduction* (Stanford, CA: Stanford University Press, 1978). Much historical evidence on the nationalization of criminal justice systems in Britain, Sweden, and Australia can be found in the case studies in Gurr, Grabosky, and Hula, *op. cit.* A comparative study of the national development of police in four European countries is Bayley, *op. cit.*

12. For an incisive study of how contemporary American institutions of criminal justice work, and do not work, see Charles E. Silverman, *Criminal Violence. Criminal Justice* (New York: Random House, 1978).

13. James Buchanan Given, *Society and Homicide in Thirteenth-Century England* (Stanford, CA: Stanford University Press, 1977).

14. On medieval versus modern attitudes toward violence see Given, *op. cit.*, chap. 1, and Norbert Elias, *The Civilizing Process: The History of Manners* (New York: Urizen, 1978, reprint of 1939 edition), 191-205. Some evidence about the moderating effect of Enlightenment thought on policies of criminal justice is reviewed in Gurr, Grabosky, and Hula, *op. cit.*, chap. VI.5.

15. Summarized in Ted Robert Gurr, "On the History of Violent Crime in Europe and America," in *Violence in America: Historical and Comparative Perspectives,* edited by Hugh Davis Graham and Ted Robert Gurr (Beverly Hills, CA: Sage Publications, 1979), 353-374.

16. Roger Lane, *Policing the City: Boston, 1822-1855* (Cambridge, MA: Harvard University Press, 1967). The incidence of homicide in Philadelphia in the nineteenth century also shows an erratic downward trend; see Roger Lane, *Violent Death in the City: Suicide, Accident, and Murder in 19th Century Philadelphia* (Cambridge, MA: Harvard University Press, 1979), chap. 4.

17. Gurr, Grabosky, and Hula, *op. cit.*

18. Lodhi and Tilly, *op. cit.*; McHale and Johnson, *op. cit.*

19. This is a summary of some of the main themes and findings about legal and criminal justice reform reported in Gurr, Grabosky, and Hula, *op. cit., passim* and especially chaps. VI.3 and VI.5. On the dismal history of prison reform in the United States see David J. Rothman, *The Discovery of the Asylum* (Boston: Little, Brown, 1971). Some indirect evidence about the contemporary impact of decriminalization of moral offenses is the steady decline in conviction rates for sexual and moral offenses in most Western societies during the last 20 years, as demonstrated in Ted Robert Gurr, "Crime Trends in Modern Democracies since 1945," *International Annals of Criminology,* Vol. 16 (Nos. 1 and 2, 1977), 41-86. The only exceptions to this decline are found in the English-speaking countries.

20. A comparative study of war's effects on homicide rates is Dane Archer and Rosemary Gartner, "Violent Acts and Violent Times: A Comparative Approach to Postwar Homicide Rates," *American Sociological Review,* Vol. 41 (December 1976), 937-963. Intensive case studies of World War I's impact on crime in Germanic Europe are F. Exner, *Krieg und Kriminalitaet in Oesterreich* (New Haven, CT: Yale Univer-

sity Press, 1927) and M. Liepmann, *Krieg und Kriminalitaet in Deutschland* (Stuttgart, Germany: Deutsche Verlags Anstalt, 1930).

21. A quantitative comparison of trends in Western crime rates since 1945 is Gurr, "Crime Trends in Modern Democracies since 1945." On Switzerland as a special case see Marshall Clinard, *Cities with Little Crime* (New York: Cambridge University Press, 1978).

22. Two studies of this phenomenon in the contemporary United States are Theodore N. Ferdinand, "Demographic Shifts and Criminality: An Inquiry," *British Journal of Criminology*, (April 1970), 169-175; and Wesley G. Skogan, "Crime in Contemporary America," in *Violence in America*, 375-392.

23. Examples of the literature on the decline of American cities are William C. Baer, "On the Death of Cities," *The Public Interest*, No. 54 (Fall 1976), 3-19; and Alexander Ganz and Thomas O'Brien, "The City: Sandbox, Reservation, or Dynamo?", *Public Policy* (Winter 1973), 107-123. The crime rates referred to in the text have been generated by the "Governmental Responses to Crime" project at Northwestern University, directed by Herbert Jacob and Robert L. Lineberry.

24. Gurr, "On the History of Violent Crime in Europe and America."

2

THE QUANTITATIVE HISTORICAL STUDY OF CRIME AND CRIMINAL JUSTICE

ERIC MONKKONEN

Counting is the major means of understanding crime and criminal justice in the past and of comprehending crime and criminal justice in the present as a part of the sweep of history. Whether historians, teachers, policy makers, social science researchers, investigators of precisely defined micro-processes or abstracted macro-processes, we all begin by conceptualization of categories and then ask, how many? how much? how many over time? across space? The next step in our inquiry is almost always to correlate the quantitative measures of two phenomena. Usually the two phenomena are related prior to the questioning by the conceptual framework, but that relationship, like the measurement, may be exceedingly vague. This is not a matter of concern at present, however. The point of which I wish to remind us is simple. Almost as soon as we begin to conceptualize about crime and the criminal justice system, questions of quantity come to the forefront.

This article descriptively and selectively surveys some of the typical work which has quantified crime and the criminal justice system in the past. It also prescriptively analyzes what should be done. Four sections follow: the first examines the range of statistical techniques which have been used to analyze historical data; the second evaluates sources, both for availability and reliability; the third looks at models, implicit and explicit, used in the research using historical data; and the fourth sketches the major areas needing more research and shows how differences in goals exert differing modes of analysis on historians and policy scientists. The paper has a two-part thesis. First, *statistical tools pose little problem to the quantitative historical researcher, but data collection does pose some problem, and model design and specification pose major problems.* The second, prescriptive part of the thesis argues that *the major focus of research should be toward the analysis and understanding of institutional behavior—the criminal justice system.* Given our data limitations and problematic models, the most useful approach for the next decade of research will be in understanding the behavior, roles, and relationships of organizations. At this point in our research, we need to know more about the processors than the processed.

ANALYTIC TECHNIQUES

The wide range of techniques used in the quantitative historical study of crime and criminal justice extends from the simplest possible counts, to percentaging, to bivariate analysis, and to multivariate techniques of some sophistication. On the other hand, it would be wrong to claim that the statistical techniques used thus far have been pushed to the limit of available skills; for example, many of the techniques analyzed in Greenberg's *Mathematical Criminology* as well as log-linear techniques, exploratory data analysis, and the various methods of analyzing categorical, multivariate models would have improved much of the existing work.[1]

Most typically, historical studies use precentages as their statistical tool. Usually, these studies analyze a set of records on individuals processed by one agency of the criminal justice system, percentaging the offenses as a part of the total sample of offenses, or percentaging social characteristics of the offender sample. Very often such elementary techniques are more than adequate for the job at hand. Michael Hindus's study of slave trials, for instance demonstrates this approach quite well.[2] In his study of slave crimes, which overturned the conventional arguments that slaves were relatively well-protected by the formal justice system, Hindus analyzed about a thousand crimes committed by free blacks and slaves in two counties of South Carolina between 1818 and 1860. His essential method was to percentage the distribution of offense types, trial outcomes, jury compositions, and some characteristics of the offenders—servile status and gender. He used these distributions to infer differences between social control of blacks and whites, to examine the quality of black justice and punishment. Not too surprisingly, Hindus found the quality of justice to be severe, erratic, and focused more on the protection of the slave system than on ameliorating the conditions of slave life. The importance of his analysis shows that rather simple analytic techniques, essentially tallying, when used with the right questions and records, can resolve historical confusion and contribute to our empirical understanding of the justice system. His study also suggests the possibility of further research. For example, the English historian Douglas Hay has argued that the legitimacy of the legal system in England depended on the equal enforcement of law.[3] Hindus makes clear that the law did not even approach equal enforcement in antebellum South Carolina, and that in fact the question of the rule of law was one argued by South Carolinians and visitors to the state. Other analyses of trial courts might well be a way to examine the day-to-day role of courts in preserving, or destroying, the legitimacy of a legal system, thus examining the questions so well studied by Hay for England.

In a sense, this is the substantive issue at the heart of an interesting debate between Lawrence Friedman, Robert Percival, and Richard Lempert which has occurred in the pages of the *Law and Society Review*.[4] While focused on civil courts as dispute settlers, and the decline or rise of this function between 1890 and 1970, both the argument and the methods could be equally or even better applied to criminal courts. Friedman and Percival originally argued that the role of the trial courts as a dispute settler declined as the court became more involved in routine administration. This conclusion came from an analysis of the mix of cases using simple percentages. Lempert's criticism of the article found an opposing conclusion using the same data: Lempert analyzed the mix but as rates based on population instead as a percentage of the total cases. Implicitly he argued that the analysis of the mix brought together two analytically different causal models, the one of the court as an actor and the other of the court as a responder to changed social conditions. Lempert also reported that he tried to reexamine Friedman and Percival's data with more sophisticated statistical tools, but without success.

More recently, Friedman has used a similar technique to analyze the trend in plea bargaining in Alameda County, California, 1880-1970.[5] In this study it appears Lempert's criticism will not obtain, for Friedman clearly focuses on the trial process, estimating the percentage of all outcomes which were the results of a plea negotiation. It is interesting to note that Friedman's study, one of four on the history of plea bargaining appearing in a special issue of *Law and Society Review* (Winter, 1979), is the only one using quantitative techniques—this in spite of the fact that all of the other authors wanted to make empirical statements concerning the presumed rise of plea bargaining. In the matter of plea bargaining, a rather simple empirical question must be answered before any further analysis takes place: What has been the historic trend in negotiated pleas? Until this question has been answered, debate on the subject, and even much of the analysis of the current situation, remains based on fairly groundless assumptions.

Two conclusions concerning method can be drawn from these articles. First, before even a description of the criminal justice process can begin, some simple counting must take place. As Friedman's article on plea bargaining and Hindus's on slave trials demonstrate, even tallies of court behavior can serve as the base for establishing an understanding of the precedents of our current criminal justice system. As Friedman observes, in reference to pleas, "the problems of criminal justice have deep roots, and reform will be difficult and slow."[6] The second methodological point to be drawn is somewhat more complex and demanding than the first. While percentages of the mix of a court's business are interesting, they are often only a preliminary step in analysis and description instead of a final outcome. Lempert quite correctly took apart Friedman's analysis. But often, more than a conversion of percentages to rates based on population must be done. Often description and analysis have implicit multivariate models, and if these are not specified and if the data are not analyzed with the relevant variables included, the outcome may well be spurious. For instance, Friedman found a rising rate of negotiated pleas, from which he inferred the subtle shift in the justice process. Yet this interpretation implicitly assumes that trials were initiated from equal beginnings over a century of court activity. Maybe prosecutors only carried through with more predictable cases. Maybe the negotiation process did not change, but the nature of the case coming to court did. A better analytic strategy might be to use logit analysis to predict the outcomes of cases, breaking down the time series into different periods. Such a procedure would at least suggest, on the court's side, if there were internally changed determinants of plea negotiation. For presumably, if the changed plea process did not come from changes external to the court, an adequately identified model of the internal process would pinpoint the locus of the rise of the negotiated plea. Such a model might have plea outcome predicted by offense type, offender characteristics, various prosecutional factors, cost estimates, court load measures, measures of plea levels in other nearby influential courts, and the like. The hypothesis that plea bargaining rose as a part of changed court procedures should find one or several powerful predictor variables changing over time. The null hypothesis, that pleas came from changed levels of defendant guilt, would be rejected if the model failed to account for any of the changed outcomes. This is not an outrageous demand, for the trial records contain enough information to make such a test possible—the sampling might not be perfect and the complete specification might have to be abandoned, but even with partial specification the results should be of interest. The outcome of a properly done analysis on changes in plea negotiation would also have policy implications, for Friedman's relatively simple analysis has policy implications—albeit negative ones. If all the determinants of the rise of negotiated pleas turn out to be historically irreversible, the reformers of the process have set themselves a stupendously difficult challenge.

Studies which percentage the mix or distribution of a single variable through time, such as Friedman's, are, of course, bivariate analyses, though we sometimes fail to conceive of them as such. More typically, we think of analyses beyond distributions as those which explicitly bring in control variables. Sometimes these control variables simply take apart a distribution, other times they bring in a control on an observed bivariate relationship. It is because Friedman's analysis of a mix over time did not proceed first by observing the mix, then controlling for time, that we properly do not conceive of his study as one with control variables.

One study which uses only percentages but which quite skillfully uses control variables to pry apart a complex set of relationships is Harvey J. Graff's analysis of the maxim put forth by nineteenth-century educators claiming illiteracy led to pauperism which, in turn, led to crime.[7] In a series of six tables, he shows for over 500 offenders the percent convicted by literacy controlling for ethnicity, occupation, gender, and offense. Graff concluded that inequality had a prior effect in determining both punishment and illiteracy and that educational reformers had confused a consequence of inequality with a cause of crime. For all of its interest, the Graff study remains inconclusive because of its failure to move beyond percentaging to genuine multivariate research. For unlike the studies which focus on the mix of outcomes of court behavior, Graff has chosen to grapple with the interaction of offender and court. While his bivariate tables with a third control variable represent a step in the right direction, it is clear that he needed a form of analysis which controlled for the simultaneous effects of ethnicity, gender, occupation, and offense type on punishment outcomes. As his analysis stands, we can only determine that these all were related—no more. His data would have allowed him to use a technique like multiple classification analysis, and the results would have undoubtedly been far more powerful and interesting.[8]

All of the relatively simple techniques discussed so far have been used on data gained with relatively high difficulty—original court dockets for Hindus and for Friedman and Percival and jail records for Graff.[9] One suspects that the time spent on data gathering precluded more sophisticated data analysis. Two studies done on European data and one on Canadian data which had been published for high levels of aggregation show the impressive statistical elegance possible when so much times does not have to be invested in archival work. (I might also point out that all three of these more sophisticated studies were multiply authored, suggesting that their methodological superiority came as a result of interdisciplinary work.) The earliest of these three studies, by Tilly and Lodhi, examined data for nineteenth-century France, posing a "structural" explanation for variation in "crime" rates, as measured by indictments ("persons accused of crimes").[10] Explicitly comparing the structural thesis to a "tension" thesis, they used path analysis to examine a model predicting, among other things, property crime, finding the proportion of a population dwelling in cities as the major explanatory variable over measures of urban change ("tension") and nonurban industrialization. Thus, they argued, the decrease in property crime over the nineteenth century came from changed structural conditions, not from change itself.

McHale and Johnson confronted the argument of Tilly and Lodhi, using an extended range of statistical techniques on conviction data from German administrative districts in the late nineteenth century.[11] Using rank order and Pearsonian correlations, multiple regression, path analysis, factor analysis, time series regressions, first difference lagged variables, and factor score coefficients, they challenged Tilly and Lodhi's finding that crime and political violence occurred in urban and industrial places, asserting the more complex argument that urbanizing places of low wealth had the high crime rates. And this developmental imbalance—the high urban growth preceding an increase in wealth or industrialization—created the social "tension" which led to high rates of crime. They argued that urban growth in an expanding economy slows crime, which locates in areas experiencing "high societal stress" rather than any particular structural characteristic.

The argument between these four scholars is quite important, both on substantive and methodological grounds. Which is it, after all, the social/economic structure or change—any kind of change—and ensuing "societal stress" which underlies the production of crime? Let me point out first that these two pieces of research do not as clearly confront one another as it first appears. McHale and Johnson's crime indicators are, at best, feeble measures of actual crime in society and their assumption that convictions measure anything but the outcomes of a criminal process puts their basic data into an unreliable position. Further, their model appears to have highly intercorrelated variables (wealth appears to be highly determined by percent urban), and a very strong probability of spatial autocorrelation.[12] Finally, the McHale and Johnson argument rests upon ecological assumptions which the argument of Tilly and Lodhi does not: McHale and Johnson say "societal stress" causes individuals to act in certain ways while Tilly and Lodhi say the structure shapes aggregate behavior. Thus, for all of its impressive array of techniques, McHale and Johnson's argument is not adequately examined, while given its assumptions, the Tilly and Lodhi argument is. And the exciting social argument between the two perspectives awaits an adequate research design with which to compare the two causal accounts.

A third, recent quantitative study of great sophistication by Blumstein et al. provides several instructive contrasts to the studies by Tilly and Lodhi and by McHale and Johnson.[13] This study, based essentially on a simple Canadian imprisonment series from 1880 to 1959, shows superior model specification and data analysis techniques more appropriate to the data and model. Parenthetically, I would add, the study conforms to the rule that the easier the data acquisition, the more elegant the models and data manipulations. Blumstein et al.'s models and analysis stay very close to the data, carefully excluding global and unmeasurable concepts such as "societal stress." First, they analyze the series using autoregressive models to estimate a second-order autoregression (with an R^2 of .79 for Canada). This done, they estimate the parameters of a second-order differential equation, against which they compare two models to account for the fluctuation in the prison population. The more satisfactory model emphasizes the reciprocal flows between three populations: prisoners, "law abiders," and "criminals"; its assumption being that a shift in the criminal and law abider populations perturbs the equilibrium of the justice system, which in turn produces the cyclical fluctuations in the prison population. The major conclusion which Blumstein et al. draw from their study is that the most effective control of the prison population is general deterrence, that is, reducing the number of people who move from the "law abider" to the "criminal" populations.

Rather than follow out the policy implications of their argument, I wish to examine the clear differences between their study and the previous examples. Any reader of these various studies will immediately realize that while all use historical data, the work of Blumstein et al. uses historical data to answer policy questions, while the others use historical data to answer questions of interest to historians and social theorists. All of the historical accounts use varying degrees of contextualist explanations—to differing extents each argument appeals to contexts of the phenomena under study.[14] Even when the intent of the authors is to make lawlike generalizations come only after an analysis of the contextual accounts of the phenomena. The disagreements focus on the proper specification of the contexts. Implicitly all agree that once accomplished, the true generalization can be expressed.

For Blumstein et al. there is no context. The Canadian imprisonment data are a time series only in the sense that they have a sequential, temporally ordered arrangement. While each unit of observation is a year, it could equally have been a month or day or decade. And no historian could resist noting the dramatic dips in the prison populations during World Wars I and II, and the equally dramatic burst in the population during the Great Depression. Further, it appears that their analysis assumes that no intended or unintended policy change affecting general deterrance occurred during the time period they selected to estimate their model. This seems a dubious assumption, and one which could probably be explicitly examined through the use of a proxy variable measuring some form of general deterrence which occurred during the time period they selected to estimate their model. But my suggestion is just the kind of contextualist suggestion one could expect from a historian, and in a sense it provides a measure of how far from a social scientific/policy analytic a historian is. There is, to be sure, a continuum of contextualism among historians, but few going much farther than McHale and Johnson toward abstracting from context.

Whether policy oriented or context oriented, none of the approaches discussed so far avoids opting at some point for vague, global concepts. Even Blumstein et al. must appeal to a Durkheimian notion of commitment to conformity, a concept meant to delineate the whole social/psychological/economic basis for social order. And their specification of this mechanism must be left at the same level of imprecision as McHale and Johnson's "societal stress" for similar reasons—incomplete understanding of society, a need to assert all else is equal, and an assumption that some aspects of human action are intuitively comprehensible.

SOURCES

There are several important points to be made about data sources for quantitative criminal justice history. Most of these points are noncontroversial but a few have been the subject of debate. (For the debate see my article and the reply to it by Harvey Graff.)[15] Before the specific detailing of sources, several observations must be made. First, as far as I am aware, there are no (even modestly) consistent indexes of criminal offenses which were not products of some formal action of the criminal justice system. As opposed to England, where data on offenses known to the police are available from the mid-nineteenth century onward, the United States has little or nothing to offer, in the nineteenth or early twentieth centures.[16] Thus the records used have been directly produced by the criminal justice system, and this fact must be taken into account in any analysis.

Second, aside from the limitation of data to that produced by the criminal justice system, a wide variety of data are available to researchers. However, unlike data for much contemporary phenomena, these data do not come on tape, ready to run. In fact, the data collection may prove to be the largest single portion of the historical researcher's time budget. Ideally, this constraint would not make any difference to the research, but it undoubtedly does. The wise researcher simply recognizes this constraint, tries for parsimony in data collection, making sure the questions are worthy of the collection effort.

Third, data collection activities must be particularly sensitive to consistency problems, which range from inconsistency in the various sources used to inconsistency within a single source. Some cities used different arrest categories for the same offense—disorderly conduct, breach of peace, and corner lounging, for instance. The researcher must keep, as a first principle, the consistency of the data set being created, so that while the data's precise relationship to a level of an actual phenomena might never be known, the variation will be consistently and relatively accurately monitored. Consistency is particularly important because certain standard adjustments often cannot be made. Offense rates cannot usually be age or gender controlled. Very often, the notion of population at risk can only be crudely estimated and not factored into the data in any precise way.

Fourth, the data typologies must be created with far more sensitivity than is usually the case with criminal justice-produced data. Some researchers have mechanically applied the seven Uniform Crime Report categories backward, with results that do not really produce the comparability such a procedure is theoretically designed to give.[17] On the other hand, some researchers have taken the opposite approach, using the common nineteenth-century typology of crimes against persons, property, and order.[18]

As mechanical in its own way as the approach which follows the Uniform Crime Report, these nineteenth-century categories fail to exploit the data to their potential. Still another group of researchers has created categories for their own purposes, more sensitively using the data for the research problem but with the unanticipated consequence of rendering the results noncomparable to other research. In spite of the comparability problem, I feel this is the best way to handle historical data, for it can make for greater consistency in aggregation, for categorization which confronts the bias in the production of the data, and for subtle insights into the indexed behavior.[19] For instance, in my research on urbanization and crime, the category of theft by trick enabled me to index a change in the kinds of offenses prosecuted in a growing or changing city, an insight no preconceived category would have produced.[20] On the other hand, my work with arrest data, which involved aggregation of over 20 cities across 60 years of change, required much broader categories.[21] Here, I opted for four simple categories which reflected the nature of the data production—total arrests, arrests which required police officer initiation, arrests initiated by victims, and homicide arrests. In no way perfect, these categories do avoid classificatory differences yet preserve indexes to different kinds of behavior. Yet they are flawed in their failure to index arrests for assaults, robberies, or burglaries.

The sources from which quantitative data can be created come in two forms, the original records or in some form of publication—what has come to be known as a "process-produced" data source. Most of the original sources can be found in agency, city, state, or historical archives. Some of these sources have been surveyed, notably the State of Massachusetts Superior Court Records Project, but most must be found by persistent inquiry.[22] When the original source is an agency which has some accountability to the state, such as a felony level court, then the sources have very often been preserved, and sometimes even microfilmed. Even the fact of publication, unfortunately, does not guarantee accessibility: for the location of the publication, changing or inconsistent agency parentage, and sheer attrition of old, unappealing, annual reports often make the location of published data sources as difficult as that of unpublished sources.[23]

Original sources for quantitative data range from arrest blotters to felony court records. Though idiosyncratically preserved and difficult to locate systematically, arrest blotters spread a wide, local net for criminal justice data. Often rich in individual level information on the petty offender, these blotters allow an almost ethnographic description of urban crime. The work of John Schnieder demonstrates the potential of these records, for he has used them to describe the nature and locational basis of the mid-nineteenth century "bachelor subculture" of Detroit, showing how the spatial differentiation of the city increased both the visibility and liability for arrest of this subgroup.[24] Jail intake records can provide a more selective but still useful sample of the offender population. Like the arrest blotters, this information source is often rich in data on individuals, allowing researchers like Graff to examine questions about literacy, for instance.[25] A third kind of local record, that from the mayor's or police or municipal courts, has potential for data on petty individual offenders. These records, like arrest blotters and jail intake records, seem to have been preserved with great inconsistency, and thus far have fueled only the most rudimentary quantitative studies.[26]

Sources of agencies dealing with somewhat more serious matters have been preserved more regularly and for this reason offer the potential of more systematic research. Roger Lane has shown, for instance, how the records of the coroner's office can be used to establish a series of actual incidence of homicides: Moreover, the series is filled with detail on the circumstances of the individual cases so more than rates can be established.[27] Felony-level court records provide an equally systematic and useful set of primary sources. My work using the criminal court of Franklin County, Ohio, established both time series as well as detailed analyses of court behavior. When linked with information on defendants from other primary sources, the minimal information of the dockets can be expanded to a study of the offenders. Experience with fuller files suggests that they do not provide a good sample of the docketed offenses, but they do provide much greater detail on the circumstances of the offense and the subsequent adjudication.[28] Lawrence Friedman's ongoing research on court behavior in California shows another important, systematic way of using felony level court records.[29] Jumping into a historical argument about the origin and increase in plea bargaining, Friedman provides the only actual empirical research to show how plea bargaining was indeed a part of the court's activities in the 1880s, and in addition demonstrates the manner in which the practice both increased and changed in the past 90 years. Given the amount of current research and significance for court policy that the discussion of the negotiated plea has generated, Friedman's work comes as a breath of good sense. And, as he suggests, that because the modern criminal justice apparatus, not crowded courts, have produced the negotiated plea, the policy implication is that any change in the plea process will be made only with great difficulty.

In contrast to original sources, the published sources do not always allow the researcher to ask as precise or as individual-oriented questions as do data from original sources. But the published, process-produced data have the virtue of consistency, both in simple terms of availability as well as in regularity of production. As a result, one could not reproduce Friedman's plea bargaining results, which depended on an analysis of changed pleas and pleas to lesser charges, but one could examine data for many places and at many points in time. Heumann's study of trials to total dispositions ratio, a surrogate measure for clear cases of plea bargaining, based on annually published court data for Connecticut, 1880-1954, loses the detail of Friedman's study, but gains considerably in scope.[30] Heumann finds a much less dramatic increase in his plea bargaining indicator than did Friedman. Is this simply because of different and more accurate measurement on Friedman's part or greater scope—one state instead of one county—on Heumann's part or regional, developmental differences? Or are the discrepancies methodological—the analysis of case mix rather than population-based rates? In any case, each study illustrates the strengths and weaknesses of original and published sources.

The simplest resolution to the substantive problem, of course, would be a study which utilized both sets of sources, examining broad, state-wide or even multistate trends, then narrowing in for a more detailed examination of representative counties. For Friedman, this would tell us just how representative Alameda County is of California; and for Heumann, we would learn if his crude measure has validity when compared to a more local analysis of actual plea bargaining. This suggestion also implies a methodological strategy—when possible, use more than one source. Not only does this strategy help locate a case study but it also validates a more broad study. In my study of Columbus, Ohio, I did just this, using both the criminal court original records and the state published summaries as well. Studies based on court records lend themselves to this particularly well, and to ignore the one source for the other is to avoid a good opportunity for a kind of reliability testing.

Other forms of data are also available as published records. Annual city reports gave a vast wealth of jail and police data.[31] The federal censuses for 1880 and 1890 had separate enumerations of imprisoned populations.[32] In general, one can assume that if a public agency had a criminal justice activity which cost an annual operating fee, then some form of accounting appeared annually, which may become the source of a data set.

MODELS

Compared to the models employed in quantitative historical research, the data sources and statistical techniques are relatively trouble free. The models tend to be vague, poorly specified, contradictory, confused, and far too grand for the actual research usually undertaken. This is due in part to the data under examination—after all, if one has clear evidence that human society is becoming more/less perfect, why bother to quibble over details?

Five grand models have informed the research: the evolutionary perfectability scheme, the modernization hypothesis, the urbanization thesis, the industrialization thesis, and the community to society thesis (Tonnies' familiar *gemeinschaft* to *gessellschaft* notion). Including the work of Blumstein et al., there are two, somewhat less grand models: the first is the more concise social control model and the second is a version of Durkheim—the constancy of punishment (rather than crime) thesis.

The first model of evolutionary perfectability (what Robert Berkhofer has called the Portestant progress myth) either believes or denies the notion that since the Renaissance, Western society has moved toward greater perfection.[33] Using some measure of the incidence of crime, holders or critics of this model read the crime index as a measure of social imperfection—the less crime, the better the society. Hobbs's classic study posed the null hypothesis: Has society "broken down" and criminality increased?[34] The answer for Philadelphia between 1790-1800 and 1937 was that crime had not increased and therefore society had not "broken down." One of the implications of Hobbs's study is that when confronted with crime data for contrasting societies—either the same society over time or different societies across space—it may be impossible to resist the urge to use crime as an index of social or moral health. Whether our interests are as policy makers or simply in understanding society, the intrinsic interest of historical data tends to pull us into the whirlpool of comparative social morality.

Progress, of course, is not an acceptable model any more, reminiscent as it is of Social Darwinism. Instead we now use the modernization model.

This model of social and economic change certainly informs more historical criminal justice research than any other one model. Further, it can subsume the urbanization, industrialization, decline of community, and even social control models. One of the clearest exemplars of this model may be seen in the work of Howard Zehr, whose study of criminal prosecution and trial rates in nineteenth-century France and Germany explicitly addresses the modernization issue.[35] Crimes of theft, he found, were higher in the cities than in the rural areas and also tended to rise over time. Crimes of personal violence, on the other hand, were associated with the traditions of particular locales or to eras of social transition. Thus, he concluded that in the modernization of Germany and France, crimes of theft were affected by the modern property relations, but crimes of interpersonal violence were not so affected. However, it is not at all clear what the modernization model predicts once a modern state has been achieved, and one wonders what the model implies for twentieth-century France and Germany. And more specific to Zehr's study, one wonders if controlling rates of theft for the amount of portable personal property and for the more accessible and pervasive criminal justice apparatus would alter the relationships he found. Further, the use of prosecution and trial rates as an index of actual crime in a sense contradicts one of the premises of modernization. We would expect that modernization to affect first the law enforcement apparatus itself. Consequently, the apparatus would act on the values of the modernizing society, thus emphasizing and rationalizing property relations far in advance of the penetration of these modern values through the whole society. I expect that the clear modernization of crime which Zehr found would disappear in a properly specified multivariate analysis, and a much more complex, less intuitive set of relationships would emerge. On the other hand, the modernization model (1) represents an improvement over the progress model, for it is more specific, (2) gives some guidance to the kinds of relationships to examine, (3) suggests a typology of crime which accords with nineteenth-century perceptions of crime, and (4) moves crime from the concept of a moral state to something which is tempered and shaped by social structure.

In certain ways the modernization model is superior to the urbanization model, even though urbanization is one aspect of modernization. Quite simply, the modernization model gives reasons to examine different kinds of criminal and bureaucratic behavior, while in its most common form the urbanization model asserts that urbanization causes anomie which in turn causes crime. This is a more specific version of the "break down of society" hypothesis tested by Hobbs. Testing the urbanization hypothesis in my study of Columbus, I found that rural people were as likely to become offenders as were urban people. As Lane has pointed out that Columbus was not a very large city, and my test did not include petty offenders,[36] we can presume a more adequate examination of this hypothesis would look at all offenders in a metropolis like New York, with a comparison examination of a rural place. However, Lane's own work rejects the urbanization hypothesis even more than mine does, so we might more sensibly wait for a study which resurrects the urbanization-causes-crime hypothesis.[37]

Like urbanization, industrialization has also been considered a component of modernization. Also like urbanization, it has been examined separately, as a mechanism deleterious both in its consequences of rigidity and destructiveness of organic society and also as a part of the rise of the bourgeoisie and the creation of modern class relations. In my study of Columbus, I found that, throughout the state of Ohio, industrialism—measured both by employment and value added by manufacturing—had little relationship to crime, as measured by court activity. Lane recently has gone further than this, finding that in Philadelphia industrial growth contributed to a decline in homicide.[38] He argues that the discipline of industrial occupations, the regularity of employment (compared to craft employment), and the growth of supervised work provided a new degree of social order both on and off the job. An analysis similar to Lane's informed the work of Hackney on homicide and suicide in the North and the South.[39] Hackney argued that the values of industrial society become internalized, resulting in less personal disputing and more self-blame, guilt, and suicide. While the validity of Hackney's empirical results has been disputed, the basic notion of his work still seems to have support.[40]

A model implicit in the urbanization-causes-crime thesis is also its obverse—this is the notion that the decline of community and rise of mass society caused a rise in crime. While the urbanization thesis focuses on anomie, the decline of community model instead concentrates on the decline of informal social control, the decreasing importance of face-to-face relationships, the disappearance of consensual standards of behavior, a failure of cooperation, and a general disappearance of an organic sense of community. As intervening variables these are all difficult to operationalize and measure, so studies using such models usually discuss crime in a time and place where there is some agreement among historians that community did go through a decline. Greenberg's book on the colony of New York exemplifies studies of this genre.[41] His analysis of the eighteenth century has clearly set upon a time when most historians would agree that community cohesiveness declined. His bringing together of the existing court records allows him to infer that crime rose and court effectiveness dropped. While most historians seem to question the validity of his findings (Lane, 1980), Greenberg's work shows clearly how the decline of community model accounts neatly, if vaguely, for a rise in crime. Like the modernization model, this model lacks measurable definition and thus tends to be tautological—if crime did not rise, then one would infer that community, in fact, did not decline.

The sixth and seventh models—social control and neo-Durkheimian "constancy of punishment"—are less global than the previous five models. The social control model fits within several larger perspectives, ranging from Marxian to some versions of modernization. It focuses first on the criminal justice system and analyzes its activities as part of a society's formal control efforts. Hindus's study of slave trials, discussed above, demonstrates this model's use at its best, for in this study Hindus first examined the court's criminal prosecutions in order to discover how a society controls slaves.[42] This does not mean he abandoned the notion of slave criminality; in essence, that variation for which the court's control policy did not account became variation Hindus attributed to slaves. Thus the social control perspective ultimately tells us about the controlled as much as the controllers. My study of police behavior begins with a similar perspective, using a time series analysis of arrest rates to understand policing.[43] Only after the police-produced component of the arrest variation has been accounted for does it move on to a discussion of other reasons for arrest rate variation. And the Levett study of the growth of policing takes a similar model of arrest data, although unlike Hindus's and my work he comes to very different conclusions, mainly attributing the variation he found to increased efforts at consciously coercive social control in industrial cities.[44] But whatever the substantive outcome, the social control model is less tautological and usually points to a far more sensitive analysis of the data than do the more global, tautological models.

The neo-Durkheimian model Blumstein used must be considered one of the more precise cases of logical model building and testing in quantitative historical criminal justice research. Comparing their favored model to another model, these researchers derived the logical consequences of each model and used simulation techniques to see how each model matched the behavior of their time series on Canadian imprisonment. The care and development of the study make it exemplary, but in some senses it is a disappointment in its very ahistoricity. In a sense, their model is only applicable in periods when no historical change has occurred, and what we want, after all, is a model which accounts for change. Presumably, the Blumstein et al. model would identify periods of change; that is, for variations which it could not predict, we would know that a genuine period of change had been identified. And then the analysis of this period of change, delineated by the model of constant punishment, would come under a more careful scrutiny, although with what models of change it is not clear.

And this leaves us at the point where many historians shove aside the vexing problems of models and do empirical research in the sources. The most precise models cannot account for elemental change; the most global and vague models account for all change, even though they cannot identify it.

RESEARCH OPPORTUNITIES

The research opportunities in quantitative criminal justice history are at a high point, for several reasons. There have been enough studies completed in the past decade to alert researchers to the possibilities and problems; major sources have been identified; the substantive questions have demonstrably far-ranging implications; interest in the work is high in many disciplines; and policy-oriented research has developed a very useful source of measures, models, and techniques to be applied to historical data. But all of this work has only scratched the surface, encouraging speculative conclusions and refutable arguments. Thus, the call is not for more research of the same kind, but for more research which builds and moves beyond what has been accomplished. And although most of the research thus far has been interdisciplinary, work in the future needs to be even more so, using more clearly specified and derived models, more appropriate statistical techniques, and exploiting sources both in greater depth and breadth.

The most important reason to pursue work in the subject further lies in the kind of interaction it examines, the relationship among individuals, society, and bureaucracies. It is here that we get into one of the most exciting and problematic aspects of the study of society and history. Do bureaucracies make differences in their social actions? How? Are these differences the same for individuals as for society as a whole? If not, then in what ways do the responses differ? And how do the pressures and demands of individuals get turned into social demands to which bureaucracies respond? Certainly, these kinds of questions lie behind the analysis of criminal behavior and attempts to control criminal behavior.

Within this broader context, the list of specific research questions seems quite large. Rather than enumerating those which I have already covered, let me add a few more questions which seem to have been relatively neglected. How has the development and behavior of criminal justice institutions related to the growth and structuring of other institutions? One might relate, for instance, the structure of the police to fire departments, to other city governmental bureaucracies and, for instance, to business structures.[45] What kind of difference did the introduction of different criminal justice organizations have on criminal behavior? On noncriminal behavior? Why did rural policing develop when it did, and did it make any difference in anything? What have been the systematic relationships between the various bureaucracies of the criminal justice system? How do political differences affect the behavior of criminal justice bureaucracies? (The comparative possibilities between Canada and the United States seem to be particularly appropriate for study, especially for places like Windsor and Detroit.) The "behavior of law," as defined by Black, has yet to be examined historically.[46] What has been the relationship between arrests and jail and prison capacities over time? All of these questions will require a substantial research investment, but all should yield results of importance and interest to a scholarly community extending across history, criminology, and the policy sciences.

This is not to imply that there are no differences between historians and social scientists who have policy decisions as an omnipresent consideration in their work.[47] The understanding of these differences should facilitate communication as the two are not mutually exclusive. Historians do their work because, ultimately, they want to understand society and the individual within it; policy makers share this goal only to the degree that they wish to control society. To this end, policy scientists use causal models while historians tend to use "reflexive contextualism"—that is, they look at the context for explanation—but with the constant consideration of their own context as a bias-producing source.[48] As a result of this methodological difference, historians produce causal accounts, while policy scientists produce accurate predictions. Therefore, historians usually read a multiple regression equation as a hypothesis test, while policy scientists look at the same equation's coefficients with an eye toward the future. These differences should not be allowed to impede the quantitative study of criminal justice in the past, but they should make the borrowers of models, data, and explanations self-conscious and reflexive.

And if the various scholars located within different disciplines can borrow self-consciously and reflexively, the work of each discipline will be the richer and more valuable for it.

NOTES

1. David F. Greenberg, *Mathematical Criminology* (New Brunswick, NJ, 1979).

2. Michael S. Hindus, "Black Justice Under White Law: Criminal Prosecutions of Blacks in Antebellum South Carolina," *Journal of American History* 63 (December 1976), 575-599.

3. Douglas Hay, "Property, Authority and the Criminal Law," in Hay et al., eds., *Albion's Fatal Tree: Crime and Society in Eighteenth-Century England* (New York, 1975), 17-64.

4. Lawrence M. Friedman and Robert Percival, "A Tale of Two Courts: Litigation in Alameda and San Benito Counties," *Lawand Society Review* 10 (Winter 1976), 267-301; Richard Lempert, "More Tales of Two Courts: Exploring Changes in the 'Dispute Settlement Function' of Trial Courts," *Law and Society Review* 12 (Fall 1978), 91-138.

5. Lawrence M. Friedman, "Plea Bargaining in Historical Perspective," *Law and Society Review* 13 (Winter 1979), 247-259.

6. Friedman, "Plea Bargaining . . . ," 258.

7. Harvey J. Graff, " 'Pauperism, Misery, and Vice': Illiteracy and Criminality in the Nineteenth Century," *Journal of Social History* 11 (Winter 1977), 246-268.

8. See Richard Jensen, "New Presses for Old Grapes: I: Multiple Classification Analysis," *Historical Methods* 11 (Fall 1978), 174-176.

9. Michael S. Hindus, "Prison and Plantation: Criminal Justice in Nineteenth-Century Massachusetts and South Carolina" (unpublished Ph.D. dissertation, University of California, Berkeley, 1975); Friedman and Percival, "A Tale of Two Courts," and Graff, " 'Pauperism.' "

10. Charles Tilly and Abdul Q. Lodhi, "Urbanization, Crime and Collective Violence in Nineteenth Century France," *American Journal of Sociology* 79 (September 1973), 296-318.

11. Vincent McHale and Eric A. Johnson, "Urbanization, Industrialization and Crime in Imperial Germany," *Social Science History* 1 (Fall 1977) 55-78; (Winter 1977), 210-247.

12. See Colin Loftin and Robert H. Hill, "Regional Subculture and Homicide: An Examination of the Gastil-Hackney Thesis," *American Sociological Review* 40 (October 1974), 714-724.

13. Alfred Blumstein, Jacqueline Cohen, and Daniel Nagin, "The Dynamics of a Homeostatic Punishment Process," *Journal of Criminal Law and Criminology* 67 (September 1976), 317-334.

14. Robert F. Berkhofer, Jr., "The Ironies of Contemporary Historical Understanding: Social Theory, Reflexivism, and Metahistory," paper presented at Hobart and William Smith Colleges (December 9, 1978).

15. Eric H. Monkkonen, "Systematic Criminal Justice History: Some Suggestions," *Journal of Interdisciplinary History* 9 (Winter 1979), 451-464; and Harvey J. Graff, "Reply," *Journal of Interdisciplinary History* 9 (Winter 1979), 465-471.

16. V.A.C. Gatrell and T. B. Hadden, "Criminal Statistics and Their Interpretation," in A. E. Wrigley, ed., *Nineteenth Century Society* (Cambridge, England, 1972), 336-396.

17. Theodore N. Ferdinand, "The Criminal Patterns of Boston since 1849," *American Journal of Sociology* 73 (July 1967), 317-334.

18. Hindus, "Prison and Plantation."

19. Eric H. Monkkonen, *The Dangerous Class: Crime and Poverty in Columbus, Ohio, 1860-1885* (Cambridge, 1975); *Hands Up: Police in Urban America, 1860-1920* (New York, 1980).

20. Monkkonen, *Dangerous Class.*

21. Monkkonen, *Hands Up.*

22. Michael S. Hindus, *Massachusetts Superior Court Survey* (Boston, 1978).

23. Eric H. Monkkonen, "Municipal Reports as an Indicator Source: The Nineteenth Century Police," *Historical Methods* 12 (Spring 1979), 57-65.

24. John C. Schneider, "Public Order and the Geography of the City: Crime, Violence, and the Police in Detroit, 1845-1875," *Journal of Urban History* 4 (February 1978), 183-208.

25. Graff, " 'Pauperism.' "

26. Arthur Hobbs, "Criminality in Philadelphia, 1790-1800 compared to 1937," *American Sociological Review* 8 (February 1943), 198-202.

27. Roger Lane, *Violent Death in the City: Suicide, Accident, and Murder in Nineteenth-Century Philadelphia* (Cambridge, 1979).

28. Monkkonen, *Dangerous Class.*

29. Friedman, "Plea Bargaining."

30. Milton Huemann, "A Note on Plea Bargaining and Case Pressure," *Law and Society Review* 9 (September 1975), 515-528.

31. Monkkonen, "Municipal Reports."

32. U.S. Bureau of the Census, *Report on the Defective, Dependent, and Delinquent Classes, 10th Census, 1880* (Washington, DC: 1888); *Report on Crime, Pauperism, and Benevolence, 11th Census, 1890* (Washington, DC: 1895).

33. Berkhofer, "Ironies." For a model relevant to the criminal justice context, see Robert F. Berkhofer, Jr., "The Organizational Interpretation of American History: A New Synthesis," *Prospects* 4 (1979), 611-630.

34. Hobbs, "Criminality."

35. Howard Zehr, "Modernization of Crime in Germany and France, 1830-1913," *Journal of Social History* 8 (Summer 1975), 117-141.

36. Roger Lane, "Can You Count on the Down and Out to Stay Down for the Count in Columbus," *Reviews in American History* 4 (June 1976), 212-217.

37. Roger Lane, "Urbanization and Criminal Violence in the Nineteenth Century: Massachusetts as a Test Case," *Journal of Social History* 2 (Winter 1968), 156-163; Lane, *Violent Death.*

38. Lane, *Violent Death.*

39. Sheldon Hackney, "Southern Violence," in Ted R. Gurr and Hugh Graham, eds., *Violence in America: Historical and Comparative Perspectives* (New York, 1969), 479-500.

40. Loftin and Hill, "Regional Subculture."

41. Douglas Greenberg, *Crime and Law Enforcement in the Colony of New York, 1691-1776* (Ithaca, NY, 1976).

42. Hindus, "Black Justice."

43. Monkkonen, *Hands Up.*

44. Allan E. Levett, "Centralization of City Police in the Nineteenth Century United States" (Unpublished Ph.D. dissertation, Universtiy of Michigan, 1975).

45. Richard B. Calhoun, "New York City Fire Department Modernization, 1865-1870: A Civil War Legacy," *New-York Historical Society Quarterly* 60 (January/April 1976), 7-34.

46. Donald J. Black, *The Behavior of Law* (New York, 1976).

47. Thomas B. Alexander and Daniel L. Yarwood, "History and Policy Studies," *Policy Studies Journal* 7 (Summer 1979), 803-810; Gerald N. Grob, "Reflections on the History of Social Policy in America," *Reviews in American History* 7 (September 1979), 293-306.

48. Berkhofer, "Ironies."

HISTORICAL ANALYSES OF CRIME

3

ILLEGAL ENTERPRISE:
HISTORICAL PERSPECTIVES
AND PUBLIC POLICY

MARK H. HALLER

There is a range of criminal activities that might best be called "illegal enterprise." Such activities involve the sale of illegal goods or services to customers who are aware that the transaction is illegal. Examples of the illegal sale of goods include the distribution of various narcotics and, during the 1920s, the bootlegging of liquor. Illegal services have included prostitution, various types of gambling, and loansharking. There are, of course, many other types of goods and services that have found illegal markets. In much of the writing on crime, the persons engaged in servicing illegal markets have been said to be involved in "organized crime," but that term has limited usefulness and will not be used here.[1]

An advantage of thinking of these crimes as illegal enterprises is that such a term focuses on them as a retail business. Those engaged in such activities are criminal entrepreneurs, with many of the problems faced by legitimate businessmen. In order to understand such activities, then, it is necessary to ask the same sorts of questions that would be asked concerning any other retail business activity. How are the entrepreneurs recruited and how do they obtain capital? How do they train and pay their staffs?

How do they advertise? How are prices set? What groups constitute the customers? What economic and noneconomic factors explain decisions concerning location of the enterprise? There is, however, an important additional question: What difference does it make that the enterprise is illegal? How do the fact of illegality and the policies of law enforcement affect recruitment, pricing, advertising, location, and customers?

Because the historian is centrally concerned with explaining change, history is a useful discipline for exploring such questions. To the extent that changes in illegal enterprises have resulted from changes in law or law enforcement policies, historical studies will involve an understanding of the interaction between law and illegal markets. It often happens, however, that factors relatively independent of law enforcement have had greater affects on the markets. These factors can include technological innovations: the impact of the telephone on sports betting or prostitution, for instance. Other factors might include changes in public attitudes and mores: the impact of changing sexual mores on prostitution or pornography. Still others include the rise (or decline) of major institutions in American society: Think, for instance, of the impact of the development of professional sports upon American betting habits. To the extent that factors independent of law enforcement altered illegal markets, the historian would be exploring the limitations of law enforcement as a means for controlling illegal markets.

At any rate, for over a decade, I have been centrally concerned with the attempt to understand the role of illegal enterprise in American urban society since the Civil War. My methodology, if it can be called such, has been the eclectic one of the historian: to seek out a variety of sources, whether stories by investigative reporters, reports by government committees and commissions, files of prosecutors and official investigative agencies, reports by "reform" organizations, or the autobiographies of criminal entrepreneurs. I have brought to the sources two kinds of questions. First, I have tried to take the criminal activities seriously as businesses and to understand criminals as businessmen. Second, I have attempted to locate urban crime within the social history of American cities. This has involved a search for the relationships of crime to political organizations, to police, to ethnic communities, to urban entertainment, to sports, and to the changing geography of American cities. The history of crime, in short, is not only important in itself but is also important as a means for illuminating the nature of American society.

In general, my stance as a historian has always been that my goal is to understand the past, not to explain how the past might provide guidance for official policy. This article does, however, provide an occasion to play with the notion that historians might have some understandings that have relevance to policy analysis.

LAW AND MORALITY

One simple lesson of history, it is sometimes assumed, is that criminal law has little impact upon behavior. It is almost axiomatic, in fact, that the failure of prohibition in the 1920s demonstrated that the state cannot legislate morality. But this supposed lesson needs further examination, for the lessons of the 1920s are more ambiguous than that. It is well to remember that the antiprohibitionists won the propaganda battle of the 1920s and secured the repeal of prohibition. Since then, we have generally perceived prohibition and prohibitionists through the eyes of their enemies. By most measures, prohibition, especially in its early years, did alter behavior and achieve key goals of antialcohol reformers: a reduction in deaths from cirrhosis of the liver, a decline in hospitalization for alcoholism, and improved work place attendance on Mondays. According to a recent study by David E. Kyvig, in fact, a comparison of per capita alcohol consumption in 1911-1915, before national prohibition, with per capita consumption in 1935, following repeal, indicates that Americans drank only 40% as much at the later date. While there may have been some unintended results of prohibition, such as a growing popularity of cocktails (once regarded as effete) or a possible increase in college student drinking, nevertheless the substantial decline in overall drinking during the period suggests that the law contributed to a significant alteration in American drinking habits.[2]

Changes in law or law enforcement have, in fact, frequently contributed, along with other factors, to substantial changes in the structure or availability of certain illegal enterprises. From 1907 to 1917, most American cities closed their wide-open redlight districts; and, while some districts made a comeback after World War I, gradually the old-time parlor houses, once the mainstay of prostitution, have joined the blacksmith and iceman in the dustbin of history. The federal Harrison Narcotics Act of 1914, following on the heels of similar state laws, accompanied the decline of the widespread middle-class use of opiates that had characterized the late nineteenth century. Thus, the critical set of questions becomes: What types of illegal markets are most vulnerable to criminal law and what kinds of illegal markets are less responsive to a law enforcement strategy?

An example is the old-time parlor house at the turn of the century. The parlor house was operated by an entrepreneur, normally called a madam or landlady. She took responsibility for hiring the staff, including the "sporting women" (who serviced the customers), the cooks and maids, and the entertainers, if any. (A fine parlor house might have a small jazz band and even a middle-class house might have a "perfessor" who played the piano.) The madam also furnished the house, greeted the customers, and arranged for referral of customers through taxi drivers, bell hops, bartenders, and others. She was responsible for necessary dealings with local politicians and with the police. The standard economic arrangement was that the madam and the prostitute split the customer's fee on a 50:50 basis. There were variations from city to city concerning whether additional charges might be levied on the prostitute, such as a fee for regular medical examination, for political or police protection, or for meals.[3]

Despite the split with the madam, the parlor house was often a desirable place to work because the efficiencies of the house made it possible for sporting women to earn more than if they worked independently. Those who solicited customers on the streets or in bars faced a problem of wasted time—the time involved in seeking customers, negotiating price, going to the place where the service would be performed, and then returning to seek another customer. In a successful parlor house, on the other hand, customers lined up and a sporting woman could service many customers without a loss of time. But, in order to enjoy these efficiencies, the madam had to invest money in a building, furniture, and the hiring of a staff. The house had to have a known location to which customers could come. Because parlor houses combined economic efficiency with vulnerability to law enforcement, they were the standard system for providing prostitution when the redlight districts were tolerated, but have now almost completely vanished from American cities in an era when the tolerance of police cannot be depended upon.

The special vulnerability of economic activities that require substantial prior investment can be seen in one of the unintended consequences of the campaign against illegal gambling in the early twentieth century—namely, the closing of legal horse tracks. After the Civil War, particularly as a result of a railroad system that made it possible to carry horses from city to city, there developed a national racing circuit. At the new tracks built around the major cities, racing fans flocked to the grounds to bet on their favorite nags and watch the races. By the 1890s, horse racing achieved its golden age in America—easily the most popular sport.[4]

Yet, although horse racing was the most popular of the newly emerging professional sports, its financing depended upon illegal gambling. At the tracks, bookmakers paid $100 per day each for the privilege of making book at the track. Fifty bookmakers, with their sheetwriters and other helpers, might set up at a major track. Western Union also paid a fee to the tracks for the privilege of telegraphing the results to subscribers, chiefly off-track bookmakers. And spectators, eager to back their favorites and cheer them on, paid admission to the tracks. Enforcement of the gambling laws would undercut the financial viability of horse racing.[5]

That is, in fact, what happened. Beginning in New Jersey in the mid-1890s and in other cities and states, especially after 1903, an anti-gambling campaign spread across the nation. Given the entrenched nature of urban gambling, the campaign had only minimal effectiveness. But a generally unintended consequence was that horse racing largely ceased in the United States. Even the threat that gambling laws *might* be enforced at the tracks was sufficient to incline track owners to cancel their seasons. Much money would have to be committed to prepare the tracks, hire the staff, and guarantee the purses for the races; such money could not be committed unless there was a near certainty that opportunities to bet would be available. Horse racing, although legal, was vulnerable to enforcement aimed at gambling, while many forms of gambling, although illegal, were less vulnerable.

During the 15 years preceding World War I, some 95 tracks closed in the United States. By the end of the period, racing continued only in Colorado, Nevada, Maryland, Kentucky, Louisiana, and (sporadically) in New York. In the decades after World War I, racing made a comeback only by adopting an entirely different system of betting. The tracks functioned with legalized parimutuel betting (thus largely eliminating bookmakers at the tracks), and in return accepted state regulation and the state's claim on a substantial portion of the tracks' income from betting. The structure of the nation's most popular professional sport was altered greatly by enforcement policies aimed at gambling.[6]

GAMBLING SYNDICATES

Although law enforcement policies can affect many illegal enterprises, it seems clear that public officials have often too narrowly defined illegal markets as problems to be dealt with by the criminal justice system and have seldom been willing to consider such activities as problems that might be dealt with, in whole or in part, by policies other than criminal law enforcement.

A particularly intractable problem has been gambling in American cities. Gambling has undergone great changes in the past 75 years, but these changes have been only minimally understood because of a narrowly law enforcement perspective. Take, for instance, the structure of gambling syndicates in American cities by the turn of the century. By 1900 both policy gambling and off-track bookmaking had become syndicated, backed by relatively wealthy gambling entrepreneurs who made arrangements with agents to take bets on a commission basis. First to become syndicated was policy gambling, a forerunner of modern numbers gambling. Policy was played with numbers from 1 to 78. Twice each day, 12 numbers were drawn, and the bettors selected 1 to 4 numbers that they wagered would be among the 12 drawn. From the point of view of the small-time policy operator, the chief economic risk was that, on any given day, a number of his customers might select winning numbers, so that he could not cover his losses for that day. However much the odds might favor the entrepreneur in the long run, that would not help if he lost his customers from a failure to make payoffs on a bad day. Most persons taking bets from customers, then, preferred to keep a straight percentage of the money bet with them and to turn over the rest to backers. The backers then assumed the risks in return for a small profit margin on large numbers of bets taken in by perhaps 100 to 300 agents.[7]

The economic risk to the small-time operator was also a basis for syndication of off-track bookmaking. The on-track bookmaker might attempt to adjust his odds and thus balance his book for each race, so that he could make payoffs no matter which horse won. But the off-track bookmaker agreed to pay at the odds prevailing at the track when the race was run. On any given race, then, an off-track bookmaker might wind up with too much money bet on a particular winning horse and be unable to cover his losses from money bet on other horses. As a result, it became common for major bookmakers to run large horse parlors, where they would have a Western Union ticker to provide up-to-the-minute information from the tracks and to take bets directly from customers. But major bookmakers also backed neighborhood bookmakers in bars, barbershops, newspaper kiosks, cigar stores, and other local outlets. The local bookmakers, like local policy writers, kept a fixed percentage of the money bet with them and passed the rest along to the backer, who assumed the risks and paid winning bettors. In addition to providing financial backing, the backers might also provide racing information to local agents.[8]

Gambling syndicates were closely tied to various aspects of neighborhood social structure. In many urban neighborhoods, people bet frequently with local bookmakers or policy writers, whom they visited regularly in the saloon, barbershop, cigar store, or other gathering place. They often established relationships of trust and friendship, so that gamblers had personal ties that ran through the neighborhoods.

There was, furthermore, a strong structural relationship to local politics. By the turn of the century, urban politics in America was often dominated by political organizations (called political "machines" by their opponents), which were organized from the grassroots up and based on the exchange of votes for favors. Such political organizations had ward leaders to mediate between politicians and city government, as well as precinct leaders in each block who kept in continued touch with voters, knew them personally, and were the backbone of the organization. Obviously, there was a considerable similarity between local political organizations and gambling syndicates—so much so, that in some neighborhoods the two overlapped. The backers of policy or bookmaking were the ward leaders and often served in city council or the state legislature; the local bookmakers or policy writers were the precinct captains, maintaining daily contact with voters. In such neighborhoods, it was not that the gambling syndicates influenced local political organizations; rather, the gambling syndicates *were* the local political organizations. And, in any event, the backers of bookmaking and policy were important neighborhood figures who had to be consulted by politicians. At a time when police departments were decentralized and strongly influenced by neighborhood political leaders, gamblers often determined law enforcement policy.

Beyond this, syndicates were linked to the neighborhood economy. Residential neighborhoods of American cities were then characterized by numerous commercial streets lined with small mom-and pop stores. Most people walked to do their daily shopping, and the stores were varied: fruit stores, vegetable stores, butchers, fish stores, flower shops, barbershops, drug stores, cigar stores, saloons, and an endless variety of other sorts. Then, as now, small retail stores were marginal ventures at best. For those proprietors who took bets on policy or horses, the small but steady income, for which they assumed no economic risk, was a welcome supplement to the fluctuating and uncertain income of their shops and stores.

Gamblers and gambling syndicates, then, had strong neighborhood ties that went beyond the fact that they provided an important and valued recreation. Gamblers participated in neighborhood politics and helped to support the local economy of small retailers. To treat gambling solely as a problem of law enforcement was to miss the place of gamblers in city life.

Gambling, especially sports gambling, has undergone major changes in the last 70 years. But these changes have generally not been the direct result of law enforcement campaigns. Rather, they have resulted from technological innovation and broad structural developments in American urban society. In a short article, it is possible merely to sketch a few of the changes.

In American city government there has been a decline in the ward as the significant unit of city government and an increasing centralization of control in city administration. This has been true for police as for other city bureaucracies. Centralization of police, combined with the decline of so-called political machines, has gradually weakened the control of local gambling over police policy.[9] At the same time, the automobile and other technologies reshaped urban geography. Residential neighborhoods were built without local shopping, with the expectation that families would drive to shopping centers for their needs. Without local shops, neighborhoods lacked institutions to harbor the numbers writer or bookmaker, so that in such neighborhoods there was virtually no neighborhood gambling. Concurrently the spread of the telephone meant that gamblers, especially those running sports betting, could operate their enterprises without fixed locations if they were willing to accept bets on credit. Finally, the growing popularity of college and professional basketball and football have meant that these sports have eclipsed horse racing in illegal betting markets. In short, the weakened role of gambling in the neighborhoods, along with the weakened control of local politicians over local law enforcement, led to the gradual decline of the old-time gambling house, horse parlor, and local bookmaking syndicates. These venerable institutions, like the parlor house, were once a standard feature of urban life but have now virtually disappeared.

LOANSHARKING AND PUBLIC POLICY

In contrast to the antigambling campaign, the campaign against loansharking in the early twentieth century took a broad view of the illegal market for small loans and pursued policies that relied only marginally on criminal law enforcement.[10]

During the first two decades of the twentieth century, the market for illegal small loans was dominated by salary lenders. Such lenders operated much like a modern small loan company. They were often located in the central business districts. Prospective borrowers, generally employees of city bureaucracies or private corporations, filled out detailed forms providing information about their employment, their family status, and their assets. If approved for a loan, the borrower received the money under the fiction that the money was advanced as a purchase of the borrower's future salary. The borrower signed complicated legal forms assigning his future salary to the lender and also often signed over power of attorney to the lender, so that, if the lender went to court to collect, the lender could also represent the borrower and confess judgment. Salary lenders often charged very high interest rates and attempted to trap the borrower into a chain debt, so that the borrower was continually paying interest but never managed to repy the principal.

Salary lending arose in a climate of opinion in which borrowing by consumers was regarded as a sign of moral weakness and was therefore to be discouraged. Usury laws set low maximum interest rates that made it impossible to operate a profitable small loan business. Banks made no attempt to change the laws, for they had no desire to enter the morally questionable business of making small loans to consumers. Most large employers had an explicit policy of firing employees whom they knew to be in debt, since employers did not wish to continue employing persons who showed such weakness of character and who might, in addition, be tempted to embezzle in order to repay a loan. Yet, despite the law and mores, there were persons who, because of family illness, vacation expenses, or other normal exigencies of life, needed to borrow money and were able to repay. There was, in short, a profitable market for small loans; and the laws were such that the market could be serviced only by illegal means.

Salary lenders had a number of collection methods. First of all, their respectable borrowers regarded the loans as moral and even legal obligations and could often be shamed into payment when they fell behind. The policy of employers to fire employees who were in debt provided perhaps the major collection leverage. A threat to inform the employer often caused delinquent borrowers to make payments. Finally, as a seldom-used last resort, salary lenders had access to the courts. Because of the close relations between salary lenders and some lower court justices, as well as the inability of most borrowers to afford attorneys, salary lenders were often able to use the courts to collect illegal loans.

Reformers, while recognizing the tragedy of borrowers being bled by high interest loans, did not define the problem to be primarily one of criminal law enforcement. They recognized, instead, that the illegal market existed because there were persons with good reasons to borrow and no legal means to do so. Thus, reformers pursued a number of policies at once. Least important, although sometimes temporarily successful, were efforts to persuade local district attorneys to prosecute salary lenders for violations of usury laws. More important, they used their influence to change the attitudes of employers toward borrowing by employees, so that employers would no longer fire employees who were in debt. Finally, they campaigned in the 1910s and 1920s for model small loan laws that would license small lenders and permit them to charge an interest rate high enough to make small loans profitable. Such laws brought into existence small loan companies, credit unions, and other sources of legal small loans. Soon large commercial banks, seeing the success of small loan activities and no longer regarding it as disreputable, opened small loan departments.

The campaign against loansharking came at a time when the United States was changing from a nation of frugal producers to a nation of borrowing consumers. The reformers' campaigns to legitimize borrowing contributed to this, both by helping to change attitudes and by creating some of the institutions that made borrowing possible. Wherever reformers persuaded employers not to fire employees who were in debt, they deprived salary lenders of a major collection tool. The model small loan laws, by allowing only licensed lenders to make small loans, deprived salary lenders of access to courts to collect outstanding loans. With their major collection mechanisms gone, salary lenders went out of business without a need for concerted enforcement of criminal laws against them.

Loansharking was again recognized as a major public policy problem in the 1960s, but the contrast with the earlier campaign against them is striking. This time the loansharks were lenders who charged usurious interest rates and used force, or the threat of force, as the ultimate collection tool. They serviced not only small borrowers, as had the earlier salary lenders, but also developed large loan markets to small businesses experiencing cash flow problems. In the 1960s the loanshark problem, discovered during the height of the "Mafia" scare, was defined almost entirely as one of law enforcement. The campaign consisted of seeking more tightly drawn laws with higher penalties and committing enforcement resources to the enforcement of such laws.

There was little attempt to explore why the antique dealers of Philadelphia, or the clothing manufacturers and jewelers of New York city, turned to loansharks for money. Nor were there concerted efforts to develop alternate, and legal, sources of credit. Indeed, the contrast between reports by enforcement agencies and government studies, on the one hand, and the few scholarly studies of modern loansharking, on the other, is interesting. Official studies emphasize the tight monopolization of the market by organized crime families, the violence of loansharks, the victimization of customers, and the danger that "organized crime" has seized control of legitimate businesses through loansharking. Scholars, by contrast, reported that the market is relatively decentralized, that violence has seldom actually been employed, that customers are often repeat borrowers, and that many appreciate the convenience of credit with minimal redtape and on short notice. Official reports support a law enforcement approach to the illegal market. Scholarly studies, on the contrary, suggest that policy makers today could learn much from the earlier campaign against loansharking and its broad definition of the problem.[11]

CONCLUSION

History, like any social science, is an imperfect guide to public policy. But history provides a perspective that is, I think, broadening. When changes in illegal markets are examined over a 50- or 100-year span, such changes are often seen to be rooted in broad societal changes and to be shaped by a variety of governmental policies. Law enforcement strategies can then be seen in perspective—both in terms of their possible strengths and their frequent weaknesses.

Clearly, illegal markets have responded to societal changes in attitudes and mores—changes in attitudes about sex, about borrowing, about drug use among various groups in American society. Markets have changed because of technologies such as the telephone. Both gambling and prostitution, for instance, have been shaped in important ways through the use of telephones to make contacts with customers. The changing geography of neighborhoods and cities has altered the markets for illegal goods just as it has altered the market for legal goods. By being aware of and sensitive to the varied factors that influence changes in illegal markets, policy makers may broaden their options. Such options may include policies that do not rely primarily on law enforcement or they may include a better ordering of law enforcement priorities and strategies.

NOTES

1. There are three main reasons why the term *organized crime* is not an analytically useful category. First of all, during the last 25 years the term has been used chiefly to label criminal behavior when engaged in by persons of Italian background. By now, the term is hopelessly compromised, so that even those who wish to use the term more broadly nevertheless find themselves using the term chiefly for Italian criminal activities or, at any rate, will be so understood by readers.

Second, the activities that are often placed within the category of organized crime range on a continuum from small-scale activities to relatively large-scale criminal syndicates. There really are neighborhood bookmakers and independent prostitutes; indeed, small scale has generally been typical of those servicing illegal markets. Yet the term *organized crime* carries with it the assumption of large and powerful enterprises. Instead of starting with that assumption, scholars should be empirical and ask the question: What has been the scale of enterprise and under what circumstances, if any, do such enterprises become large and powerful?

Finally, the term *organized crime* carries with it the implication of a particular type of coordination: a hierarchical and bureaucratic types of organization. Often organized crime is compared to large corporations as parallel examples of modern bureaucratic structures. Yet, among illegal markets as well as legal markets, there are many systems of coordination, of which hierarchical organization is just one. The term *organized crime* assumes one sort of coordination and hinders the exploration of other forms.

What is needed, then, is a term, like *illegal enterprise*, that identifies a type of illegal activity and then allows the exploration of size and methods of coordination without prior assumptions concerning the enthnicity of illegal entrepreneurs, the scale of the enterprises, or the methods of market coordination.

2. Kyvig, *Repealing National Prohibition* (Chicago: University of Chicago Press, 1979), esp. chap. 2; John C. Burnham, "New Perspectives on the Prohibition 'Experiment' of the 1920's," *Journal of Social History*, II (Fall 1968), 51-68.

3. For a summary of studies of prostitution before World War I, see Howard B. Woolston, *Prostitution in the United States Prior to the Entrance of the United States into the World War* (New York: Century Co., 1921); also Charles Washburn, *Come into My Parlor: A Biography of the Aristocratic Everleigh Sisters of Chicago* (New York: National Library Press, 1936); Investigators' reports in Committee of Fifteen papers, University of Chicago Library; Investigators' reports and papers, Teasdale Commission files, Series No. 2/3/1/3-8, Wisconsin Historical Society, Madison.

4. John R. Betts, "Organized Sport in Industrial America" (Ph.D. dissertation, Columbia University, 1951), chap. 3 & pages 200-206; Dale A Somers, *The Rise of Sports in New Orleans, 1850-1900* (Baton Rouge: Louisiana State University Press, 1972), chap. 5; William H.P. Robertson, *The History of Thoroughbred Racing in America* (New York: Bonanza Books, 1964), Part III; Hugh Bradley, *Such Was Saratoga* (Garden City, NY: Doubleday, 1940); Frank G. Menke, *The Story of Churcill Downs and the Kentucky Derby* (New York, 1940).

5. See Haller, "Rise of Urban Crime Syndicates" (unpublished paper); [George E. Smith] *Racing Maxims and Methods of "Pittsburg Phil"* (1908; republished by Gambler's Book Club, 1968).

6. Charles B. Parmer, *For Gold and Glory: The Story of Thoroughbred Racing in America* (New York, 1940), chaps. 9, 10; Henry N. Pringle, *The Facts about Race Track Gambling*, pamphlet (Washington, DC [1916]); Frank G. Menke, *Down the Stretch: The Story of Colonel Matt J. Winn* (New York: Smith & Durrell, 1945), chaps. 5 & 6.

7. David R. Johnson, "A Sinful Business: The Origins of Gambling Syndicates in the United States, 1840-1887," chap. 1 of David H. Bayley, ed., *Police and Society* (Beverly Hills, CA: Sage, 1977), pages 29-35; Herbert Asbury, *Sucker's Progress: An Informal History of Gambling in America from the Colonies to Canfield* (New York: Dodd, Mead, 1938), pp. 88-101; Chicago *Tribune*, Dec. 22, 1881; Citizens' Association of Chicago, *Bulletin* No. 11 (July 31, 1903); Haller, "Rise of Urban Crime Syndicates."

8. Haller, "Rise of Urban Crime Syndicates"; Rufus Jarman, "The Great Racetrack Caper," *American Heritage* XIX (Aug. 1968), 24-27.

9. Robert M. Fogelson, *Big-City Police* (Cambridge, MA: Harvard University Press, 1977), chaps. 1, 9, & *passim*.

10. Discussion of the history of loansharking based on Haller and John V. Alviti, "Loansharking in American Cities: Historical Analysis of a Marginal Enterprise," *American Journal of Legal History* XXI (1977), 125-156.

11. For scholarly studies of loansharing, see John Michael Seidl, " 'Upon the Hip'—A Study of the Criminal Loan-Shark Industry" (Ph.D. dissertation, Harvard University, 1968); Annelise Graebner Anderson, *The Business of Organized Crime: A Cosa Nostra Family* (Stanford, CA: Hoover Institution Press, 1979), esp. pages 64-73; and an important, but as yet unpublished study of New York loansharking by Peter Reuter and Jonathan Rubinstein.

4

URBAN HOMICIDE IN THE
NINETEENTH CENTURY:
SOME LESSONS FOR THE TWENTIETH

ROGER LANE

This article was commissioned in the hope that a knowledge of the history of urban criminal violence might be helpful in understanding the problem of urban violence today. Historians do not usually frame their questions with public issues directly in mind, but in this case the hope may be at least partially justified. An examination of the incidence and patterns of nineteenth century homicide may provide, if not detailed policy proposals, at least some perspective on current problems, and some suggestions about the approaches which may work in reducing current levels of violence.

What follows is based on my own work on homicide in 19th century Philadelphia which, with the help of twentieth century studies of the same city, enables further speculation about some of the changes which have occurred over nearly 150 years.[1] If we assume that homicide is an index of individual and nonrational violence in general—"successful assault," in James Q. Wilson's phrase—and that Philadelphia is a typical city, then the findings—about police efficiency, the gun culture, the connections among behavior patterns, employment, race, and murder—all have significant implications. Some of these are already obvious, apparent to observers of contemporary violence; others require the longer historical perspective provided below.

I.

What is most notable about the rate of criminal homicide in the nineteenth century city is that, in contrast to the modern experience, it was going down, raggedly, over time. In Philadelphia, the rate of indictment for homicide per 100,000 population, between 1839 and 1901, is shown in Table 1.[2]

To argue that the rate of crime was falling through the nineteenth century, not only for homicide but for most other violent felonies, was once controversial. The conventional academic wisdom long held that there was a positive correlation between urban growth and criminal behavior of all kinds. But although there are still considerable problems involved in measuring the phenomenon, the contrary evidence is by now overwhelming. Every single study of nineteenth century Britain, the most

TABLE 1 No. and average annual rate per 100,000 population of episodes resulting in homicide indictments, by period.

Years	No.	7-yr. rate	No.	21 yr. rate
1839-1845	73	3.7		
1846-1852	85	3.1		
1853-1859	138	4.0	296	3.6
1860-1866	100	2.4		
1867-1873	156	3.3		
1874-1880	205	3.7	461	3.2
1881-1887	159	2.4		
1888-1894	167	2.2		
1895-1901	231	2.7	557	2.5

SOURCE: Roger Lane, *Violent Death in the City: Suicide, Accident and Murder in Nineteenth Century Philadelphia.* Copyright 1979 Harvard University Press. Reprinted by permission.

rapidly urbanizing society in the world, shows that "serious" crime was declining, whatever the methods or definitions used and whatever the period or area covered.[3] And with some exceptions and ambiguities so do longitudinal studies in American jurisdictions—states and cities much more complicated by urban-rural, black-white, native-immigrant, and preindustrial-industrial differences than the British, all of which obscure the basic patterns.[4] The key question then about the trend in homicide is not what but why, and in particular why the pattern in the nineteenth century city is so strikingly different from that in the late twentieth.

While comparisons across time are extremely difficult, Philadelphia is the best place in which to attempt them simply because Marvin Wolfgang's classic *Patterns in Criminal Homicide* was based on all cases known to the police in that city between 1948 and 1952. Frank Hartleroad, a student of Wolfgang's, has updated this for 1972-1974, using basically the same methods and sources. My own study of all indictments between 1839 and 1901 employs the same questions, whenever possible, in addition to several others of my own design. But its differences with the two modern studies are themselves revealing.

Homicide is generally considered one of the firmest indices of criminal behavior, least subject to the vagaries of differing "labelling" procedures and definitions. Barring the relatively rare, calculated, offense—the perfect crime beloved of mystery writers—it may be assumed also that all but a handful of killings become "known to the police." Neither assumption holds true for the previous century, however, as the best official statistics available greatly underestimate the actual number of homicides committed.

The "best available" figures for three eras indicate, on paper, a composite murder rate for Philadelphia of 3.0 for the 1839-1901 era, as compared to 5.9 for 1948-1952, and 25.7 for 1972-1974.[5] But the official comparison is radically misleading in that the gap between the "real" and the "officially recorded" homicide rate in the nineteenth century was far greater than in the mid or later twentieth, meaning that the "real" rate was proportionally much greater than shown.

This is true first because the "best available" statistics for the earlier period are neither "crimes known to the police" nor arrests but the number of indictments presented to the Grand Jury, and many cases were and are lost between discovery of a homicide and an indictment. Second, very few of the indictments include a form of murder still very common in the previous century but very rare in our own: that is infanticide, usually committed by unmarried women or others for whom birth control or abortion were inaccessible. Virtually undetectable by the forensic techniques then available, infanticide was easy to hide under cover of any number of infantile diseases or mishaps. Some fraction of the total, however, may be measured by the number of anonymous new borns found unburied in the city's streets, lots, and privies. These tiny corpses were typically listed as having died from "unknown causes"; some 12.3 per 100,000 cases were reported annually in the 1870s, 5.0 in the 1890s. If counted as homicides, they would have multiplied the "best available" figures severalfold.

Even if the rather special case of infanticide is discounted, it remains clear that nineteenth century murder totals were systematically undercounted at the source, as the result of weaknesses in the operations of the justice system. Much evidence, some of it quantitative—an increase in the severity of sentences, for example; and some of it qualitative—an insistence upon prosecuting preadolescents, and on bringing obviously accidental killers to the dock—suggests that the system in the later nineteenth century was far stricter about homicide than it had been earlier, or is indeed today. But despite a continual lowering threshold of tolerance for violence which accentuates the finding about the falling rate of indictment, prosecutors even during the last decade of the century never succeeded in convicting as many as half of those for whom indictments were drawn. One reason may be that among those indicted, the modal killing—a fight started in saloon or similar public place and reaching its denouement in the street—involved no guns, knives, or any other weapon normally considered lethal. Middle-class juries were fully aware that drunken violence was commonplace in the City of Brotherly Love. Given "X" number of brawls, most of which resulted in no permanent damage, a few "winners" would land lucky blows in an unluckily sensitive spot, or pursue their fury through one last and deadly kick in the head. The plea of self-defense in these affrays was easy to bring and hard to deny. The result however was a natural sense of prosecutorial futility, a futility felt throughout the system of criminal justice.

One important source of this futility was the ineffectiveness of the detective system. The city acquired its first fulltime police officers in 1845, its first detectives shortly after. In the modern city, anywhere, the homicide unit is a prestigious and efficient body. But Philadelphia's nineteenth century detective service—and as late as 1898 it had only 15 men—was geared almost entirely to the recovery of stolen property, usually from an underworld with which the detectives enjoyed a number of profitably corrupt connections. Wholly without technological aids—no photos, fingerprints, or laboratory analysis—and more important without incentive or interest, the police were often impotent. The nineteenth century homicides indicted include a number of bizarre cases, with weapons, for example, ranging from a ship's cannon to a scrap of flannel. But in terms of motive, only one man was tried for a sex slaying, and only a handful for robbery—murder; the explanation is not that either type was so rare but that any attempt at flight or concealment was often enough to baffle an "investigation." Moreover, of Wolfgang's list of circumstances which make detection relatively difficult—such as killings by strangers, or in the streets—most were more characteristic of the previous century than of our own.[6]

The impotence of the detective system was manifest, ultimately, in the operations of the coroner's inquest, the intake end of the machinery. From the viewpoint of the coroner himself, neither the time nor the effort involved made "homicide" findings as rewarding as the "suicide" or "accident" alternatives. And from a wider, functional viewpoint, the society as a whole presumably had no wish to be reminded of the existence of problems its institutions were unable to solve. In the absence of a "smoking gun" or its equivalent, then, and an obvious and easily arrested suspect, there was considerable indirect pressure at the inquest for verdicts other than homicide. This was sometimes impossible given witnesses to a street fight, say, or a corpse full of bullet holes. Nevertheless, coroners' juries time and again came up with accident or suicide verdicts in cases which at this date seem highly implausible. By comparison with modern figures, an enormous number of Philadelphians were "drowned" each year, particularly in the early and middle parts of the century; in about 40% of these cases, evidence for "drowning" was merely that the body had been found in the water; the fact that both hands were found tied behind the back was no sure key to a "homicide" verdict. Similarly, a number of men were found with skull fractures in streets or alleys outside of saloons and declared to have "fallen on the pavement while drunk"; a dying declaration about "robbers" and "blackjacks" might well be ignored.

All together, these factors make it clear that the nineteenth century murder rate was far higher than was officially measured. How much higher it is impossible to say, but some estimate may be attempted. The "best available" figures—number of indictments—yield a composite rate of 3.0 per 100,000, as stated. In the six years for which full coroners' reports are available, however—1854-1857 and 1878-1880—there were just 101 indictments prepared but 33 other cases in which murder verdicts were returned at inquest. If this figure—the equivalent of modern "crimes known to the police"—may be extrapolated for the century as a whole, the rate would be over 4.0 per 100,000. More dramatically, the conservative Philadelphia *Public Ledger* for the years 1839-1841, 1870, and 1900 raised the possibility of foul play in more than *twice* as many deaths as resulted in indictments. This count of what may be homicides for some reason "mislabelled" by the coroner does not include infanticides, murder-suicides, unwitnessed skull fractures, or routine "found drowned" cases, but it comprises 92 "suspect" cases beyond the 82 indictments listed for the five years. If extrapolated it would suggest a murder rate over 8.0. If the anonymous dead newborns were counted in, the overall rate would be in the 15.0-20.0 range. In short, any comparison between the nineteenth century and more recent rates is likely to be misleading, since those for the earlier period are far higher than any official sources are likely to show.

II.

More revealing than raw quantitative comparison—full as it is of treacherous figures and guesswork—is a comparison of the *patterns* of nineteenth and twentieth century homicides, patterns which may bring us closer to an explanation of changing rates of violent behavior.

One simple comparison already suggested is of weapons used, as shown in Table 2. (Note that the nineteenth century figures are taken of necessity from trials only, and as successful prosecution was more likely when weapons were used, they overestimate the real proportion of homicides with weapons.)

The history of handguns—revolvers small enough to carry hidden on the person—is clearly associated with changes in the murder rate. They became available first in the 1850s and help account for the jump shown in Table 1 for that decade. But it appears also that their use was confined largely to street toughs and others constantly alert to the possibility of deadly violence. Not until the 1880s did suicides—a more representative sample of adult males—come to prefer handguns to hanging, the pattern which has prevailed in this country ever since and reveals much about its weaponry. Even then it seems guns were not commonly stashed in the home; one clue is the markedly lower rate of homicides by nineteenth century women,

TABLE 2   Weapons used in all criminal homicides,
by percent in 3 periods.

Weapon	1839-1901	1948-1952	1872-1974
Firearms	25	33	56
Sharp Instrument	25	36	31
Blunt instrument	17	9	3
Fists, Feet, Body	21	16	5
Other	12	6	5

SOURCE: Roger Lane, *Violent Death in the City: Suicide, Accident and Murder in Nineteenth Century Philadelphia.* Copyright 1979 Harvard University Press. Reprinted by permission.

only 9.8% of those indicted (just 5.6% if infanticides are omitted), as compared to 17.6% in 1948-1952 and 13.2% in 1972-1974. Without deadly weapons readily at hand, fewer arguments in bedrooms and kitchens were likely to end in death—or to be "won" by women. The increase in their availability has continued, however, to multiply the deadly potential in angry encounters of all kinds; a man in a car, street, or taproom with a hidden weapon is a kind of booby trap, capable of unexpected explosion when crossed, transforming what in an earlier age might have been a drunken shoving match into a fatal incident. What handguns have done is not directly to increase the violent *inclinations* of the population but the ability to translate these inclinations into sudden deadly action—often regretted within moments. Had they been as common in the last century as in 1970 or even 1950, the murder rate would have been sharply higher; had they been less common in recent years, conversely, the rate would as surely have been lower.

But if it is useful to ask technological or "how" questions about changes in the murder rate, as above, the most significant answers result from asking "who" did the killing, and "when" the rate changed most sharply. If the concern is with the propensity for violent behavior, the figures for homicide itself may give no clear answers since so many other variables are involved. One is the technological, as sketched above. Given the same or even a lower number of violent encounters in the 1850s as the 1840s, more killings would result simply because of the introduction of handguns. Changes such as differing prosecutorial standards—an insistence upon prosecuting simple accident as manslaughter in the late nineteenth and early twentieth century—may exaggerate official figures in relation to "real" behavior, so may improvements in police or coroner's procedures. Immigration may also distort matters, as in the 1900-1920 era, when an influx of foreign and domestic newcomers from more violent places obscured the fact that the settled population was growing less violent. Thus in asking both "when" and "who," it may be useful to investigate the clues provided, somewhat more clearly, by two phenomena which are in varying ways linked with homicide—that is accident and suicide.

The nature of the link between homicide and suicide has been suggested most strikingly by the social psychologist Martin Gold, inventor of the "Suicide-Murder Ratio." A number of social scientists—notably Andrew Henry and James Short, Jr., in 1951—had previously noted a connection, largely negative, between the propensity toward directing aggressive impulses either inward or outward, but Gold's is the most useful and economical statement.[7] His argument is that the process of socialization inclines individuals and, by extension, groups toward either the internalization or the external expression of aggression, and thus in extreme situations toward either suicide or homicide. Those individuals inclined to be suicidal are trained to be cooperative, rational, and at the extreme repressed.

Those inclined to be homicidal, remain spontaneous, impulsive, or reckless. The "Suicide-Murder Ratio" for any group is the suicide rate divided by the sum of the suicide rate plus the homicide rate; a low decimal indicates a propensity for homicide, a high decimal for suicide. The analysis tends to work for such variables as class and race, with Short and Henry indicating that suicides tend to occur among people of high status and murders among people of low status. Gold's formulation accounts for sexual and ethnic differences also; some groups, traditionally men (most strikingly young black men), tend to be high in both homicide and suicide, a result explicable in terms of higher levels of anger, or frustration, and evident when the full ratio is given rather than the single decimal which expresses its result.[8] Accident rates are easily explicable in terms of the concept, if not so easily fitted into the formula or ratio per se. Accident tends to result from the same habits—alcoholic recklessness and impulsiveness—which in special circumstances may lead to manslaughter. And studies have repeatedly shown that the accident-prone are typically quarrelsome, disruptive young people, as likely to be found smashing faces as telephone poles.[9]

The figures for nineteenth century Philadelphia and the northeastern United States generally tend to confirm both the usefulness and the validity of the "Suicide-Murder Ratio." All group differences were more sharply defined then than now, and those high in homicide—blacks, Italians, Irish, and natives—tended to be low in suicide, and in the same rank order, a situation precisely reversed for German and Eastern European immigrants generally. Just as the rate of homicide was going down in the aggregate population, so too was the rate of "simple" accident—that is accident not essentially a function of technology. Suicide, at the same time, was rising. And more clearly than with homicide, the accident and suicide figures show just when, and with further analysis just why, the change in the pattern of aggressive behavior occurred.

The change in the indices of violent death is quite striking, and the best explanation is that it is connected with the most fundamental of nineteenth century social processes, the urban-industrial revolution. More specifically, and from the present point of view most significantly, it was the changed work habits demanded by the new economic order which account for the decline in recklessness, for the substitution of internally directed for externally directed aggression. For these purposes what distinguishes the traditional from the modern industrial economy is not productivity or income per se—violence is not directly the result of poverty—but pacing and discipline. The work of farmers and artisans, while often difficult and in spurts brutally so, is highly variable, with intense activity alternating with long slack periods. There are tasks to do rather than hours to be filled; most activity is unsupervised, and there is rarely anything that cannot be interrupted for a distraction, or perhaps a drink. Both factory and bureaucracy, in contrast, require order and cooperation, a steady pace insured by constant supervision and equally constant awareness of the clock. Neither the hours nor the nature of the job typically permit spontaneous interruption, or the easy workaday consumption of alcohol; what they demand instead is control enough to endure long stretches of boredom and frustration without external signs of rebellion. Those who can do this successfully are those whose socialization has made this second nature, who have become in E. P. Thompson's phrase "their own slave drivers." Their habits, also, may extend well beyond those directly exposed to the discipline exacted in factory or bureaucracy. The behavioral norms in the modern city are rational, cooperative, and orderly, whatever the previous experience of most of those who exhibit them in public; Erving Goffman has shown in a series of studies that an urban population acquires these norms through some process of contagion or example which makes living in the city itself an education.[10]

In the nineteenth century, the behavior most useful to the new economy was inculcated most directly in the public schools. Americans had earlier acquired a high level of literacy in a variety of ways; the point about public schooling was that one learned above all to sit still, take turns, hold your water, mind the teacher, and listen for the bell—all perfect training for later factory or bureaucratic employment. And from the present point of view, what is most striking about such behavior is that it is precisely what Gold defines as inclining people toward suicide rather than homicide. Conversly, studies of accident-prone children, whose attitudes and behavior might later make them violent teen-agers or adults, defines them neatly in terms of their degree of resistance to the classroom and its discipline.

School, factory, and bureaucracy, then, with mass supervision and discipline, are the kinds of influences which in theory might account for falling rates of interpersonal violence, homicide and accident, accompanied by rising rates of suicide in the same aggregate population. And much evidence confirms such an interpretation for nineteenth century Philadelphia, and by extension urban United States generally.

The first clue involves the timing of change. The figures for suicide and for drowning (the latter technologically the "simplest" of accidents) are given in Table 3. Both, after a period of no decisive movement, "broke" sharply in the years around 1870. (The homicide rate would show the same "break"—see Table 1—if it were not for the introduction of revolvers, which swelled the number of killing in the 1850s, as compared to the 1840s, and the distorting effects of the Civil War in the 1860s.) From about 1870 to the end of the century, while the murder rate dropped significantly *despite* the growing availability of handguns, and a continually lowering threshold of tolerance for violence, the suicide rate nearly doubled while the drowning rate more than halved.[11]

The key period in the death indices, about 1870, is also a key period for the national figures on employment and schooling. (Given the great mobility of the nineteenth century, when few adult residents of Philadelphia had been born there, national figures on these points are more useful than are local figures).[12] The greatest historical increase in those employed in factories and bureaucracies occurred during the 1860s, and the proportion increased steadily after that.[13] Educational figures run precisely parallel. Public schools in the North and West were typically authorized in the 1840s and proliferated in the 1850s; while enrollment

TABLE 3   No. and average annual rate of officially reported
deaths from drowning and suicide, by period.

Years	Annual Suicide Rate	Annual Drowning Rate
1839-1845	5.0	16.5
1846-1852	3.2	16.6
1853-1859	4.8	19.8
1860-1866	4.3	19.5
1867-1873	5.6	18.0
1874-1880	7.0	15.0
1881-1887	9.0	10.6
1888-1894	10.0	8.8
1895-1901	11.8	7.8

SOURCE: Roger Lane, *Violent Death in the City: Suicide, Accident and Murder in Nineteenth Century Philadelphia.* Copyright 1979 Harvard University Press. Reprinted by permission.

figures are not available directly, the greatest increase in public funding occurred during the same decade, 1860-1870, parallel to the increase in factory and office jobs.[14] The first significant number of graduates entered the workforce, then, shortly before 1870, and from that date on there was a steady increase in both enrollments and time annually spent in school.[15]

A closer analysis of the effect of schooling and occupation on the murder-suicide ratio may be obtained from the suicide rates of all occupied males in the northeastern United States, as provided in the special study for the 1890 census (see Table 4). While Table 4 omits some crucial variables—notably immigration, which is highly associated with suicide and helps account for the anomalously high rates in the "laboring and servant" category—its import is clear. The line between men with high rates and those with low does not clearly divide rich from poor, or those with high status from those with low, or even the self-employed from the wage-earning. The division is rather between those engaged in traditional work—requiring little public schooling, supervision, or external discipline—and those engaged in the newer kinds of work. This conclusion is clearer when the aggregate groups in Table 4 are analyzed more closely. Thus the low-suicide "entertainment" and "mercantile and trading" groups were made up almost entirely of convivial unsupervised types such as bartenders, innkeepers, traveling salesmen, and hucksters. Among the leaders, little divided the richest bankers, in the "clerical and official" group, from

TABLE 4   Age-standardized suicide rates for all occupied males
over 15 in registration states of 1890 census

Occupation Above Av. Rate	No. in 1000's	Suicide Rate
Personal service,		
police and military	78	28.6
Professional	117	23.7
Clerical and official	324	21.2
Laboring and servant	469	17.6
Manufacturing and		
mechanical	1,168	17.0
Av. Rate For all		
Occupied	3,491	15.6
Below Av. Rate		
Entertainment	55	12.9
Mercantile and Trading	291	12.7
Agriculture, Transport,		
other outdoor	990	10.4

SOURCE: U. S. Census of 1890; Reported earlier in Roger Lane, *Violent Death in the City: Suicide, Acident and Murder in Nineteenth Century Philadelphia.* Copyright 1979 Harvard University Press. Reprinted by permission.

the lowliest clerks and copyists, repressed bureaucrats par excellence. Among those wearing blue collars, the traditional aristocrats, cabinet-makers and carpenters, stood at the very low end of the suicide scale, while the highest was occupied by the newest, most regimented, and most carefully supervised of all—operatives in mills and factories.

The occupational profile of those indicted for homicide in Philadelphia—a sample of some 881 fully adult males—is precisely the opposite, as Gold's thesis would suggest. Then as now, those who did have listed occupations typically held some of the least attractive jobs in the socio-economic pecking order. Most strikingly, however, a growing proportion of them, cumulatively about two-thirds of the total, cannot be located in the Philadelphia *City Directory* at all; even those who can seem typically to have stayed in the city only a couple of years, as compared to the 10 or so years characteristics of urban males generally.[16] Thus the great majority of nineteenth century murderers were not truly urbanites at all but drifters, transients working at the most casual of jobs if indeed they were legally employed at all. As a group, then, they were almost wholly beyond the reach of the new economic order as represented by office, school, and factory.

III.

The significance of this finding about homicide, behavior patterns, and employment is best illustrated by an analysis which briefly surveyes the trend in homicide *since* the nineteenth century and attempts to relate the industrializing, the fully industrial, and the postindustrial city together.

The materials for such a survey are not easily available, since there are no trustworthy figures anywhere for the time between the end of the nineteenth century and 1933, when the FBI began publishing its index. A few of the scattered official figures, for various jurisdictions, show rising rates during this period, but these are often the effect of a number of variables which increased the number of homicides *recorded* but not those actually *committed* by the urban population. These variables include improved policing, as departments acquired new priorities, telephones, automobiles, and radios; the prosecution of auto accident as manslaughter—very important after 1900; and as mentioned, the distorting effect caused by the in-migration of native and foreign ethnic groups with high levels of violence. In any case, after 1933 when these variables had levelled out considerably, the FBI figures show a generally downward trend until the later 1950s.

In Philadelphia, and probably in all major urban-industrial centers, the analysis in sections I and II suggests, then, that the "real" trend in homicide was down for a very long time, dropping not only through the nineteenth century but most of the twentieth. How, then, do we account for the dramatic rise over the past generation?

One simple, but in itself misleading, explanation for rising homicide rates is that it has been almost entirely a black phenomenon. The black rate was high historically, and in contrast to the white was almost always rising, while Philadelphia has become increasingly a black city. (The black population, cumulatively about 4.3% of the whole between 1839 and 1901, was 18% in 1950, and 34% in 1970.) And as Table 5 shows, the white rate was clearly dropping between the nineteenth century and the

TABLE 5   Black and white homicide rates per 100,000
          population in 3 periods.

	1839-1901	1948-1952	1972-1974
Black	7.5	24.6	64.2
White	2.8	1.8	2.8

Total is of persons indicted for 19th century, arrested for 20th; see text.
SOURCE: Roger Lane, *Violent Death in the City: Suicide, Accident and Murder in Nineteenth Century Philadelphia.* Copyright 1979 Harvard University Press. Reprinted by permission.

mid-twentieth, even if the misleading "best available" sources are used. Only very recently, as the better educated have "fled" the city for the suburbs, to be replaced increasingly by Latin immigrants, has the white rate turned up.

What, then, accounts for the difference between the black and white trends in homicide, one rising as the other falls, so that the former is now over 20 times the latter?

For the nineteenth century the explanation is clear. While neither Africans nor southern slaves were notable for interpersonal violence, urban blacks through much of the period—constant victims of race riot, forced into illicit occupations and dangerous neighborhoods—found that carrying weapons was an indispensable survival mechanism. Proportionately far more black than white killings involved knives and, later, guns. And the result was that, however necessary as protection, the carrying of weapons, as suggested earlier, tended to escalate otherwise harmless arguments into deadly affairs.

But what is distinctive about the black rate is not that it started high—during 1839-1859, for example, at 6.1 per 100,000, it was not dramatically higher than that for the Irish or later Italian immigrants—but that it continued to climb. And the reason for that is simply the obverse of the reason why it tended to fall within the dominant white population. The habits demanded by factory and bureaucracy are the key—and factory and bureaucratic employment were systematically denied to blacks. In the absence of the kind of jobs which made public schooling and the attendant behavior patterns relevant (and many were denied schooling as well), there was nothing working in the black population to counteract the fact that guns were ever growing cheaper and more common. Not until World War II were plants and offices generally opened to blacks—and ironically it was just too late.[17] For many, the mixed benefits of the Industrial Age lasted only through the postwar into the Korean boom. Then came the "postindustrial" era of the later 1950s and after. Opportunities for the unskilled and poorly educated closed up in the cities. And the results of that closure—in itself more important than poverty, per se, in its effects on behavior patterns and lifestyle—have been apparent ever since in the level of inner city violence.

This analysis is confirmed by one last table. In retrospect it appears that the 1948-1952 period studied by Marvin Wolfgang, the period of postwar and Korean full employment, represents the urban-industrial era at its successful height, a period during which interpersonal violence reached a low point. The nineteenth century had been a time of transition, a time in which industrialization was still in process, when rates were high but dropping. The 1970s have been the opposite—a period of postindustrial stagnation, in which rates are high and climbing. When the three periods are compared, the result is a kind of univers curve, in which the homicide patterns of this latest era have come in many ways to resemble those of the earliest. As shown in Table 6, the specific ethnic group involved is less important than the structure of the urban economy, and consequently the kind of socialization and employment experienced in particular by young men. The presence in large numbers of those with irregular habits and little to do tends to increase the proportion of killings outside of the family, those by strangers, males, across racial lines, on the streets, and by multiple assailants. Perhaps above all, since one day looks much like the next to those not working steadily, murder and manslaughter tend to be spread more through the week and less concentrated on weekends, the time when a fully employed population gets its paychecks and does its drinking, visiting, socializing, and fighting.

IV.

What can be concluded from all of this? The basic lesson of the nineteenth century is that it is possible for a city, and an economy, to grow and prosper while its rate of homicide declines. But this is not a

TABLE 6　Some patterns of homicide in three periods, by percent
tried, for 19th century, percent arrested, for 20th C.

	1839-1901	*1948-1952*	*1972-1974*
Location			
Home	31	51	32
Street	39	30	37
Saloon, bar	12	8	10
Other	18	12	16
Relationship			
Family	22	25	19
Acquaintance	48	61	50
Stranger, unknown, or other	30	14	31
Percent male accused	90	82	87
Percent killings on weekends	50	67	50

SOURCE: Roger Lane, *Violent Death in the City: Suicide, Accident and Murder in Nineteenth Century Philadelphia.* Copyright 1979 Harvard University Press. Reprinted by permission.

lesson easily put into practice. What it yields, when analyzed, is one obvious positive suggestion, one negative suggestion, and one area in which to keep looking for a more fundamental solution to the problem of modern urban violence.

First, the obvious suggestion is to limit handguns. Historically the growing availability of these weapons has helped to transform otherwise harmless anger into higher death rates; it should be equally possible to throw the equation into reverse.

Second, the negative suggestion is that increase in police efficiency alone will have little effect on homicide rates. The police, like such other agents of "urban discipline" as public schools and campaigns to encourage orderly behavior, were introduced in the early or middle nineteenth century, when they "fit" the needs of urban-industrial system. They seemed, then, to accomplish their goals in progressive fashion. But clearly they no longer do; the virtues of orderly behavior are not self-evident, and the process of imposing them is not only painful but may be regarded as irrelevant, even tyrannical, when they no longer "fit" the needs of the population at which they are directed. Furthermore, the police are doing about all that can reasonably be asked. During the previous century, when the justice system had difficulty in dealing with homicide at every level, there was much room for improvement—and the rates dropped nonetheless. Since that time dramatic advances have been made; already by the mid-twentieth century, some 90% of all killings were "cleared by arrest." This is a figure which leaves little room for improvement—and yet the murder rate is climbing.

Third, the experience of the nineteenth century suggests that fundamental behavior patterns are the key to explaining long-term changes in the rate of interpersonal violence. The basic trend in the rate of such violence was down, from the earliest available records through the late 1950s, the result of the more disciplined behavior demanded in a modern economy and enforced by the schools and similar agencies. This in turn increased the propensity toward internalized aggression—suicide at the extreme—and decreased that toward external aggression—homicide and accident at the extremes.

Fourth, the urban black population, however, frozen out of bureaucratic and factory employment, developed unique patterns of violence as a result, with a continually rising homicide rate. Jobs in plants and offices were opened too late, just before the "postindustrial" period of the late 1950s and since. Frustration and the homicide rate have thus risen especially in the past generation, the result of the availability of guns and the nonavailability of productive jobs, the kinds which affect behavior patterns as well as providing pocket money.

Fifth, the study of history offers no direct solution to the problems posed by the current level of inner city violence. We cannot repeat the past; the industrial city may well be dead beyond recall; we cannot impose on the inner city the kind of discipline earlier imposed on the dominant white population. Indeed we would not if we could, given the high price which that process exacted in suicide, repression, and other forms of human misery.

Nevertheless, we can at least look to the past for the suggestion that long-term change in the homicide rate is a function of long-term change in the nature of employment and socialization in the society. And what we need most is an end to the separate path of economic development which was forced upon the urban black population, and some more humane and inclusive substitute for the socialization once provided by regular productive employment, and an educational system and other public agencies fully relevant to that system of employment.

NOTES

1. This article is largely based upon my study of *Violent Death in the City: Suicide, Accident and Murder in Nineteenth Century Philadelphia.* (Cambridge, MA: Harvard University Press, 1979). The principal sources used are the stories behind more than 1500 criminal indictments for homicide, all those issued between 1839 and 1901, plus the Philadelphia *Public Ledger* and the official reports of police, coroners, and health department. All footnote references to these and other primary sources from the book will be omitted. The same is true for references to the two major sources for homicide in the twentieth century, Marvin Wolfgang's classic *Patterns in Criminal Homicide* (New York: Wiley, 1966), and a study by Frank Hartleroad based on a half-sample of all homicides known to the police between 1972 and 1974. Both studies are described in the text; I am especially indebted to Hartleroad for the use of his materials in manuscript.

2. There are a number of possible ways to count the "homicide rate." For technical reasons the best available for nineteenth century Philadelphia are of "episodes," regardless of number killed or number of killers per episode, and are obtained through the official indictments, a problem discussed below in the text.

3. For a recent survey of the British studies, see David Phillips, *Crime and Authority in Victorian England: The Black Country, 1835-1860* (London: Roman and Littlefield, 1977), Ch. 2.

4. For review of American studies, see Eric Monkkonen, *Police in the Urban Social Structure 1860-1920* (forthcoming).

5. Note that for the purpose of greater comparability, this count is not of episodes, as in Table 1, but of number of persons indicted, for the nineteenth century, or arrested, for the twentieth. The effect of this procedure, as explained, is to exaggerate the twentieth century figures as compared to those for the nineteenth.

6. See also Table 6. The nineteenth century materials do not permit direct comparison with all of the characteristics which make detection difficult, such as an aged victim. See Wolfgang, *Patterns in Criminal Homicide,* pp. 290-294.

7. Martin Gold, "Suicide, Homicide, and the Socialization of Aggression," *American Journal of Sociology* 62 (May 1958), 651-661. See also Andrew F. Henry and James Short, Jr., *Suicide and Homicide: Some Economic, Sociological, and Psychological Aspects of Aggression* (New York: Free Press, 1964), *passim.*

8. Very recently, as discussed in Appendix C to *Violent Death in the City,* the age-adjusted suicide rate of black males, in Philadelphia and elsewhere, has come to approach or surpass that of whites, an "advance" led by an unprecedentedly high rate among young men. The use of the Suicide-Murder Ratio not only helps to show and explain this, in terms of despair, frustration, and aggression, but also makes it clear that because of the enormously high homicide rate in the same group, the black-white differences in this ratio have continued to grow.

9. Julian A. Waller, "Accidents and Violent Behavior: Are They Related?", in *Crimes of Violence: A Staff Report Submitted to the National Commission on the Causes and Prevention of Violence* XIII, (Washington, DC: Government Printing Office, 1969) surveys the relevant literature.

10. See, for example, Erving Goffman, *Relations in Public: Microstudies in the Public Order* (New York: Basic Books, 1971).

11. The study of accident rates is highly technical; in fact, with a number of changes accounted for, such as population movement away from the water and decreased accessibility of the city's rivers, the change in the drowning rate would be less than shown, but the later rate would still be less than half of the earlier. The suicide rate is of course always a matter of suspicion, but after elaborate checking I am confident that the relative change in the rates, if not their absolute accuracy, is roughly correct. See *Violent Death in the City*, Chs. 2 and 3.

12. Ideally of course, were they available, figures from such places as Ireland, Germany, Italy, and Eastern Europe would be necessary to complete the picture.

13. See table on "Industrial Distribution of Gainful Workers: 1820 to 1940," in *Historical Statistics of the United States* (Washington, DC: Government Printing Office, 1960), p. 74.

14. Albert Fishlow, "Levels of Nineteenth Century American Investment in Education," *Journal of Economic History*, 26, no. 4 (December 1966), 418-456.

15. *Historical Statistics of the United States*, p. 207.

16. Typically some 75% of adult males should be locatable in a City Directory: see Stephan Thernstrom, *The Other Bostonians: Poverty and Progress in the American Metropolis, 1880-1970* (Cambridge, MA: Harvard University Press, 1973), appendix B. Thernstrom also surveys the literature on nineteenth century mobility, finding that "persistence rates" varied between about 40% and 60% a decade, meaning that the *other* 60%-40% had died or moved.

17. On black employment see William Robert Fogel and Stanley M. Engerman, *Time on the Cross: The Economics of American Negro Slavery*, I (Boston: Little, Brown, 1974), 260; Thernstrom, *Other Bostonians*, 214.

5

HOMICIDE IN THE TWENTIETH CENTURY UNITED STATES

MARGARET A. ZAHN

This article is a review of extant information on homicide in the United States from 1900 to 1979. This descriptive review is seen as a necessary prelude both for a historically grounded theory of homicide and for a set of workable social policies to deal with this type of interpersonal violence. This review establishes not only the changing trends but also a portrait of the dominant types of homicide existing in different periods of American history.

METHODOLOGICAL CONSIDERATIONS

Establishing a portrait of homicide through an entire century, using existing studies, poses a variety of problems. The first is lack of comparability across studies. Studies on homicide lack comparability in a number of ways. One way is in how homicide is defined. In some studies, homicides include those cases killed by officers of the law or those occurring in self-defense, that is, justifiable. In other studies they do not. Those studies in the 1920s, for example, seem more likely to include justifiable homicides than do those in the 1960s.[1] Further, in some periods abortion and/or infanticide are included as separate types of homicide, while at other times they are not included or defined as criminal homicide. Further, while many studies discuss victim-offender relationships, there is no consistent definition across studies of the various types of victim-offender relationship, for example, what constitutes an acquaintance or a stranger. In fact, in many studies, there is no definition at all. Further, in some studies only cases in which the offender is known are included while in others those with both known and unknown offenders are included. Additionally, some studies use offenders as their research base, while others use victims and sometimes the two are confused with each other. In all, there are many ways in which the available studies are not comparable and thus difficult to use.

Additional problems revolve around data sources, their availability at different time periods, and biases and difficulties specific to each source. There are, for example, no fully national homicide statistics prior to the early 1930s. Thus, data in the early part of the twentieth century are essentially local in character. The major types of data sources available for use include arrest, conviction, or execution data from local units of government; coroners' data also from local units of government; and newspaper accounts. A brief nonexhaustive review of some of the kinds of problems with two of these data sets follows.

POLICE DATA

It has generally been concluded that police data are more useful than correctional system data for studies of crime since the police have first contact with the original criminal events upon which the statistics are based.[2] While this may be true in establishing trend data, it may be less valid for victim-offender relationship, motive, or manner of death. In effect, initial police reports may convey a different motive from either subsequent police reports or court reports. Further, manner of death and presence of alcohol and drugs are more accurately reported by a Medical

Examiner than a police report. This kind of data may be especially important in tracing the impact of illegal substance use and laws governing it on homicide types and rates. The point is that, while "experts" agree that police reports are most useful, they do not specify for what and it seems that the usefulness depends on the question about homicide that we want answered.

Despite this caveat, review of the literature on police statistics indicates that these statistics may reflect as much about the activity, size of the police force, ability to do detective work,[3] and tolerance level of the community[4] as they do the actual criminal phenomenon itself. A victim-offender relationship may remain "unknown" as a result of police inactivity, inadequate police work, or lack of interest in the victim. Lack of interest, in turn, may stem from the social characteristics of the victim (a skid rower or junkie in modern urban America; an Indian or black in earlier American towns) or from organizational restraints on police investigative departments. For example, lack of systematic investigation may result from assessing that the community does not want the investigation done or from low morale occurring when the police feel that their work will not result in prosecution. A systematic review of how police organization and police practice impinge specifically on homicide has not, to my knowledge, been done. It certainly seems credible that official police data may be fairly accurate on the actual occurrence of a homicide event. Our understanding of the types of homicide or of motives, however, may directly reflect the size of the force, the connections its investigative units have to the community, the priorities of the departments, and other organizational variables.

Other problems such as changes in legal code also may affect police data. At the present time, people dying as a result of faulty car design would not be classified as murder victims. While their cases might be investigated by accident investigation units, they would not likely be investigated by the homicide unit. Should pending court cases establish that deaths due to faulty design intentionally put out by a car company are homicide, a new type—that is, corporate homicide—would emerge as would changed police organization to investigate and report it. For an interesting discussion of this, see Swigert and Farrell, "Corporate Homicide: The New Criminality."[5] Other limitations of police statistics and of Uniform Crime Report data which are based on police statistics can be found in Savitz (1978).[6]

CORONERS' DATA

Mortality data are produced also by coroners and/or medical examiners' offices who forward their results, via death certificates, to the Division of Vital Statistics of the National Center for Health Statistics. While this article does not review all problems with data at the local coroners level, it should be noted that, as with police departments, patterns and practices of the coroners' offices will affect data collected by them. Some examples support this. The coroner, an appointed or elected official, is responsible for determining cause and/or manner of death. Coroners, as opposed to medical examiners, require no medical training. In some places the only requirement for holding office is that they be of legal age to hold office, and be living. Early in the century, and in the late nineteenth century, there was a fee-for-service system among coroners which directly affected their reporting of homicides. Coroners received a set fee for each death that they investigated and for which they established cause of death. The fee paid was the same no matter how much difficulty the case involved and the fee was, in cases of murder, often to be collected from the convicted offender. If, then, it was likely that the offender could not be found, as when a victim was found with a slit throat on the highway, or if the victim was of low social value, for example, an infant, these deaths were not likely to be reported as homicides but rather as a ruptured aorta in the case of the slit throat and suffocation for the infant.[7]

Further, the thoroughness of the investigation and detailed determination of cause of death is directly affected by the size, training, and funding of coroners' and medical examiners' staffs. Doing autopsies and establishing and maintaining toxicology units is expensive. Some offices, for example, large Medical Examiner (ME) offices, have such equipment and thus can tell actual cause of death, drugs in the blood stream, and the like. Many other smaller units cannot.

The factors noted above affect data collection at the local level; additional ones affects its reporting at the national level, that is, in the Vital Statistics reports. Changes in definition and coding affect the reports. For example, the ME determines intent of death during the course of investigation. If he/she calls it a homicide, it is; otherwise, it may be called an accident. If the medical examiner cannot determine which cause this suspicious death is, he/she can then call it undetermined. Prior to 1968, however, there was no possibility for calling a case undetermined. If an ME was unsure, the case was assigned, through a series of complex procedures, to either the accident or homicide categories.[8] The impact of such shifts in coding schemes on homicide rates is unclear but it is certainly plausible that such changing classification procedures have a decided effect on the data produced.

Added to this problem is the fact that states entered the national reporting system at different times. While Vital Statistics were available for some states from around 1900, they did not become fully national until the 1930s. Prior to the 1930s, the data available depended on which states and cities were included. Boston was the first entrant and, in general, there were data from East Coast cities very early. Boston had death data in 1880, Pennsylvania in 1906, and Washington, D.C., in 1880. Other states, however, for example, Georgia and Texas, entered the registry much later, in 1922 and 1933, respectively. In establishing the homicide trend, then, we have difficulty with obtaining national data prior to 1930 and, throughout the century, there are the forementioned data-reporting difficulties which affect the quality and the nature of the data.

In general this rather extended discussion of police and coroners' data has been included since almost all studies of homicide are based on one or the other of the two. While there are numerous problems with the data at both the local and national levels, it is somewhat reassuring to note that when comparing Uniform Crime Reports (UCR) and Vital Statistics rates of homicide through time, they are consistently in the same direction. In general, vital statistics rates are usually somewhat higher than the UCR for the same year.[9] This is due largely to the fact that Vital Statistics use a medical definition of homicide, that is, the intentional taking of another's life and UCR uses a legal definition, that is, the willful killing of another. Justifiable homicides, then, for example, police officers killing felons, are included in Vital Statistics while they are not in the UCR.

In the following sections all major studies of homicide from 1900 to 1979 are reviewed. The review attempts to establish a clear pattern of both the volume and type of homicide existing in each time period.

HOMICIDE: 1900-1930s

Despite the limitations of Vital Statistics noted earlier, these data were the basis for two major studies of early twentieth century homicide: Brearly, *Homicide in the United States* (1932) and Hoffman, *The Homicide Problem* (1925). Brearly and Hoffman were concerned with rates and showed that there was a steady increase in homicide rates from 5.0 in 1906 to 8.5 in 1929 (8.8 in 1926 and in 1928 were the highest years reported in their studies).[10] Higher victimization rates existed among blacks, among the young, and among men in certain regions of the country. The South and its northern neighbors (Ohio and West Virginia) had the highest rates while the New England states and the northern part of the Midwest had the lowest. The majority (71.46%) of the homicides were completed with a gun (Brearly, 1932: 68) with the general tendency being toward an increase in the use of guns throughout the early 1900s. Brearly explains part of the increasing homicide rate by inclusion of the western and southern states into the mortality data, and perhaps to some extent the impact of prohibition.

Local studies of specific cities using police and court data support the general trend established by Brearly. Sutherland and Gehlke (1933), based their arrest data from Baltimore, Buffalo, Chicago, Cleveland, St. Louis, and the state of Massachusetts, show increasing homicide rates from 1900 to the late 1920s with the peak for the five cities occurring in 1928. For Massachusetts the peak was in 1925.[11]

Boudouris's (1970) study of Detroit 1926-1968 using police records also shows the late 1920s to have a higher homicide rate than any of the other periods he studied. Boudouris's is one of the few studies for this time period that classified data into victim-offender relationships. Based on police record data for both victim and offender, Boudouris classified homicides into (1) domestic and love affairs; (2) friends and acquaintances; (3) business relationship, for example, landlord-tenant and prostitute-pimp; (4) criminal transaction, that is, homicide resulting from violation of the law, for example, bootlegging; (5) noncriminal, that is, killing of a felon by police or private citizen; (6) cultural-recreational-casual; (7) subcultural-recreational-casual; (8) other; and (9) unknown. He found that for the years 1926-1933, the largest percentage of homicides were noncriminal or justifiable, that is, killing of a felon by a police officer or a private citizen. When these were removed from the analysis, there were almost equal proportions of homicide involving domestic relations (18.2%), friend and acquaintances (18.2%), and criminal transactions (16.6%).[12] Many of the criminal transactions during this period (up to 1933 and the repeal of prohibition) were related to gang wars to control bootlegging. Forty of the 130 criminal transaction homicides in 1926-1929 or 71 out of 236 in 1926-1934 were of this variety. An additional 18 of the homicides were police killed in the line of duty, often in the process of enforcing prohibition law.

An analysis of 883 homicides in Chicago for the years 1926-1927 showed a somewhat similar pattern to that shown in Detroit. Like Detroit, a large percentage of homicides during this period were justifiable. While these Chicago data do not specify criminal transactions as a type of homicide, the data do suggest that when justifiables are removed from the analysis, the two major categories of homicide were gang and criminal related (approximately 33.3%) and altercations and brawls (30.4%). Domestic homicides were quite low being only 8.3% of the total.[13]

These two sources, then, suggest that to speak of one modal type of homicide for the 1900-1933 time period would be inaccurate, for there were a number of types. The occurrences of friends or acquaintances killing each other in arguments were frequent; however, homicides resulting from criminal transactions and those considered justifiable took on equal if not paramount importance. These latter two types, furthermore, were both apparently highly related to bootlegging and to the attempted enforcement of prohibition laws.[14] The extent to which family-related homicides were of importance varied with the city studied. It shared almost equal importance with criminal and friend homicides in Detroit but was of lesser importance in Chicago.

In sum, when we look at available data for the period of 1900 to the early 1930s, we find there was an increasing rate of homicide from 1900, peaking in the late 1920s and early 1930s. While the friend-friend homicide persisted as a major category, the category of criminal transaction and justifiable homicides became of equal or sometimes greater importance in terms of the amount and type of killing that was going on. The repeal of prohibition affected the rate, and the mid-1930s began to see a decline in rate and change in type which became pronounced in the next period of history.

HOMICIDE: THE MID-1930s TO THE MID-1960s

The mid-1930s began to see collection of fully national data on homicide both in the Vital Statistics and the UCR. These data reveal a steady decline of the homicide rates from the high of the late 1920s and early 1930s (Vital Statistics data) to a low and fairly steady rate of 5.6 in the 1940s and 4.8 in the 1950s (see Figure 1). The low rate of the 1950s persisted until the mid-1960s.[15]

In terms of the relationships in which people were killed, there were a number of studies of this period representing both southern and northern

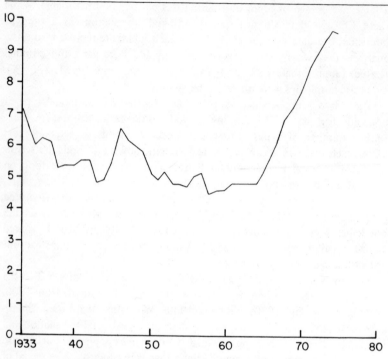

SOURCES: Uniform Crime Reports 1933-1965 as listed in Crimes of Violence
Marvin Wolfgang, 1967, p. 47.
Uniform Crime Reports 1965-1977 for each separate year.

FIGURE 1: Homicide Rates Per 100,000, U.S.A. 1933-1977

cities: Bullock (Houston), 1955; Harlan (Birmingham), 1950; Bensing and Schroeder (Cleveland), 1970; Boudouris (Detroit), 1970. Wolfgang's (1958) classic study of Philadelphia was also done during this time. All of the studies seem to show that during this period, domestic and love-related homicides became a more important category than in any preceding time and that males killing males in quarrelsome situations continued to be an important form of homicide, while homicides related to criminal transactions decreased to a small percentage.

Bullock (1955), using police records for the 489 cases of criminal homicide in Houston 1945-1949, found the highest rates of homicide clustered among low-income, black, and Hispanic people, 67% of whom were laborers and domestic servants. The homicides occurred most frequently between people who knew each other (in 87% of the cases the victim and offender were acquainted with each other) and arguments were the prime precipitating factors. Bullock does not indicate the number killed in domestic quarrels but indicated marital discord as a third most important reason for death. The three most frequent patterns precipitating homicide were: (1) arguments originating out of a variety of situations; (2) love triangles produced by jealousy between friends; and (3) marital discord. The most frequent place of death was a rooming house (42.1% of the victims were killed there) followed by a tavern (28.6%) and the street (21.1%).[16]

Birmingham, Alabama, was studied by Harlan (1950) during this same period. In his analysis of 500 cases of criminal homicide in that city from 1937 to 1944, he found that the majority of the victims were black males (67.8%) and that 45.2% of the cases were black males killing other black males. In all but 4.7% of the cases, the victim and the offender knew each other. The modal category was a black male killing a black male while arguing in a private residence. Murders stemming from such arguments (e.g., arguments over dice or money) were the prime circumstance surrounding homicides in Birmingham; marital discord, jealousy, and quarrels over lovers ranked next in frequency as the basis for murder.[17]

In northern cities of that time, Cleveland and Detroit, a similar pattern prevailed. Bensing and Schroeder (1970), using 662 cases of homicide from 1947 to 1953 in Cleveland, found that the majority of homicides involved black males who knew each other. In only 4.5% of the cases were the victim and offender unknown to each other. While Bensing and Schroeder's study does not permit establishing the predominant motive for homicide, they do list the following three motives as important: (1) quarrels of a petty nature; (2) marital discord; and (3) love or sex disputes in which the deceased is slain by one other than a spouse or common law mate.[18]

The importance of marital and love disputes is further documented in Boudouris's study of Detroit. He examined police reports on homicide in Detroit from 1926 to 1968. Analysis of his data shows the 1940s and especially the 1950s to be a time when domestic relations and love affairs claimed most of the homicide deaths. Recomputing his data to combine domestic relations and love affairs into one category indicate that in the 1920s, 21.9% of the homicides were domestically related; that figure rose in the 1930s to 29.3%; to 32.6% in the 1940s; and to a high of 38.4% in the 1950s.[19]

The friends and acquaintance category remained in a steady second place to domestic and love relations as lethal during the 1940s and 1950s.

Criminal transactions, which were of importance in the late 1920s and early 1930s, declined to a total of 19.2% of Detroit's criminal homicides in the 1940s and 9.2% in the 1950s.

Wolfgang's classic study further demonstrates the importance of close relationships in homicide during the 1940-1960 period. Wolfgang (1958) examined the universe of 588 criminal homicides in Philadelphia which occurred in 1948-1952. He used primarily police records which included the investigation reports of the Police Homicide Unit, witnesses' statements, and the like. The data for the 1948-1952 period indicated an overall criminal homicide rate of 5.7 per 100,000. The homicide rates for blacks and males were many times greater than for whites and females. The rate was 22.5 for blacks; 1.9 for whites; 9.0 for males; and 2.6 for females. Taking race and sex together, black males had a rate of 36.9 per 100,000; black females 9.6; white males 2.9; and white females 1.0. Further, a significant association was found between age and homicide. Those in the age group 25-34 were most likely to be victims, and offenders were likely to be in the 20-24 age group.

In terms of homicide setting, Wolfgang found that the single most dangerous place in Philadelphia in 1950 was inside a home (50.5% of the victims were slain there). Furthermore, the methods used to kill varied, with stabbing being the major means of death (38.8%) followed closely by shooting (33%), beating (21.8%), and other means (6.4%).

Wolfgang classified the cases both in terms of the victim-offender relationships and in terms of motive recorded by the police for the slaying. The relationships were coded into those of family; close friend, that is, frequent direct intimate contact over time; acquaintance, that is, direct contact as a result of personal knowledge but devoid of intimacy or frequency; stranger; paramour, mistress, prostitute, that is, a love object other than a spouse; sex rival; enemy; paramour of offender's mate; felon or police officer; innocent bystander; homosexual partner. (In 38 of the cases, the offender remained unknown.)

When adding together those involving a love object or sexual relationship, that is, family, paramour, and homosexual partner, we find that 35.1% of the victims were in a close love or sexual relationship with the killer. Further, when adding close friend and acquaintance, 28.2% and 13.5%, respectively, we find an additional total of 41.7% of the victims knew their killer.

Motives were classified as being the ostensible police recorded motive and included altercations of a "relatively trivial origin" (35.0%); domestic quarrels (14.1%); jelousy (11.6%); altercations over money (10.5%); robbery (6.8%); revenge (5.3%); accidental (3.9%); self-defense (1.4%); halting a felon (1.2%); escaping arrest (1.0%); concealing birth (1.0%); other (3.4%); and unknown (4.8%).[20]

In sum, the 1940s and especially the 1950s were a time with a relatively low and stable homicide rate. It was a time, further, when two types of murder seemed most prevalent, that between family members—usually husband and wife or lovers—and that between two males known to each other who were arguing at the time. In some cities, for example, Detroit, the family and love relationship murder was predominant, while in other places the male killing a male was the more frequent. But in all instances these two types were the dominant ones and, unlike an earlier period, the family and love relationship murder became a more highly dominant form in relationship and motive.

HOMICIDE: THE 1960s and 1970s

The trend of homicide in the 1960s and 1970s, as indicated by UCR data, shows the rate to remain fairly low and stationary from 1960 to 1965 (4.6, 4.8, 4.8, 4.8, 5.1, respectively). The rate began to increase in 1965 and 1966 (the rate was 5.6 in 1966) and continued steadily upward throughout the latter half of the 1960s and into the 1970s, with a peak rate occurring nationally in 1974 at 9.7. (The average UCR rate in the 1960s was 5.5, and in the 1970s 8.9.)

In terms of specific studies of homicide, there are more studies in this period than was true of earlier times. The most comprehensive study during this time was the Violence Commission Report (1969) and subsequent analyses by Curtis (1974).[21] A series of local studies included Zahn (1975), Zahn and Bencivengo (1973), Zahn and Nielson (1976), Zahn and Snodgrass (1978), Riedel and Katzanelson (1977), Block (1974, 1977), Hirsch (1973), Mumford et al. (1976), and Lundsgaarde (1977).[22]

The Violence Commission Report and subsequent analyses by Curtis (1974) was a national survey, using a 10% random sample of 1967 arrest reports, of 17 large U.S. cities.[23] The Commission found criminal homicide to be intrasexual in nature (63% of the cases where the victim-offender relationship was known involved a male killing another male) and intraracial (when race of both the victim and the offender is known only

10% of the murders are interracial). It is suspected, however, that the increase in stranger killings represents also an increase in interracial murders, especially black on white. In terms of victim-offender relationships, the 17 American cities in 1967 showed husband and wife killings to account for 15.8% of all criminal homicides; 8.9% were other family members; 9.0% were other primary relations, that is, close friends and lovers; 29.8% were nonprimary but known to each other; 15.6% were strangers; and in 20.9% of the cases the offender remained unknown (thus likely to be a stranger).

Regarding motive, the survey revealed that minor altercations were the most frequent reasons for the death (35.7%); followed by unknown reasons (21.0%); other reasons (10.6%); and robbery (8.8%). Family quarrels accounted for only 7.7% of the homicide deaths. In terms of weapon, 46.6% were killed with a firearm, 29.2% with a knife, and the remainder by other means.

Other local studies reveal similar homicide patterns although with some variation based, apparently, on differences between northern and southern cities. Studies of northern cities for the 1960s and 1970s include: Block, Chicago (1974, 1977); Riedel and Katzenelson, Washington, DC (1977); Zahn and Bencivengo and Zahn and Nielsen, Philadelphia (1973, 1976); and Hirsch, Cleveland (1973). Studies of southern or southwestern cities include: Mumford et al., Atlanta (1976); Lundsgaarde, Houston (1977); and Zahn and Snodgrass, Dallas (1978).

Block (1974, 1977), using police records, studied 7045 criminal homicides occurring in Chicago from 1965 to 1974. He found that the homicide rate doubled in that period of time from 11.4 per 100,000 in 1965 to 29.2 in 1974. The number of homicides in which the victim and offender did not know each other increased dramatically from 95 to 410 and, in fact, the most common offender is one whose identity remains unknown to the police. Much of the increase in homicide could be accounted for by an increase in the number of homicides related to robbery. There are, according to Block, essentially two patterns of homicide, one of altercation homicide based on domestic feuds or arguments with friends and the second based on robbery. The second increased much more rapidly than the first in the time period studied. Further, there was an increase in homicides using guns.

Riedel and Katzenelson (1977), using arrest data for 3411 homicides in Washington, DC, from 1957 to 1974, found an increasing rate for the time period, from 12.2 in 1957 to 31.3 in 1974. They found an appreciable decrease in the age of offenders. Homicide remained an intraracial event, primarily between nonwhite offenders and victims. While they did not do an analysis based on victim-offender relationship, they do note a decrease in the percentage of homicides occurring in homes. In 1957, 58.0% of the homicides occurred there, while in 1972, 32.7% did. One of the largest changes was in method used to kill: In 1957, 35.9% of the homicides were committed by firearm, by 1974 this had increased to 82.8%.

The findings for Chicago and for Washington, DC, are similar to those in Cleveland (Hirsch, 1973) and in Philadelphia (Zahn, 1975; Zahn and Nielsen, 1976). Hirsch, using coroners' records, found that the homicide rate in Cleveland rose gradually in the early 1960s and then dramatically in the latter half of the 1960s. The rate of increase was great for both nonwhite and white males, although the increase for white male victims were much greater, 600% compared to 200% for nonwhites. While they do not study victim-offender relationships, they note a higher percentage of homicides occurring by firearms than in the preceding time periods.

Zahn, also using medical examiners' records, studied 1935 homicide victims in Philadelphia from 1969 to 1973. When comparing her results with those of Wolfgang, who studied Philadelphia in the late 1940s and in the 1950s, she found a much higher rate of homicide in 1970, 19.2 per 100,000. There are more offenders in the youngest age groups. Data showed that over half (50.4%) of the homicides occurred with a gun, and 35.3% occurred at home. Further, in terms of reasons for the homicide, the most frequent category was arguments: 34.9% of the homicides resulted from such circumstance. This was followed by unknown (fully 24.3% of the homicides occur for unknown reasons, usually by unknown offenders) and this was followed by domestic quarrel (15.4% of the homicides occurred for domestic reasons). In general, while the dominant form may be an acquaintance killing another acquaintance in an argument, it is closely followed by a stranger killing someone, with the circumstances immediately surrounding the event remaining unknown.[24]

Findings from studies of northern cities, then, show a consistent picture of an increasing homicide rate in the late 1960s and into the 1970s; an increase in homicides by gun; and an increase in homicides with unknown assailants who may be murdering for money or for reasons other than direct argument. The stranger is, indeed, a more fearful figure in northern American cities in the 1970s than he was earlier.

Studies of southern and southwestern cities for the same time period show a somewhat different pattern. Mumford et al. (1976), using police and medical examiners' records for 591 victims in 1961-1962 and 1971-1972, found that there was an increasing rate of homicide, increasing for both black and white males. The pattern of homicide varied somewhat, however, for the blacks and the whites. While most blacks and whites were killed at home by relatives or acquaintances, more blacks were killed in such a situation than whites. Whites were more likely than blacks to be killed in a public place and this tendency seemed to increase from the 1960s to the 1970s. In both situations, however, firearms were the main mode of attack and there was an increase in the use of firearms from the 1960s to the 1970s.

Lundsgaarde (1977), studying 300 murders in Houston in 1969, found murder was largely intraracial, with only 6% of Houston killers crossing racial boundaries. The categories of relationship and kinds of situation have not, he claimed, changed significantly over the past 40 years, with the exception of a slight increase in the number of killings involving strangers (in 17.5% of the cases the killer was a total stranger to the victim). In his sample the vast bulk of victims knew their killers—in 31% of the cases they were in the family group. In Houston most were killed by guns (86%) and more were killed outside the home (60%) than inside.

Zahn and Snodgrass (1978), studying 202 homicide victims in Dallas, found, as in Houston, that most victims were males; that 33.6% of the killings were family related; and 24.5% involved acquaintances, 17.3% strangers, and 13.4% unknown. About equal numbers were killed inside as outside the home, and the primary motive for killing was domestic quarrels. Of the murders, 38% were a result of domestic quarrels. As in all other cities, the gun was the main instrument of death.

Taking all studies from the 1960s and the 1970s, there is some commonality. There is a higher rate of homicide than in the time period immediately preceding it. By and large homicide is, as in other time periods, intraracial and intrasexual, although there is some slight increase in interracial (black on white) homicide and guns are the most frequent mode of attack. There is an increase in stranger murders and in cases where the offender remains unknown, although this increase is much more pronounced in northern cities. In southern or southwestern cities domestic violence remains a significant category while in the North the stranger and the unknown assailant homicide is now a dominant (if not the dominant) murder relationship.

SUMMARY

From a review of the foregoing information, it seems warranted to suggest the following regarding homicide in twentieth century America.

THE HOMICIDE RATE

The homicide rate has fluctuated through time. The trend was relatively low at the turn of the century (Lane, 1978) but started to increase in the early twentieth century, reaching one peak in the 1920s and early 1930s. The course went down, with occasional exceptions, in the 1940s and remained low and stable during the 1950s and early 1960s, A sharp and steady rise began to occur around 1965, peaking in 1974 (the rate was 9.7 in that year). The rate for the final two years (8.8) remains high, however, and is the same as the high rates found in the 1920s (8.8 in 1926, 8.7 in 1927, and 8.8 in 1928).

THE SEXUAL CHARACTER OF HOMICIDE

Homicide has remained intramale in character through time. Generally speaking, when comparing across studies, approximately 60% of the cases involve a man killing another man. Very few women kill another woman.[25] In cross-sex killings, while men and women (usually husbands and wives) have been killing each other for some time, it seems that there is more likelihood for men to kill women than the reverse. (Research which I am currently beginning will determine whether this is true even during times of increasing attempts at female liberation.)

THE RACIAL CHARACTER OF HOMICIDE

The extent to which homicide is intraracial or interracial is somewhat difficult to assess, since white frontiersmen killing Indians and the Ku Klux Klan killing blacks may not be generally contained in information on homicide. Using conventional sources on homicide, however, it seems that homicide is consistently an intraracial rather than an interracial event. While the predominance of homicide within racial groups is consistent through time, there has been some increase in interracial homicide since the mid-1960s. In 1967, 10% of the homicides were interracial (Mulvihill et al., 1969) with the percentage being higher than that in some cities (Chicago, Block, 1974; 1977).

THE VICTIM–OFFENDER RELATIONSHIP

The comparison between studies on victim-offender relationship is the most difficult to accomplish. This is due to the fact that there is no consistent definition of what constitutes an acquaintance or a stranger relationship and, further, many studies use motive as the basis of classification, for example, criminal transaction, but do not indicate whether the criminal transaction involved an acquaintance or stranger relationship.

After trying to make the data comparable, however, the following seems supportable. Throughout the century a male killing another male with whom he is acquainted is a regular and persistent form of homicide. During the time of greatest homicide, however, the stranger or economic relationship murder predominates. In the late 1920s the murder related to prohibition and in the 1960s and the 1970s the murder by unknown persons for unknown reason and/or the murder for profit (robbery) are of importance. In contrast, when homicide rates are low such as in the 1950s, family and acquaintance homicides are dominant, with family murders especially so.

In general it seems that the percentage of family-related murders does not fluctuate dramatically through time. The stranger and unknown categories of relationship and so-called economically motivated homicides, however, do. They are the main contributors to the times of highest rates.[26] In all events, while some categories of victim-offender relationship remain throughout time, the prominence of these types varies in different time periods.

MANNER OF ATTACK AND HOMICIDE

Many current researchers point to the increasing use of guns as the reason for the increase in the homicide rate generally (e.g., Block, 1974) and, more specifically, for the increase in homicides where the victim's assailant remains unknown. The data from existing studies suggest that deaths by firearms do not show continuous progressive rise throughout the century, but rather that a high percentage of deaths by gun occur at the same time as high homicide rates. Since we have seen that the homicide rate fluctuates decidedly, so, too, does the use of guns.

Prior to the twentieth century, Lane (1978) indicates that a person in Philadelphia was as likely to have been killed by a gun (25%), a sharp instrument (25%), or fists and feet (21%). In the 1924-1926 period, the overall rate of firearms used in homicides rose sharply. Brearly (1932) reports that 70.2% of the nation's homicides were gun related. Boudouris (1977), writing of Detroit 1926-1929, also indicates high use of firearms, with 60.9% of the victims killed that way. His figures, interestingly, almost duplicate those of the most recent UCR which show 62.5% killed by guns, 19% by a sharp instrument, 12.9% by a blunt instrument, and 5.5% by the body. The findings from the 1920s and from the 1970s contrast sharply with Wolfgang's findings in the 1950s in Philadelphia where the major means of death was a knife.

Time series studies, further, support the notion of the fluctuating use of guns (Riedel and Katzenelson, 1977; Block, 1974, 1977). Riedel, for instance, traced death by guns in Washington, DC, from 1957 to 1974. The percentage killed by guns remained low and steady from 1957 to 1966 (e.g., 35.9% were killed by firearms in 1957). These percentages jumped to 82.8% by 1974, with the percentages for each year since 1966 being the following (52%, 60%, 70%, 73%, 66%, 65%, 76%, and 82%, respectively).[27]

Block also reported an increase in killings by guns as it attended an increase in murder during robberies and by unknown assailants. Interestingly, however, in Chicago, killings of women victims were about equally likely to be killed by gun or other method, while gun killings of black and Latin males increased especially fast.

The point is that guns do bear a relationship to the murder rate; in times of highest homicide rates, the 1920s and early 1930s and since 1968, the percentage of people killed by gun is also high. Yet it would not seem that availability of guns alone is the answer to the high U.S. homicide rate. It seems unlikely, for example, that the number of guns available were appreciably less in the 1950s than in the 1920s, or that the number changed drastically in Washington, DC, from one year, 1968, to the next, 1969. What may change is not only availability but also the readiness to use guns and the definition of when and for what purpose the use of firearms is desirable.

From the foregoing we might ask of what importance it is to know these facts; to know that the rates of homicide fluctuate with very high peaks in the late 1920s and early 1930s and the mid-1970s; to know that the major types of victim-offender relationship are somewhat variable with the high rate times being characterized by more guns, more stranger, and unknown homicides; and that, while family killings and males killing their male acquaintances remain types, the importance of family-related homicide is relatively stable through time and significant when the overall homicide rate is low. The importance lies in two areas: the research questions they trigger and their implications for social policy.

While a complete statement of new research directions and all the policy implications derivable from them is beyond this current attempt, a few beginning statements may prove helpful.

In terms of research directions, this historical review would suggest that closer attention be paid to the connection between markets for illegal goods and the overall rate of homicide violence. It seems possible, if not likely, that establishing and maintaining a market for illegal goods (booze in the 1920s and early 1930s; heroin and cocaine in the late 1960s and early 1970s) may involve controlling and/or reducing the competition, solving disputes between alternate suppliers, or eliminating dissatisfied customers. The resolution of such problems in illegal markets is not easily done by resorting to use of legal sanction (although payoffs may occur). There may, then, be more likelihood of resorting to force to settle differences. This resolution has the added advantage of silencing the victim and thus preventing unwanted information from leaking to official sources.

The use of guns in illegal markets may also be triggered by the constant "fear" of being caught either by a rival or by the police. Such fear may increase the perceived need for protection, that is, a gun, thus may increase the arming of these populations and a resulting increased likelihood of use. For the overall society this may mean a higher homicide rate.

All of this supposition, of course, begs the larger questions of why substance use is sanctioned at certain times and why so many people at certain periods want these substances. Both questions may also be related to research foci necessary for understanding homicide.

If this historical survey might prompt different research directions, so, too, might it prompt new considerations of policy issues. For example, these findings have direct implications for the deployment of criminal justice resources. The very allocation of resource systems may be affected by such knowledge, for with careful monitoring of types of homicide that are occurring, differing allocations to solve the problems associated with these types might occur. As robbery-related homicides increase, for example, the allocation of resources to improve robbery detection equipment in stores or on the streets and educating the citizen in self-protection (without arming himself/herself) might result. Further, additional resources to increase crime lab work, for example, ballistics, would seem a reasonable approach. Because of the prohibitive cost of such labs, they might be set up on a county or regional base, thus allowing not only better detection but cost-effective detection as well.[28]

When family homicide is dominant, additional resources to family courts; more training to help people solve domestic disputes; educating people to not reach for a gun if they argue; or, if they have guns in the house, to make sure they are not loaded, might be done. And, if homicides are linked to illegal market activity, attempting to draw people out of the illegal markets and into legal ones would seem necessary.

Further, gun control has often been proposed as a way to reduce the homicide rate. Since the data here indicates a correlation between a high homicide rate and a high use of guns, this approach seems justified. However, those persons using guns and their reasons for doing so must also be closely examined. Perhaps, if my previous analysis has any validity, taking profit out of illegal substance markets would also reduce the use of guns in some populations and, thus, the homicide rate overall.

Many more research and policy considerations suggest themselves. I hope that these few illustrate sufficiently, however, the direct relevance of history to our current endeavors and that they provide some illustration of why a firm grounding in history is necessary for both the understanding of and the solution to the problem of homicide.

NOTES

1. This difference is at least partially attributable to differences in data sources. In the 1920s Vital Statistics were used as a base of homicide studies and they include justifiable homicides within the overall homicide statistic. Police date (Uniform Crime Reports) which are used more frequently in later studies do not so classify it.

2. Donald J. Mulvihill and Melvin M. Tumin with Lynn A. Curtis, *Crimes of Violence*, Vol. 11 (Washington, DC: Government Printing Office, 1969), 14-16.

3. See Leonard D. Savitz, "Official Police Statistics and Their Limitations," in Leonard D. Savitz and Norman Johnston, eds., *Crime in Society* (New York: Wiley, 1978) and M. Hindelang, "The Uniform Crime Reports Revisited," *Journal of Criminal Justice* Vol. 2:1 (1974) 1-17.

4. See Roger Lane, *Violent Death in the City: Suicide, Accident, and Murder in Nineteenth Century Philadelphia* (Cambridge, MA: Harvard University Press, 1979); and L. J. Center and T. G. Smith, "Criminal Statistics–Can They Be Trusted?", *American Criminal Law Review* 11: (1973), 1046-1086.

5. Victoria Lynn Swigert and Ronald A. Farrell, "Corporate Homicide: The New Criminality" (Unpublished paper presented at the American Society of Criminology meetings, Dallas, 1978).

6. Leonard D. Savitz, *op. cit.* This article and other sources indicate that the number of police agencies cooperating in the voluntary Uniform Crime Report reporting system has changed over time from 400 in 1930 to 8500 in 1968, representing 92% of the national population. National data, then, are not available from police sources until well after the 1930s which makes establishing the homicide trend for the early part of the century difficult.

7. Roger Lane, *op. cit.* (1979).

8. Information regarding this classification change was obtained from a telephone conversation with the former head of the Mortality Unit of Vital Statistics.

9. Examples of homicide rates from both Vital Statistics and Uniform Crime Reports sources: Vital Statistics homicide rates for 1971, 9.1; 1972, 9.4; 1973, 9.8; 1974, 10.2; 1975, 9.8. UCR data homicide rates for 1971, 8.5; 1972, 8.9; 1973, 9.3; 1974, 9.7; 1975, 9.6.

10. H. C. Brearly, *Homicide in the United States* (Chapel Hill: University of North Carolina Press, 1932) and Frederick Hoffman, *The Homicide Problem* (San Francisco: Prudential Press, 1925). Vital Statistics data reported subsequent to the publication of Brearly and Hoffman's studies showed the homicide rate continued to rise and peaked in 1933. (The rate in that year was 9.7.) These Vital Statistics are summarized in *Historical Statistics of the United States: Colonial Times to 1970* (Washington, DC: Government Printing Office, 1975) p. 414.

11. Edwin H. Sutherland and C. E. Gehlke, "Crime and Punishment," in *Recent Social Trends in the United States* (New York: McGraw-Hill, 1933) 1114-1167.

12. James Boudouris, *Trends in Homicide, Detroit 1926-1968* (Unpublished Ph.D. dissertation, Wayne State University, 1970) and James Boudouris, "A Classification of Homicides," *Criminology* 11 (1974, 525-540.

13. For detailed analysis of the Chicago data, see H. C. Brearly, *op. cit.,* p. 58 and also, Arthur V. Lashly, "Homicide (In Cook County)," Chapter XIII, in *The Illinois Crime Survey* (Chicago: Illinois Association for Criminal Justice, 1929).

14. For an interesting discussion of how violence became associated with bootlegging, see "Bootleggers and American Gambling 1920-1950" by Mark Haller (unpublished manuscript, Temple University, 1979).

15. The rate for the decades were computed by averaging the UCR homicide rate figures for the 1940-1949 and 1950-1959 periods, respectively.

16. Henry Allen Bullock, "Urban Homicide in Theory and Fact," *Journal of Criminal Law and Criminology,* 45 (1955), 563-575.

17. Howard Harlan, "Five Hundred Homicides," *Journal of Criminal Law and Criminology* 6 (1950), 736-752.

18. Robert C. Bensing and Oliver Schroeder, Jr., *Homicide in an Urban Community* (Springfield, IL: Charles C Thomas, 1970).

19. James Boudouris, *op. cit.* (unpublished Ph.D. dissertation, Wayne State University, 1970). Data for the 1920s do not encompass a whole decade but only the years 1926 to 1929. All figures represent an average of the percentages.

20. See Marvin E. Wolfgang, *Patterns in Criminal Homicide* (Oxford, England: Oxford University Press, 1958).

21. The Violence Commission Reports are found in Donald J. Mulvihill and Melvin M. Tumin, *Crimes of Violence: Staff Reports to the National Commission on the Causes and Prevention of Violence,* Vols. 1, 11, 12, 13 (Washington, DC: Government Printing Office, 1969). See also, Lynn A. Curtis, *Criminal Violence* (Lexington, MA: Lexington Books, 1974).

22. The following is a fairly comprehensive list of local studies done of homicide in the 1960s and 1970s. Margaret A. Zahn, "The Female Homicide Victim," *Criminology* 13 (1975), 400-415. Margaret A. Zahn and Mark Bencivengo, "Violent Death: A Comparison between Drug Users and Non-Drug Users," *Addictive Diseases: An International Journal*, Vol. 1:3 (1973), 283-296. Margaret A. Zahn and Kathleen E. Neilson, "Changing Patterns of Criminal Homicide: A Twenty Year Follow-Up" (Unpublished paper presented at the American Society of Criminology meetings, Tucson, Arizona, November 1976). Margaret A. Zahn and Glenn Snodgrass, "Drug Use and the Structure of Homicide in Two U.S. Cities," in Edith Flynn and John Conrad, eds., *The New and Old Criminology* (New York: Praeger Press, 1978), 134-150. Marc Riedel and Susan Katzenelson, "Homicide Trends in the District of Columbia 1957-1974" (Unpublished paper presented at the American Society of Criminology meetings, Atlanta, 1977). Richard Block, "Homicide in Chicago: A Ten Year Study, 1965-1974" (Paper presented at American Society of Criminology meetings, Chicago, 1974) and Richard Block, *Violent Crime* (Lexington, MA: Lexington Books, 1977). Charles S. Hirsch, "Homicide and Suicide in a Metropolitan County: Long Term Trends," *Journal of the American Medical Association* 223 (1973), 900-905. Robert S. Mumford, Ross S. Kazer, Roger A. Feldman, and Robert R. Stivers, "Homicide Trends in Atlanta," *Criminology* 14 (1976), 213-232. Henry P. Lundsgaarde, *Murder in Space City* (New York: Oxford University Press, 1977).

23. The cities surveyed included: Atlanta, Boston, Chicago, Cleveland, Dallas, Denver, Detroit, Los Angeles, Miami, Minneapolis, New Orleans, New York, Philadelphia, San Francisco, Seattle, St. Louis, and Washington, D.C.

24. Additional studies by Zahn and by Zahn and Bencivengo, *op. cit.* (1975, 1973) also show a connection between illegal drug use and homicide in the 1960s and 1970s. In a high percentage of Philadelphia cases (approximately one-third in 1972), homicide victims have drugs, usually heroin, in their systems at time of death. Further, 14% of these users died in drug-related arguments. How many of the "unknown assailant" homicides may involve drug-related arguments remains, of course, a mystery. The connection between illegal substance use and homicide victimization in the 1960s and 1970s, however, warrants closer attention.

25. The problem of infanticide in which women are more usually involved than men complicates this statement somewhat. The complication may be especially important in the early part of the century.

26. Whether the increased volume leads to more police and coroner classification of homicides as unknowns or whether the higher percentage means a real change in the nature of social relationships and the object of attack warrants close examination.

27. For the complete analysis, see Marc Riedel and Susan Katzenelson, "Homicide Trends in the District of Columbia 1957-1974" *op. cit.* (1977).

28. Thanks to Chief Inspector John Craig of the Philadelphia Police Department for this idea.

HISTORICAL ANALYSES OF CRIMINAL LEGISLATION AND POLICY

6

THE POLITICS OF CRIMINAL JUSTICE REFORM: NINETEENTH CENTURY FRANCE

THOMAS J. DUESTERBERG

I

The casual observer of modern politics knows that the "crime problem" is an issue charged with political importance. A standard salvo in any political campaign is that one's opponent either exhibits indulgence toward the criminal or that repressive measures are weighted unjustly against him. Similar charges have been a regular source of political currency since the late eighteenth century.[1] What is perhaps less evident is that the repressive practices of a given regime inevitably reflect its most deeply rooted political beliefs and reveal much about the nature of its political arrangements. In this article I would like to explore the history of criminal justice reform in modern France and to show the ways in which political considerations have tempered and shaped them.

The French case offers a unique perspective on this question for two reasons. First, the history of criminal justice reform in France recapitulates the Western experience in modern times. Each successive stage in the development of the contemporary system of criminal justice in the advanced Western world is clearly demarcated and articulated in French history. From the campaign against the "barbarism" and "inhumanity" of the Old Regime practices, through the world-wide movement of prison reform in the early nineteenth century, to contemporary practices of "social defense" and scientific management of deviance, the French have been in the forefront of criminology and penal practice. Second, French political life in the period from 1760 to 1900 (by which time the contemporary system of criminal justice was largely in place) was more mercurial than that of other nations. More pertinent, the principal changes in criminal law and penal practices in France occurred invariably as the result of profound political transformations, that is, soon after revolutions or *coup d' états*. The coincidence in the histories of political regimes and criminal justice reform allows us to gauge the deep political grounding of each type of repressive practice developed in modern times.

My purpose in delineating the relationship between political change and reform in the system of criminal justice is of course to show the political limitations inhibiting or promoting certain types of criminal justice policy. But I would also like to suggest that familiarity with some features of the French experience is useful to those reflecting on the strengths and weaknesses of the American justice system. An understanding of the process by which the contemporary French justice apparatus took form will illuminate some problems facing American justice officials. For the French have, since the end of the nineteenth century, resolved some of the political difficulties inherent to the implementation of a policy designed to prevent crime (1) by regulating some features of social life, (2) by implementing social scientific correctional strategies to treat deviants and potential deviants, and (3) by taking precautionary measures against habitual offenders. These programs, which contemporary criminology recommends, have not been fully implemented in the United States due to the deeply rooted respect for individual liberty lying at the heart of the American political consensus. Consequently, an examination of the way in which the French have approached this problem may prove useful.

II

Before beginning a discussion of the political meaning of criminal justice reform, it is necessary to give a brief overview of the major stages marking the development of the contemporary program of criminal justice in France and to describe in a cursory manner how each stage is linked to a particular phase in the evolution of modern French democracy. I might add that I regard this process as teleological only in the sense that each of its stages has contributed to the constitution of the present system of justice in France. I will also make a few remarks describing the manner in which reform has been accomplished. This will provide a preliminary indication of the symbiotic relation between political change and justice reform.

Four essential components comprise the contemporary French criminal justice system:[2] (1) retribution, the punishment of offenders; (2) deterrence, the attempt to discourage potential offenders through the threat of retribution; (3) correctional or rehabilitative treatment, the use of methods devised by scientific experts to modify antisocial or criminal tendencies in the offender; and (4) prevention, the implementation of programs intended to combat those psychological and social conditions thought to be conducive to criminal behavior. As is well-known to students of the history of criminal law, modern theories and institutions of criminal justice first appeared in the latter half of the eighteenth century in the context of the campaign to reform the inhumane and ineffective repressive practices of the absolute monarchy. During the great age of reformist thought and revolution in Europe, legislators and social critics devised a new method of controlling crime which relied primarily on the powers of retribution and deterrence.[3] The greatest single monument to the reformist spirit of the eighteenth century is the Napoleonic Code (1808-1810).

Supporters of the Code (a preliminary version of which was introduced in 1791) hoped both to control crime and to limit the absolute authority of the executive power. The repressive system employed by the Old Regime had become a symbol of its arbitrary authority and its ineffectual rule. Contemporary observers were shocked by what they perceived as an invasion of criminals. The basic assumption underlying the Code was that crime could be deterred most effectively by assigning a specific quantity of punishment to each socially harmful act (which is the utilitarian definition of crime). Proponents of the rule of law also reasoned that liberty could be protected best by a criminal code with a fixed universe of crimes and punishments and by rules of procedure establishing the rights of individuals against arbitrary arrest and punishment. The purpose of the Napoleonic Code, then, was to deter crime through a reasoned scale of proportionate penalties while at the same time protecting the freedom of the innocent.

Soon after the fall of the Napoleonic Empire (1915), however, politicians and social thinkers began to question the efficacy of the Napoleonic system, which had been maintained largely intact by the restored Bourbon monarchy (1815-1830).[4] Impetus for the asault on the deterrent system the Emperor bequeathed to modern France came primarily from a group of liberals who were eventually to take power after the Revolution of 1830. Despite the liberal intentions of the philosophers who first elaborated the utilitarian theory of deterrence, the pristine rule of law envisioned by eighteenth century reformers was never definitively established in France before 1830. Napoleon and the last two Bourbon kings abused the intent of the Codes by replacing the legally constituted tribunals with military jurisdictions and employing blatantly arbitrary methods of political repression. Napoleon also modified the original liberal codes to employ a harsher scale of penalties than the principles of proportionality and humanity warranted. Furthermore, by the late 1820s, it had become apparent that criminal activity was increasing, leading liberal critics to the empirical conclusion that a system of harsh repression and deterrence was ineffective.[5]

When the liberal critics of the 1820s assumed power in 1830, one of the first and most publicized of its reforms altered the nature of the criminal justice system.[6] The liberal social thinkers, some of whom now were legislators and administrators, who engineered the reforms reasoned that crime could be reduced and personal liberty better protected by eliminating authoritarian impediments to the rule of law and by perfecting methods of punishment. The 1830s and 1840s mark the heroic age of prison reform in the Western world, and the liberals of the July Monarchy made a significant contribution to the movement.[7] One change implemented in the 1830s had the effect of individualizing punishment by giving judges and juries the right to determine sentences within fairly broad limits. More important to contemporaries, however, was the transformation of prisons into "penitentiaries" capable of effecting the moral rehabilitation of inmates. Consequently, the French began to rely on an individualized, corrective prison regime as a necessary supplement to the deterrent effect of the criminal code.

In 1848 the Constitutional Monarchy fell to a revolutionary upsurge, and in 1851 Louis-Napoleon imposed an authoritarian regime on the French. The new Emperor, like his uncle and most dictators, attempted to win prestige and maintain order by shoring up the forces of repression and by imposing harsh criminal penalties on political and common-law offenders.[8] He terminated the program of prison improvement, choosing instead to alter criminal law and procedure to permit stiffer sentences. Napoleon thus reversed the trend of the previous 20 years by increasing penalities and reducing emphasis on rehabilitative treatment. His policy of achieving order through the use of blunt force was especially clear in his harsh treatment of political dissidents and of petty recidivists. The justification offered by the Emperor's supporters for the new repressive regime, whose single lasting accomplishment was improving the training and tripling the size of the police forces, gives an unusually clear insight into the political nature of criminal justice reform. The leading penal theorist of the Second Empire (1851-1870) made the following claim in his analysis of the justice reforms of the July Monarchy:

> One can also be certain that the 1832 revision of the penal code, however one interprets it (either as an abdication of the rights and duties of authority, or as a concession to disorder and the violation of laws, or as the complete enervation of the penal system) was the most direct, if least noticed, causes of the moral anarchy which brought the Revolution of 1848![9]

Apart from its decision to gut the liberal reforms of the July Monarchy, the Second Empire made no lasting contribution to modern ideas or policies in the field of criminal justice. What Napoleon did accomplish was to break the stranglehold of classical liberal thinking in all fields, including that of criminal justice. After 1848, theorists and practitioners began to contemplate repressive correctional and preventive policies which challenged, at least implicitly, the principle of inviolability of individual liberty which informed the thinking of the *philosophes* and the practice of the July Monarchy. By challenging the classical liberal and penal philosophy of his predecessors, Napoleon opened the path to further innovations by the first stable democratic regime to rule France, the Third Republic (1871-1940).

During the first three decades of the Third Republic, the French criminal justice system took its contemporary form. As with the other changes of regime in nineteenth century France, the Third Republic was born on the heels of violent events. It was only after their forces had decisively turned back the conservatives' efforts to reinstate dictatorial rule (that is, after 1879) that the republicans were able to initiate the series of social reforms which included profound changes in methods of repression and crime control.[10] The republicans perceived that social reform was imperative if they were to maintain political power in the face of conservative and authoritarian opposition. One means of solidifying political support was to find new, more effective means to restore the social and moral order so gravely compromised by the revolution and social crisis of the 1870s.[11] A new approach to the crime problem, whose unacceptable growth a government study in 1880 confirmed, proved to be an important component of the reform program.[12]

The justice officials of the Third Republic developed a multifaceted program to counter what they now labelled an "epidemic" of crime.[13] One of the first major policy changes of the Third Republic was to reinstate and perfect the program of prison improvements (1875). The major thrust of prison reform was to provide more adequate correctional treatment and postliberation care for petty offenders who spent less than two years behind bars.[14] The minister of justice also overturned those Napoleonic statutes which had undermined some rights and procedures guaranteeing due process and proportionality of punishment.[15] Next, a series of laws intended to permit the forces of repression to protect society against such "dangerous" individuals as alcoholics, violent revolutionaries, the criminally insane, and habitual offenders was passed into law between 1873 and 1894. A law of 1885, for instance, allowed judges to sentence habitual offenders to penal colonies for life. These laws mark a significant evolution in legal thinking, as their intent was to punish a dangerous *state* rather than a specific *act*.

Another important body of legislation passed between 1885 and 1891 introduced parole and probation into sentencing procedures and made the "legal pardon"[16] much simpler and easier to obtain. The effect of these laws and sentencing practices was to reduce the prison population by one-half between 1870 and 1910.[17] By this time criminologists had come to believe that the most effective means to correct criminal behavior was to effect the social reintegration of the offender, hence to treat him outside the enclosed walls of the prison. In close contact with an internal movement to improve the judicial regime for juveniles, reformers also gradually developed and implemented a separate regime of tribunals and correctional facilities for youthful offenders (completed in 1912).[18] In this instance, too, the effect of the new procedures was to keep juveniles out of prisons and to effectuate their reform in the context of the community rather than the asylum.[19]

What was truly innovative in the penal reforms of the Third Republic, and what links them to contemporary policy, is that they were conceived as part of a much broader program of social reform. The political leaders and social thinkers of this period spearheaded a series of reforms which inaugurated the age of the welfare state in France.[20] The most important innovations included the creation of the modern system of secular education, economic stimulation and labor regulation programs, an expansion of public welfare services, regulation of dangerous substances, public health programs, and the first of the modern series of social security programs (all introduced between 1874 and 1900). Republican politicians intended these measures to supply the degree of social justice required to consolidate support for the new democratic state, while at the same time breaking the stranglehold of the Catholic Church and the conservative elites on education, the economy, and public welfare services.[21]

Criminologists viewed these programs as a means to combat crime and social disorder in general.[22] They reasoned that it was the "breakdown" of social organization, rather than simply the moral defects of the offender, which explained the "crisis of civilization" whose clearest indicator was the growth of crime. Both legislators and social theorists wanted to restore social order by regulating social institutions and providing those services deemed necessary to the maintenance of strong and healthy social ties.

The evolution of the contemporary juvenile justice system in the Third Republic provides the most striking example of the links drawn between social reform and changes in criminal law.[23] Laws passed in 1889 and 1898 radically altered the regime of juvenile justice and at the same time effected a profound change in the most sacred of modern social institutions, the family. These two laws declared that in any case of a crime committed "by or against" a child, the court could rule the *family* had failed in its duty to educate its offspring. In such cases, the laws gave the presiding judge power to revoke the legal authority of the parents over their child. The laws then charged the bench with seeing to the proper education and/or correctional treatment of the child, be he victim or offender. Even a child victimized by his parents could be sent to reform school if the judge found his behavior antisocial in any way.

The laws on child abuse and juvenile delinquency illuminate several trends in the social and criminological thought of the Third Republic. They demonstrate, first, the degree to which legislators linked social and penal reform. Second, they show how legislators invoked the threat of crime as a justification for broad social reform. Finally, they give proof of the shift in criminal thought which has caused modern social thinkers to combat delinquency through the regulation of social relations rather than through retribution or correctional education alone. The use of parole, probation, and legal pardons, and the decline of imprisonments likewise illustrate the same policy. For these new programs to succeed, it was necessary to exert some degree of control over the social networks burdened with the task of achieving the social reintegration of deviants and potential deviants.

III

Thus far I have shown that the modern history of the French criminal justice system can be divided into three principal phases, that these phases describe a progressive evolution in which the contemporary strategy of repression has unfolded, and that each successive period of innovation can be linked to a specific political regime. My brief descriptive history is the first indication of the political grounding of criminal justice reform. An examination of individuals (and political movements) taking the lead in the various efforts at reform provides evidence of a different sort to corroborate my thesis. In the interests of brevity, I will restrict my observations to the first two waves of reforms and reformers.

Preceding each wave of progressive criminal justice reform in modern times (I use the term *progressive* to describe those reforms which have proved lasting and which are still incorporated in contemporary strategies) was a sophisticated campaign of research and publicity by social reformers who were, at least partially, politically motivated. The classic example of such a campaign is of course the theoretical and political agitation conducted by the *philosophes* for the purpose of terminating the "barbarism" of monarchical justice.[24]

What is most relevant to my argument is the source of criticism and its content. The source of innovation in the late eighteenth century (and throughout the nineteenth) was the political opposition to the existing regime. Many of the *philosophes,* who were later to become revolutionaries, seized upon the crime problem as a point of attack against the Old Régime. Mirabeau and Mably, for example, insisted that any legal system, such as that of Bourbon France, which was both unjust and inefficient was by definition corrupt and inhumane. Marat, Brissot, Linguet, the Encyclopaedists, Voltaire, LeTrosne, and Robespierre all wrote treatises condemning the criminal laws and tribunals of the Bourbon monarchy.

The works of eighteenth century reformers and revolutionaries were also an important source of the utilitarian theory holding that crime could best be controlled by imposing a strictly delimited rule of law and by regulating punishment according to the principles of proportionality and humanity. Adherence to these principles would, in effect, place limits on the absolute authority of the monarchy, whose political ascendancy the *philosophes* challenged. Hence the social and political critique of the *philosophes* combined theoretical and political arguments against the Old Regime and the system of justice it employed.

The bond joining penal reform to political opposition is even more evident in the era of the July Monarchy.[25] In the 1820s and 1830s, the theoretical and political impetus for progressive reform originated in the liberal opposition to the restored Bourbon monarchy. Social thinkers collaborated with liberal political actors in reform groups such as the Royal Prison Society, the Society for Christian Morality, and (in the 1830s) the Academy of Moral and Political Sciences. Social critics of this era were even more sophisticated than the *philosophes* in that they used modern scientific studies to demonstrate the inability of the criminal justice system to maintain social order and protect the lives and liberty of the citizenry. Studies undertaken by liberal reformers drew attention to both the magnitude of the crime problem, by producing the first reliable times series data on crime, and the inadequacy of current methods of punishment to correct aberrant social behavior, through a multitude of reports on prison conditions and recidivism. In an age dominated by the "positive" scientific spirit, the studies of liberal reformers tended to show that the system of harsh repression and inhumane methods of incarceration only served to create new sources of crime and to erode personal liberties.[26] As in the eighteenth century, the new theories of criminal behavior (in this case the new "penitentiary science") served to condemn a political regime and a particular strategy of repression.

What is particularly revealing in this period is that most of the important criminological studies were either conducted or supported by liberals who were to hold important positions in the July Monarchy.[27] François Guizot was a minister under Louis Philippe. Charles Lucas, Louis Moreau-Christophe, L. R. Villermé, and G. Ferrus all became prison inspectors during the July Monarchy. A. M. Bérenger, the duc de Broglie, and P. Rossi occupied influential positions in the Institut de France and as advisers to Louis Philippe. Tocqueville was of course an academician and legislator, but was sent abroad on one of the five missions to study the most advanced prison systems. Louis Philippe himself was a patron of the liberal reform agencies: the Royal Prison Society and the Society of Christian Morality. After the Revolution of 1830, liberals used government machinery to stimulate research supporting efforts at reform. The regime sent missions abroad, supported studies by academicians, and directed the department of justice to collect statistics and conduct research on criminal behavior and methods of punishment. The July Monarchy was the patron of the type of scientific research which is at the origins of scientific criminology, and which has provided scientific legitimacy for reforms introduced for political reasons. In the next section I will show the positive political reasons stimulating liberals to such a vast reform effort.

IV

To understand the politics of criminal justice reform fully, a final aspect of the question must be explored, for the reforms I have associated with specific regimes and specific political actors were also integrated with positive political goals and philosophies. Reformers have always been more than critics of their political opponents. They have always attempted to implement new programs as a means of consolidating political support and guaranteeing social order. Furthermore, French politicians have exhibited an acute understanding of the philosophical (or ideological) aspects of the issues they confront, and this is apparent in their approach to criminal justice reform.[28] In this section, then, I will show how two regimes, the July Monarchy and the Third Republic, have integrated their strategy of justice reforms with their most fundamental political beliefs and institutions.

The Revolution of 1830 brought to power a wealthy and highly sophisticated elite which had been schooled in the precepts of classical liberal political and economic thought.[29] The Constitution of the July Monarchy limited the franchise to the wealthiest 2% of the popualtion, and power was shared between a "citizen king" and a two-tiered legislature. The political philosophy of the regime was intended as an antidote to the high-handed and reactionary tactics of the last Bourbon kings. The ruling political class was determined to limit the authority of the executive power and the central government, to protect the political liberties of the citizens (at least of the full citizens), and to create a political climate fostering economic prosperity and social stability.

A key maxim of the ruling elite held that to govern less was to govern better. Consequently, the government adhered to a laissez-faire policy in economic and social affairs. Education and public welfare were left largely in the care of private individuals or groups. Professional philanthropists preached the doctrine of self-help and personal responsibility. The government took few initiatives to stimulate the economy, provide measures of social security, build public housing, or promote social and economic equality. Finally, the July Monarchy strove to maintain public order and to protect liberty by adhering to the doctrine of a rule of law. New laws assured fairness in criminal and civil procedure, reduced the scale of punishments, abolished most "religious offenses," eliminated most remaining physical and public punishments, and worked to protect against political repression. The government also recognized the rights of prisoners to adequate care while incarcerated and sponsored programs to aid in their rehabilitation.

I noted earlier that the two most important penal reforms of this regime had the effect of individualizing punishment and of introducing a modern penitentiary program. The scrupulous application of the rule of law went far toward protecting the liberal political ideal of the July Monarchy, but the ruling elite reasoned that these additional improvements were necessary if their political credo was to be realized.[30] The law of 1832, which individualized punishment by charging the presiding judge with the task of determining punishment according to the degree of responsibility and the motivation of the offender, was informed by the belief that the individual alone was responsible for his act and that the purpose of punishment was, consequently, to correct his aberrant character.[31] These principles also informed the great prison reform of the 1830s and 1840s, which attracted the strong support of great liberal thinkers of the quality of Tocqueville, Guizot, and Charles Lucas.

In a liberal state intent upon restricting the authority of the central government and the executive, the scope of action of the criminal justice system must necessarily be restrained. The criminal justice reforms of the July Monarchy had just this effect. The new laws forbade, in most cases, the punishment of religious and political dissidents, assured that only those found guilty of offenses against the written statutes would be punished, and limited the extent of punishment. Furthermore, reliance on individual punishment and rehabilitation in the prison placed the burden for protecting social order squarely on the prison. As a consequence, the government found it unnecessary to embark on a program of broad educational, social, or economic reform as a means of assuring social stability. The liberals of this period concluded that the existence of the modern prison (and other asylums to treat the insane and the physically ill) largely obviated the necessity of any other social reform destined to preserve public order and stability.[32] The modern penitentiary became the focus of the criminal justice system in the classical liberal era precisely because it offered a solution to the problem of social order which did not entail massive social and economic reform, or the brand of harsh repression characteristic of authoritarian regimes. Thus it helped accommodate the liberal political ideal of governing better by governing less by finding a better form of punishment.

After 1848, the central government in France began to assume an ever-larger role in the regulation of economy and society. The trend took form during the populist, plebiscitary regime of Louis-Napoleon and gained speed during the Third Republic. France's first stable democratic regime was dominated by the parliament, in reaction to the authoritarian tendencies in French political culture.[33] The most pressing political question facing the nascent regime was to attract the type of broad popular support needed to preserve democratic rule in a country long dominated by conservative elites and the military. To achieve this goal, republican legislators introduced the social reform program discussed earlier. Supporters of the program intended it not only as a means of consolidating popular support for the republic but also as a means of preserving the social order so gravely compromised by the revolution of 1871, endemic political unrest in the 1870s, and the frightening growth of criminal activity.

I explained earlier how the social and economic programs inaugurated by the Third Republic were coordinated with reforms of the criminal justice system. By arrogating the right to educate the youth of France, regulate business and labor, manipulate social institutions, and make compensation for the underprivileged social and economic classes, the French state explicitly assumed at least limited authority to control society when national interest so demanded.[34] (In effect, the concept of a "national interest" or a "social good" first became meaningful with the establishment of a true democracy.) Criminal theory propounded in this era had advocated strengthening and improving social ties as a means of combatting deviance. Many of the reforms mentioned earlier necessitated the adjustment of social and economic institutions. Laws tending to sanction the states of drunkenness or of "dangerousness" (habitual offenders act) involved a breach in the previously sacrosanct principle of individual liberty preached earlier in the century. If, as contemporary criminologists argued, crime resulted from improper socialization or from economic deprivation, then only a strategy involving the regulation of society and economy could hope to contain the spread of deviance. In fact, the programs to combat juvenile delinquency, to reeducate convicts and first offenders, and to reintegrate ex-convicts into society could only be successful if the government exercised some control over the social milieu into which these categories of offenders were often released.

The doctrines of classical liberalism were fundamentally incompatible with the developments in social, economic, and repressive policy in the Third Republic. Political thinkers, aided by the sociological theories of Durkheim and other criminologists, soon filled the ideological void created by this dissonance. The politician Leon Bourgeois, the social thinker Charles Gide, and Durkheim all contributed to the elaboration of the doctrine of solidarism, which became something of an "official philosophy'' of the Third Republic.[35] The new social and political philosophy argued that the rights of the community supersede those of the individual in many circumstances. The sociological works of Durkheim gave a scientific grounding to the theory of communal solidarity by showing the irreducible necessity of communal life to individual fulfillment and to social order.

The doctrine of solidarism legitimated the social reform practice of the Third Republic and also provided a rationale for the new focus of the criminal justice system. I noted earlier that criminologists frequently faulted social organization in seeking to explain crime, and in turn sought to combat deviance by reinforcing what they considered to be healthy social ties. Analysis of the crime problem, furthermore, provided a stimulus to the elaboration of solidarism by demonstrating the extent of communal responsibility in the genesis of deviance. The theory of punishment developed at this time also shows the extent to which solidarist theories penetrated criminology. Theorists such as Tarde and Durkheim no longer considered the purpose of punishment to be simple retribution or rehabilitation, but rather the reinforcement of the sense of communal responsibility and justice among the noncriminal population.[36] As in the period of classical liberalism, then, the theory and structure of the criminal justice system both reflected the prevailing political consensus and provided one sort of legitimation for that consensus.

V

What can the contemporary observer learn from this brief survey of the political meaning of criminal justice reform? It is clear that significant reform occurs in the wake of profound political transformation. Equally obvious, at least in the case reviewed here, is that criminal justice reform has always been, in modern times, a highly politicized issue. This is true not only in the sense that the crime problem evokes partisan passions but also in the sense that particular reform schemes, whether progressive or reactionary, are normally associated with specific political and/or ideological movements. One can also note that the scientific expertise associated with progressive reforms of the criminal justice system has usually come directly from a political party or has enjoyed the support of some such group. Reform results from the coordinated efforts of politicians, social thinkers, and justice officials.

As a final point of interest, I think that the particular circumstances associated with the modern history of criminal justice reform has some relevance to contemporary America. While not wanting to press the argument too far, I would hazard the observation that the United States has not yet squarely faced the political problems associated with the implementation of reforms designed to control crime by regulating social and economic institutions. Perhaps the reason for this is that the political price, in terms of the inroads that would be made on the sacred doctrine of individual liberties, is too high for the American system to pay. The revival of the theory and practice of retribution and deterrence seems to be associated with the current distrust of government intervention. As I noted earlier, a retributive (or even correctional) strategy does not entail manipulation of the lives of third parties or innocent citizens. While there is much demand for changes along the general lines of the preventive practices undertaken by the French and others, a full commitment to such a policy will probably remain a vague dream until we resolve the accompanying political questions.

NOTES

1. See, for example, E. P. Thompson, *Whigs and Hunters: The Origin of the Black Act* (New York: Pantheon Books, 1975); G. F. LeTrosne, *Mémoire sur les*

Vagabonds et les Mendians (Soissons: Simon, 1764); and Voltaire, "Prix de la justice de de l'humanité," in *Oeuvres Completès* (Paris: Garnier, 1880), XXX, 533-586.

2. Among the best works on criminal justice in contemporary France are J. Léauté and R. Vouin, *Droit Pénal et Criminologie* (Paris: Presses Universitaires de France, 1964); and P. Bouzat and J. Pinatel, *Traité de Droit Pénal et de Criminologie,* second ed. (Paris: Dalloz, 1970), 3 vols.

3. Recent works on this subject are Pierre Deyon, *Le Temps des Prisons* (Paris: Editions Universitaires, 1975); and Michel Foucault, *Surveiller et Punir: Naissance de la Prison* (Paris: Gallimard, 1975).

4. For criticism of the system created by Napoleon, see the pages of the *Journal de la Société de la Morale Chrétienne* (1822-1830); A. M. Berenger, *De la Justice Criminelle en France* (Paris: l'Huillier, 1818); and Charles Lucas, *Du Système Pénal et du Système Répressif en Général: De la Peine de Mort en Particulier* (Paris: Charles-Béchet, 1827).

5. Contributing to the perception of a rise in crime in France was the publication of a serial record of criminal statistics beginning in 1825. The *Compte Général de l'Administration de la Justice Criminelle* confirmed some of the fears of the critics of the Napoleonic system, especially concern with the rate of recidivism, thus adding fuel to the debate on reform.

6. See Jean Bancal, "L'oeuvre pénitentiaire de la Restauration et de la Monarchie de Juillet," *Revue de Science Criminelle et de Droit Pénal Comparé,* VI (1941), 219-243; and Michelle Perrot, "Délinquance et système pénitentiaire en France au XIXeme siecle," *Annales; Economies, Sociétés, Civilisations,* No. 1 (1975), 67-91.

7. Foucault, *Surveiller et Punir,* has chronicled this movement. Among the most influential contemporary works were: G. de Beaumont and A. de Tocqueville, *On the Penitentiary System in the United States and Its Application in France* (Carbondale: Southern Illinois University Press, 1964); Charles Lucas, *De la Réforme des Prisons, ou Théorie de l'Emprisonnement* (Paris: Legrand & Bergounioux, 1836-38), 3 vols.; and L. M. Moreau-Christophe, *De la Réforme des Prisons en France* (Paris: Huzand, 1838), 2 vols.

8. See Arnould Bonneville de Marsangy, *De l'Amélioration de la Loi Criminelle* (Paris: Cotillon, 1855-64), 2 vols.; Perrot, "Délinquance et système pénitentiarie"; and H. C. Payne, *The Police State of Louis-Napoleon Bonaparte* (Seattle: University of Washington Press, 1966).

9. Bonneville de Marsangy, *De l'Amélioration,* I, 22-23.

10. See especially J. P. Azéma and M. Winock, *La Troisième République* (Paris: Calmann-Lévy, 1976), 85-123.

11. See J. T. Joughlin, *The Paris Commune in French Politics: 1871-1880* (Baltimore: Johns Hopkins University Press, 1955).

12. France; Ministere de la Justice, *Compte Général de l'Administration de la Justice Criminelle* (Paris: Imprimerie Nationale, 1882),"Résumé rétrospectif."

13. It was during this period that the science of criminology was perfected. Among the many activities of the criminological experts was the production of time series studies confirming the overall growth of crime in the nineteenth century. Criminologists also gave widespread (and often alarmist) publicity to the crime problem.

14. See Comte Othenin d'Haussonville, *Les Etablissements Pénitentiaries en France et aux Colonies* (Paris: Lévy, 1875).

15. There is no single secondary source which gives a good overview of the reforms of this period. The best means to follow the course of change is in the annual volumes of the legal journal, *Dalloz: Jurisprudence Générale,* 1873-1900.

16. In French jurisprudence, a *réhabilitation légale* meant only. that the consequences of a conviction, which normally included loss of certain civil rights and the existence of a criminal record (a *dossier judiciare*), were eliminated. The pardoned offender normally served his sentence before the pardon was considered.

17. See France; Institut National de la Statistique et des Etudes Economiques, *Statistique Générale de la France,* CVIII (Paris: Imprimierie Nationale, 1951), 97. The total incarcerated population dropped from 53,461 in 1852 to 25,679 in 1910.

18. See J. Donzelot, *La Police des Familles* (Paris: Minuit, 1977), and H. Gaillac, *Les Maisons de Correction, 1830-1945* (Paris: Cujas, 1971).

19. It is instructive to observe that psychiatric thinking at this time also tended to emphasize treatment in a communal setting rather than in the isolation of the asylum. The historian of asylums in France has labelled this period that of the "revolt against the asylum." See Robert Castel, *L'Ordre Psychiatrique,* (Paris: Minuit, 1976), chapter 7.

20. See H. Hatzfeld, *Du Paupérisme a la Sécurité Sociale: 1850-1940* (Paris: Colin, 1971).

21. Prior to the 1880s, welfare and education were dominated by the church and wealthy philanthropists. Religious and philanthropic organizations also played a large role in the penal system, especially in the areas of juvenile reform schools, female prisons, and convict-aid societies. The third Republic extended the regulatory power of the state over such private organizations as part of its program to break the power of the conservative elites.

22. See Emile Durkheim, *De la Division du Travail Social,* eighth ed. (Paris: Presses Universitaires de France, 1967), and E. Durkheim, *Suicide* (New York: Free Press, 1951).

23. See Donzelot, *Police des Familles;* and Gaillac, *Maisons de Correction.*

24. See Foucault, *Surveiller et Punir, passim.*

25. See especially L. R. Villermé, *Des Prisons telles qu'elles sont et telles qu'elles devraient être* (Paris: Mequignon, 1820); Lucas, *Du Système Répressif;* and François Guizot, *De la Peine de Mort en Matière Politique,* in his *Mélanges Historiques et Politiques* (Paris: Lévy, 1869), 239-434.

26. See the works of Tocqueville, Bérenger, Lucas, Moreau-Christophe, Guizot, and Villermé.

27. See T. J. Duesterberg, "The Origins of Criminology in France," in *Theory and Research in Criminal Justice: Current Perspectives,* ed. by John Conley (Cincinnati: Anderson, 1979).

28. See Gabriel Tarde, *Penal Philosophy* (New York: Little, Brown & Co., 1912); and Emile Durkheim, *Moral Education* (New York: Free Press, 1961).

29. See A. Jardin and A. J. Tudesq, *La France des Notables,* 1815-1848 (Paris: Seuil, 1973); and René Rémond, *The Right Wing in France: from 1815 to De Gaulle* (Philadelphia: University of Pennsylvania Press, 1969).

30. See the works of Guizot, Bérenger, and Lucas; and P. Rossi, *Traité de Droit Pénal* (Paris: Sautelet, 1829), 3 vols.

31. See France; Chambre des Députés, *Procès-Verbaux,* Session 1831, "Exposé des motifs du projet de loi tendant à introduire des réformes dans les lois pénales," (Paris: Imprimerie Royale, 1831), I. 414-428.

32. For example, see Charles Coquerel, "Note sur la question de la réforme des prisons," *Journal de la Société de la Morale Chrétienne*, III, No. 17 (1824), 214.

33. See Azéma and Winock, *La Troisième République*, 159-200; and J. M. Mayeur, *Les Débuts de la Troisième République, 1871-1898* (Paris: Seuil, 1973), *passim*.

34. See Hatzfeld, *Du Paupérisme a la Sécurité Sociale, passim.*

35. See L. Bourgeois, *Solidarité* (Paris: Colin, 1896); Ch. Gide, L'idée de Solidarité," *Revue Internationale de Sociologie*, I (1893), 385-400; and J.E.S. Hayward, "The official social philosophy of the Third Republic: L. Bourgeois and Solidarism," *International Review of Social History*, IV, No. 2 (1959), 261-284.

36. See Tarde, *Penal Philosophy;* and Durkheim, *Moral Education.*

7

HISTORY AND POLICY IN JUVENILE JUSTICE

THEODORE N. FERDINAND

This article traces the development of juvenile justice in the United States from the early decades of the nineteenth century to the present era. It will illustrate how historical events can shape current policies and set up political tensions that affect fundamentally the administration of the juvenile justice system today. It will demonstrate that those who form current juvenile policy and guide the debate that swirls around juvenile justice must also examine its historical development if they are to understand and cope with the political crosscurrents they encounter at every turn.

Before the modern era, public policy regarding young people was relatively simple. Serious youthful offenders were punished formally in the criminal courts, and dependent children were cared for at public expense as circumstances permitted. All others were dealt with informally. Since then, the scope of juvenile justice has broadened considerably; the means for achieving juvenile justice have become truly variegated; and controversy surrounds both the mission and the means of juvenile justice.

AUTHOR'S NOTE: I wish to thank Mary Bularzik, James Inciardi, and Nicolas Hahn for commenting on an earlier version of this article.

The debate has assumed a distinct right versus left polarization.[1] Without detailed knowledge of the historical development of juvenile justice, however, it has been difficult for either side to pinpoint persuasively which purposes of juvenile justice are legitimate and what methods are needed. A better understanding of the history of juvenile justice, however, can clarify the origins of pesent-day policies and help identify which purposes are still appropriate, and where they are no longer geared to today's problem and are therefore properly discarded.

To give some substance to these very general phrases, let us turn back to the early part of the nineteenth century when the legal foundations of juvenile justice were still being laid.

THE EARLY FORMS OF JUVENILE JUSTICE

At first, there were no legal distinctions between adult and juvenile offenders: Both were punished in basically the same way. Terrible penalties were attached to serious violations of the criminal law, and they were applied to everyone, adults and children alike.

The early law did make a distinction between adults and children but only in equity courts and mainly in cases where guardianship or inheritance were at issue. Where there was no clearly identified guardian, or where the heirs to important estates were not clearly designated, the court was obliged to look after the interests of those who could not do so themselves (e.g., children) as the rights of the various parties were sorted out. Such intervention by the court in behalf of children was justified in law by the ancient doctrine *parens patriae;* that the king as father of the country had the ultimate responsibility for protecting his subjects.

There was an obvious need for court intervention in many disputes involving children, and *parens patriae* served this need very well. It also provided, however, an opening through which the court could intervene in the lives of children in other ways where the need was less obvious. In England two landmark cases illustrate nicely the ease with which *parens patriae* was used to broaden the role of the courts in the lives of children.[2] Percy Shelley, the poet, sought to gain custody of his children from his wife's family, the Westbrooks, after her death. The case was ultimately heard in Chancery Court in 1817, and the judge's decision rejected Shelley's suit on the ground that he was not a fit father to raise his children. He was accused of being an atheist, and because his attitudes and behavior were equally unconventional in other areas, he was denied custody of his children.

The second case in 1827 was similar in that Long Wellesley was also seeking custody of his children from his wife's relatives. Like Shelley, when Wellesley's scandalous social behavior was revealed in court, his suit was denied. In both cases *parens patriae* was used in a novel way to justify the courts' intervention to protect children from an unconventional parent.

In the United States *parens patriae* was being extended in similar fashion. During the colonial period, poor laws had been used extensively to control the behavior of poor people, and under these laws the children of poor people were apprenticed out to protect them from the social effects of their poverty. The connection between this use of the poor laws provided a kind of precedent for extending the concept of *parens patriae* to permit court intervention not only where the child's economic interests were threatened but also where his or her social welfare was in jeopardy.[3]

By the early nineteenth century a variety of situations combined to invite a further strengthening of the court's authority in this area. In 1824 New York City established a House of Refuge to supervise dependent, vagrant, and delinquent children. To justify taking costody of the children, a doctrine not unlike *parens patriae, in loco parentis*, was introduced. The state acting *in loco parentis* committed the children to the House of Refuge in their own best interests and subjected them to a mixture of educational, vocational, and religious instruction.

A few years later in the 1830s when public schools were being established in the Northeast, there was deep concern that a successful challenge to the authority of the courts to commit children to the House of Refuge would also weaken the authority of the community in requiring children's attendance in the public schools.[4] The courts appreciated the wider significance of a challenge to their *parens patriae* authority, and when it came, they brushed it aside with little hesitancy.

Mary Ann Crouse had been committed to the House of Refuge in Philadelphia on a complaint by her mother. When her father learned of her commitment, he challenged it on the ground that she had been incarcerated without a jury trial. The Pennsylvania Supreme Court rejected his appeal in *Ex parte* Crouse (1938) on the ground that the purpose of the House of Refuge was to reform and improve the child, while holding her in wholesome restraint.[5] Since the House of Refuge was an environment wherein Mary Ann Crouse might be suitably educated and socially formed, the court reasoned, it was in her best interest to be there instead of at home. The action of the court conformed to the requirements of *parens patriae* and needed no further justification.

The ultimate significance of this new use of *parens patriae* was to justify a much deeper penetration of the equity courts into the life of the family. Initially the courts had entered cases only to defend children when their economic interests or the rights of guardianship required it. In order to justify the court's committing children to Houses of Refuge and requiring their attendance at public schools, however, *parens patriae* became a more general doctrine and the equity courts found themselves almost untouchable as they set out to remold the poor families of urban America.

As *parens patriae* became the cornerstone of juvenile justice in the nineteenth century, it drew the courts unwittingly into a highly charged issue: the formulation of an ideal against which American families might be weighed. Under *parens patriae,* court intervention was permitted only when the child's best interests were endangered; but in order to determine exactly what the child's best interests were—particularly where his or her social welfare was involved—the court was obliged to make very subtle and often controversial decisions. Several authors have suggested that the courts regularly used overly narrow and conventional criteria in evaluating families. The issue here is not which criteria are best for this purpose, but rather that the equity courts were obliged to set standards of family life that could not help but be politically controversial. It is relatively easy to determine what a child's best economic interests are, but who is to say which set of social conditions is sufficiently destructive to warrant separating the child from its natural parents?

An important decision in Illinois, *People v. Turner,* confronted this issue directly in 1870.[6] Daniel O'Connell was committed to the Chicago Reform School under an 1867 statute which permitted the commitment of any child who is "a vagrant, or is destitute of proper parental care, or is growing up in mendicancy, ignorance, idleness or vice." Daniel's father challenged the commitment on the ground that Daniel had committed no crime. The Illinois Supreme Court heard the appeal, ruled that the statute was hopelessly vague, and ordered that Daniel be released from the Chicago Reform School. In defending its ruling, the court argued that the parent-child relationship should be disturbed for only the most serious of reasons.

The ease with which it may be disrupted under the laws in question; the slight evidence required, and the informal mode of procedure, make them conflict with the natural right of the parent. Before any abridgment of the right, gross misconduct or almost total unfitness on the part of the parent, should be clearly proved.[7]

To repair the law relating to juveniles, the Illinois legislature passed a statute in 1879 that required a detailed description by the court of the grounds for any action concerning a juvenile and adequate notice to the parents. It also permitted court-appointed counsel and a trial before a jury of six. This statute was ruled constitutional *In re Ferrier* (1882), and although it required more specific justification by the court for any intervention in family life, it did not relieve the court of the politically sensitive task of setting minimal standards of family life.[8] Indeed, it made the court's position more vulnerable by forcing it to spell out more clearly the criteria it was using in evaluating families.

The decision, *People v. Turner* (1870), also touched upon another serious defect in *parens patriae*, one that was to plague the juvenile court into the mid-twentieth century. As we have seen, *parens patriae* emerged primarily in the equity courts largely isolated from the traditions of the Common Law and criminal due process. Indeed, since *parens patriae* assumed that the court was acting in behalf of children, there was no need to build into its procedures the same web of restrictions curbing the state's prosecutorial power that is an integral part of the criminal courts. To be sure *People v. Turner* took issue with the flimsy evidence and informal procedures whereby Daniel O'Connell had been committed to the reform school. But *In re Ferrier* simply reaffirmed that in acting in behalf of the child, the court need not observe due process as found in the criminal courts. Later decisions by the U.S. Supreme Court would not dismiss this issue so lightly.

THE JUVENILE COURT IS FOUNDED

In 1899 the traditional but uncodified authority of the equity courts over children was drawn together and institutionalized in the form of a juvenile court and a formal juvenile code, but with one significant extension. In addition to dependent and wayward children, which the equity courts had long dealt with, the juvenile court also assumed jurisdiction over delinquent children, which the criminal courts had previously mainly

dealt with. The juvenile court brought *parens patriae* to bear on delinquents, and in the beginning the court was viewed in Illinois and elsewhere
as a defender of children with little need for due process or the adversary
proceedings of the criminal courts. It exercised wide powers over children
and their families, and it could enforce its orders with little fear of
reversal.

These powers were challenged in Pennsylvania in *Commonwealth v.
Fisher* in 1905, and *parens patriae* emerged for a third time unscathed.[9]
Frank Fisher, 14, was arrested for larceny and pleaded not guilty. His case
was tried in the Philadelphia Court of Quarter Sessions, an equity court,
under the Pennsylvania juvenile code adopted in 1903. He was subsequently adjudicated a delinquent and committed to the House of Refuge,
but the court's order was appealed to the Pennsylvania Supreme Court. In
rejecting this appeal the Pennsylvania Supreme Court provided as broad an
interpretation of *parens patriae* as the most ardent champions of the
juvenile court could possibly have wished. It argued that

> as the welfare of the state requires that children should be guarded
> from association and contact with crime and criminals, and as those
> who, from want of proper parental care or guardianship, may
> become liable to penalities which ought not to be imposed upon
> them it is important that the powers of the court, in respect to the
> care, treatment, and control of dependent, neglected, delinquent,
> and incorrigible children, should be clearly distinguished from those
> exercised by it in the administration of the criminal law.[10]

It further pointed out that the court

> is not for the punishment of offenders but for the salvation of
> children, and points out the way by which the state undertakes to
> save, not particular children . . . but all children under a certain age,
> whose salvation may become the duty of the state, in the absence of
> proper parental care or disregard of it by wayward children.[11]

With regard to the absence of due process in the juvenile court, the
decision held that

> the natural parent needs no process to temporarily deprive his child
> of its liberty by confining it in his own home, to save it and to shield
> it from the consequences of persistence in a career of waywardness;
> nor is the state, when compelled, as *parens patriae,* to take the place
> of the father for the same purpose, required to adopt any process as

a means of placing its hands upon the child to lead it into one of its courts.[12]

The juvenile court was the culmination in the twentieth century of all that *parens patriae* had come to stand for in the nineteenth century. It was designed to reform and ultimately to restore the juvenile to his or her family and community; it was expected to act with an enlightened, benevolent spirit in the best interests of the juvenile, even in the face of determined opposition by the juveniles or their families; and it was to do so within a largely informal framework.

Its champions were well-placed in America. Judges Ben Lindsey in Denver, Julian Mack in Chicago, and Harvey Baker in Boston pushed ardently for its success, and child-saving in the larger sense became something of a mission for a small but significant group of progressives in the late nineteenth and early twentieth centuries.[13] Indeed, the child-saving movement had gathered sufficient momentum by the early decades of the twentieth century to override the many obvious deficiencies of *parens patriae* as applied to the problems of children. With the support of such fervent advocates, the juvenile court matured (one could almost say, hardened) during the next 50 years with scarcely any significant changes in form or substance.

Its defects, however, were obvious and could not be ignored indefinitely. The most apt candidate for juvenile court action was the disorganized and mildly deviant child, that is, the nuisance child, who needed some slight degree of judicial action to reinforce the parents' authority.[14] Such children when confronted with the authority of the court and the surveillance of a probation officer were often persuaded that further deviance was unwise.[15] Intervention by the court was shallow in such cases, and the child's social restoration was easily and painlessly achieved. These children were abundant, if not in the majority, in most urban juvenile courts.

These same courts, however, were ill-equipped to handle children who for whatever reason were determinedly delinquent and posed thereby a serious threat to the community. Neither were they prepared to defend their *parens patriae*-based authority in the face of substantial evidence that those who took custody of serious delinquents in institutions had little interest in reforming them or in restoring them to their families and communities. These two problems ultimately proved the undoing of the juvenile court as conceived in the early years of the twentieth century, and they forced substantial revisions in its goals and procedures in the 1960s and 1970s.

There is ample evidence that seriously criminal juveniles abounded in America throughout the nineteenth century. Herbert Asbury has documented the gangs of young thugs that dominated the streets of lower Manhattan in the antebellum period, and the escapades of dozens of youthful desperados in the Old West have become legendary.[16] In the nineteenth century they were handled for the most part by the criminal courts as criminal offenders and, therefore, posed no problem to the equity courts that had authority primarily over dependent and wayward children. In the twentieth century, however, when the juvenile court assumed jurisdiction over nearly all children below the age of 16 or 17, seriously criminal children were largely diverted from the criminal court to the juvenile court and imposed upon it a clientele with which it was entirely unprepared to cope.

There have been few critical studies of the early juvenile court (i.e., from 1900 to 1940), but it seems likely that serious delinquents confronted the juvenile court with two insoluble problems. First, serious offenders and those immediately linked with them—that is, their victims and their relatives—were concerned with much higher stakes than were minor offenders. Considerable property and sometimes life and limb themselves were involved, and in spite of the child-saving mission of the court, there were often heavy pressures from those immediately affected urging the court to protect them and the community before all else.

When the juvenile court struggled bravely to reform the child criminal, its efforts more often than not accomplished little, for the child either ignored or exploited the social services offered him by the court. When the court responded to community pressures, however, and placed the child in secure custody, it found itself violating one of the basic dicta of *parens patriae*, namely, that its authority to commit children to juvenile facilities was grounded on its mandate to *help* these children. In dealing with seriously delinquent children the court was made to seem either ineffective or inconsistent with its *parens patriae* mandate. Moreover, insofar as it acted in behalf of the community, it was assuming the stance of a criminal court vis-à-vis the child.

The second problem that the court was forced to deal with was the slow transformation of nearly all facilities designed to reform delinquents from institutions committed to their benevolent resocialization to institutions committed basically to secure custody and little else. This transformation seems to have affected virtually all kinds of juvenile institutions from Houses of Refuge in the early nineteenth century to training schools and youth centers well into the twentieth.[17] This transformation often meant that their inmates actively resisted—sometimes with violence—the staff, and that the staff were profoundly disillusioned with the rehabilitative goals of such institutions. The situation had deteriorated seriously in Houses of Refuge by the 1850s, and by the 1870s and 1880s juvenile training schools were similarly beset with riots, fires, and scandalous conditions.[18] Training schools suffered chronically from these same problems well into the 1950s, and as such posed another difficulty for the juvenile court acting as *parens patriae*.[19]

If the juvenile court was required to act in behalf of the juvenile as it exercised its considerable authority over him and his family, the utter incongruity of committing him to a juvenile institution where the inmate culture was seriously criminal, where inmate interaction was exploitative, and where the staff were punitive could not be easily ignored. The more serious delinquents tended disproportionately to be sent to training schools, to be sure, with the result that those groups which supported a punitive judicial response were not likely to complain about the inconsistency. Several legally trained observers of the juvenile court, however, did note the incongruity and suggested that insofar as the juvenile court was assuming the functions of a criminal court, it should also assume the procedures of the criminal court.[20]

By the 1950s, then, the juvenile court was dealing with many seriously delinquent children in a patently punitive fashion and committing them to seriously corruptive institutions. All of this was done in the name of *parens patriae* in equity courts without due process protections.

THE DEBATE ABOUT JUVENILE JUSTICE

By the 1950s two camps were beginning to form in juvenile justice: those who condemned the arbitrary and punitive climate in many juvenile courts and those who defended the social orientation of the juvenile court.[21] The former pointed up the contradictions between the ideal of *parens patriae* and the practice of juvenile justice in America; the latter regularly excused the prisonlike training schools and punitive judges as human failures and not directly a result of the humane principles guiding juvenile justice.[22] As the debate sharpened, however, cries arose for abandoning the socialized juvenile court altogether and transferring its social functions to nonlegal agencies.[23] Proponents pointed out that the Scandinavian countries already utilized this kind of division of labor in dealing with youth problems, and they suggested that a similar arrangement in this country would work equally well.[24]

As the debate unfolded, however, it assumed a curiously ahistorical and superficial tone. Little consideration was given to the historical basis of the existing juvenile justice system in America, and no careful thought was given to the deeper sources of its difficulties in the contemporary nature of delinquency. In order to devise a reasonable alternative to the present approach to juvenile justice, a careful diagnosis of its deficiencies is essential.

Let us attempt such a diagnosis. As we consider the historical sources of the existing juvenile court together with its current liabilities, we will be in a better position to weigh the merits of any proposals for change and also, thereby, to see the benefits of a historical perspective for policy formation.

EVALUATING PARENS PATRIAE

The main problem with the *parens patriae* doctrine over the years is that it has been expanded over successively wider segments of the juvenile population. The enthusiasm of its early champions blinded them to growing evidence that not all juvenile problems could be solved by court intervention—no matter how well meaning. A good idea need not always be extended until it becomes irrelevant or even harmful.

As we have seen, *parens patriae* was used initially to authorize the courts' intervention in matters involving children's inheritance and guardianship. By the early decades of the nineteenth century it had been extended to include children exposed to unwholesome influences in their families, and at the beginning of the present century *parens patriae* was used to justify the court's custody over delinquent children. In a little over a hundred years, three successive segments of the juvenile population came under the control of the equity courts, and in each case the court was permitted by *parens patriae* to separate children from their natural parents, if necessary to protect their economic, social, or legal well-being.

A good argument can be made in each case for court intervention, but in the last two cases—that is, where the child is exposed to unhealthy social influences, and where the court assumes custody of delinquent children—court intervention also contains great potential for mischief. Not many would question the right of a juvenile court to intervene, for example, if the parents of an adolescent girl were forcing her to participate in incest. The court would be derelict if it failed to take custody of the girl in such cases. The court's authority to intervene when circumstances demand it is not in serious contention. The problem lies, however, in defining when circumstances are sufficiently hazardous for the child to warrant court intervention.

There are a few family situations that nearly everyone would agree require court intervention, and there are many more family situations that nearly everyone would agree should be left alone. There is also a middle area where the issue is not clear-cut, and when the court intervenes in such cases, it is likely to provoke bitter criticism from one or more segments of the community. A consensus has not been reached here, and when the court strays into this area, it wanders into a minefield.

The court needs explicit guidelines to insure that it avoids a parochial perspective in determining when conditions in the family are sufficiently unwholesome for a child to require court intervention. In the absence of such guidelines, the court will be forced to learn the sensitivities of the community in a very unpleasant fashion.

By the same token, a good argument can be made for judicial intervention when the child is following a delinquent path in the community. In such cases, however, should the court be governed by the best interests of the child or of the community in coming to a decision regarding the child? With minor delinquents where the problems are not severe, much can be accomplished by only a shallow intervention, and the best interests of the child should in such cases be the primary consideration. Where the child is already seriously delinquent, however, heavy pressures for retribution and community protection develop, and the court is often obliged to apply strict measures to the child regardless of its mandate from *parens patriae*. In such cases, however, the court is embarking upon a punitive path that is well beyond its authority and jurisdiction.

At first, defenders of the court insisted that the punitive measures were, in fact, benevolent regardless of their appearance.[25] It was not enough, however, simply to deny that a punitive philosophy was creeping into certain segments of the juvenile justice system. The facts were unimpeachable. Many training schools were not basically different from adult institutions, and delinquents in many courts were imprisoned more readily than most of their adult counterparts.[26] The result was that *parens patriae* juvenile courts were losing their legitimacy, and as their credibility waned, their benevolence both in spirit and in practice was challenged.[27]

The solution, however, does not need to be an entirely fresh start along different lines. That is the prophet's solution, but it does not always lead to the promised land, or even to clear improvements in social or legal institutions. Rather, I prefer a tailoring of the court's jurisdiction to those segments of the juvenile population that genuinely need its social services. Some children need protection from a variety of destructive forces, and a court with *parens patriae* authority and flexibility seems best suited to a certain type of child, that is, the nuisance child whose delinquency is minor and whose difficulties stem basically from troubled relationships with adults. Since the court must involve itself in a very sensitive area— adult-child relationships—court authority is probably indispensable. Voluntary compliance cannot be assured and it will be necessary occasionally to utilize the inherent authority of the law to gain cooperation. Hence, the social functions of the court need a legal basis to be performed adequately.

Where the child is seriously delinquent, however, the situation is changed fundamentally. The most basic issue here is not the parent-child relationship (even though it may be seriously disturbed), but the child's behavior before the laws of the community. This issue must be settled before the question of the child and its parents can be approached constructively. The child's rights and obligations in the face of criminal charges are prior to his or her rights as a child vis-à-vis the parents. Since the *parens patriae* court is not structured to protect the rights of children as defendants, a new court with due process protections is needed at this level.

In dealing with seriously delinquent children, the new court needs an unimpeachable authority to withstand the retribution pressures of victims and others against criminal defendants, and it needs clear due process safeguards to protect juvenile defendants from the awesome power of the state in criminal prosecutions. At the same time, this new court will be dealing with children who often can benefit from a variety of social programs that adults who have already settled into a life pattern could not. Thus, even though this court should partake of the traditions of the full criminal court, it should also have access to social facilities specifically geared to defendants who are still children and who, while presenting a serious threat to the welfare of the community and sometimes needing to be segregated in secure facilities, are still worthy of the best efforts of the community to divert them from a confirmed criminal path.

The Youth Courts of Chicago, New York, and Philadelphia provide a model for the kind of court I am describing here.[28] They are usually organized as criminal courts with full due process protections, but they are permitted some flexibility in sentencing defendants of a youthful age, that is, up to 21. Such courts regard the administration of justice according to the criminal code as their first responsibility, but they also have access to social programs and custodial facilities geared to the youthful age of their clientele.

In essence, then, I am arguing for a narrowing of the *parens patriae* court's jurisdiction to those children whose problems are personal and who pose little threat to the community. Those children who have committed serious offenses should have their charges adjudicated justly in a full criminal court oriented to their peculiar situations as children, that is, a children's court. Such courts could still utilize the social programs of the traditional juvenile court to shape as far as possible the maturation of these children into full adulthood. Nevertheless, the legal responsibilities of these courts would still be prior to their social responsibilities to the defendants, and their inability to achieve dramatic success with the children they encounter should not seriously undermine their legitimacy in the legal community. Moreover, their adherence to due process should reinforce their legitimacy in the eyes of the defendants. Thus, these courts would avoid the arbitrary quality of the *parens patriae* court which damaged its authority in the eyes of both the legal community and most defendants.

Even though the children's court is certain to contain flaws of its own, it represents an attempt to deal with some of the problems of the traditional juvenile court and therefore deserves consideration. At the same time we should be aware of its deficiencies and modify it accordingly—unlike the champions of the early juvenile court who nurtured a fervor not unlike that of the Crusaders as they marched to liberate Jerusalem from the infidels. Such enthusiasm is needed, no doubt, to establish a new social institution like the juvenile court, but it can also lead to an overestimate of its capacity to deal with the problems it confronts. We must avoid a similar error with the new court.

A LESSON FROM HISTORY FOR POLICY MAKERS: JUVENILE JUSTICE

The final question that we must consider is, perhaps, the most important: In what ways is an understanding of history useful to policy makers in the contemporary world? This all too brief survey of the development of the juvenile justice system over the last 180 years suggests that in order to understand the strengths and weaknesses of a particular doctrine, it is important to be aware of the historical circumstances that gave it birth as well as the pressures that contributed over the years to its maturation. *Parens patriae* illustrates this point very well.

The circumstances that led initially to its application to juvenile problems differed fundamentally from the pressures that contributed to its gradual extension to most forms of juvenile deviance. The early legal deficiency that *parens patriae* satisfied offered it an easy legitimacy in juvenile problems—and since this was a rapidly developing area with broad legal needs and few established doctrines, *parens patriae* was pressed into service in nearly every area of juvenile difficulty. Its champions failed to see the dangers of an overly broad application to the problems of juveniles in a complex urban-bureaucratic society. They were probably not unusual in this regard, but by appreciating the sources of their commitment to *parens patriae,* we can understand better their motivation in supporting the court even today and, thereby, be better able to persuade them of the need to modify it to reflect the nature of delinquents today.

The critics of the *parens patriae* court fully understood the legal and social dilemmas that ultimately proved its undoing. But they also failed to recognize the real contributions made by the court to the solution of a narrow portion of the problems juveniles encounter. A knowledge of the history of the court points clearly to those areas where the court proved effective and where its continued functioning is needed. By describing these areas in specific terms, it should be possible to phrase persuasive arguments to these critics demonstrating the need for a limited *parens patriae* court serving certain kinds of juveniles.

The policy maker who has a historical perspective will find it much easier to pinpoint confidently the strengths and weaknesses of his or her domain and, therefore, understand basically its limits as well as its potential strengths. Not only will he or she be more effective as an administrator but also more persuasive in answering critics from both the right and the left. Policy makers may not always be aware of the advantages of a historical perspective. When a skill is almost uniformly underdeveloped, its benefits cannot be widely appreciated. But national organizations—both public and private—that mold and support policy in juvenile justice have a responsibility to cultivate in policy makers the abilities that will enhance their effectiveness. Clearly, a historical perspective falls within this area and deserves meaningful support from those national organizations that hope to improve juvenile justice in America.

NOTES

1. For a discussion of the substance of the right-left polarization in criminal justice, see W. B. Miller, "Ideology and Criminal Justice Policy: Some Current Issues," *Journal of Criminal Law & Criminology* Vol. 64 (1973), 141-162.

2. N. H. Cogan, "Juvenile Law, Before and After the Entrances of 'Parens Patriae,' " *South Carolina Law Review*, Vol. 22, (1970), 179-181.

3. D. R. Rendleman, "Parens Patriae: From Chancery to the Juvenile Court," *South Carolina Law Review*, Vol. 23 (1971), 217.

4. See S. L. Schlossman, *Love and the American Delinquent* (Chicago: University of Chicago Press, 1977), 10.

5. Ex parte Crouse 4 *Whart.* 9 (1838).

6. *People v. Turner* 5 Ill. 2800 (1879).

7. *Ibid.*

8. *In re Ferrier* 103 Ill. 367 (1882).

9. *Commonwealth v. Fisher* 213 Pa. 48 (1905).

10. *Ibid.*

11. *Ibid.*

12. *Ibid.*

13. *Schlossman, op cit.,* Chapter 4.

14. M. Rosenheim, "Notes on Helping Juvenile Nuisances," in M. Rosehheim, ed., *Pursuing Justice for the Child* (Chicago: University of Chicago Press, 1976), 43-66.

15. According to Schlossman, the "nuisance child" is the kind of lad most warmly embraced by Judge Ben Lindsey in his Denver court in the early 1900s. See Schlossman, *op.cit.,* 56.

16. H. Asbury, *The Gangs of New York: An Informal History of the Underworld* (New York: Blue Ribbon Books, 1939).

17. See Schlossman, *op. cit.,* 34-36, and C. Perrow, "Reality Shook: A New Organization Confronts the Custory-Treatment Dilemma," *Social Problems,* Vol. 10 (Spring, 1963) 374-382.

18. Schlossman, *op. cit.,* Chapter 6.

19. See A. Deutsch, *Our Rejected Children* (Boston: Little, Brown, 1950).

20. See, for example, P. Tappan, "Treatment Without Trial," *Social Forces* 24 (1946), 306-317; R. G. Caldwell, "The Juvenile Court: Its Development and Some Major Problems," *Journal of Criminal Law, Criminology, and Police Science* 51 (1961), 493-507; and F. A. Allen, *The Borderland of Criminal Justice* (Chicago: University of Chicago Press, 1964).

21. Jerome Miller is probably the most outspoken critic of juvenile training schools, and defenders of the court's social orientation include Murray and Adeline Levine in *A Social History of Helping Services: Clinic, Court, School, and Community* (Englewood Cliffs, NJ: Prentice-Hall, 1970).

22. For an example of the former see Justice Fortas's majority opinion in *Kent v. United States* 383 U.S. 541 (1966); and an example of the latter is contained in Justice Stewart's minority opinion in the same decision.

23. See T. H. Rubin, "The Juvenile Court's Search for Identity and Responsibility," *Crime and Delinquency* 23 (1977), 1-13.

24. T. S. Dahl, "The Scandinavian System of Juvenile Justice: A Comparative Approach," in M. Rosenheim, ed., *Pursuing Justice for the Child* (Chicago: University of Chicago Press, 1976), 327-347.

25. See *Commonwealth v. Fisher, loq. cit.*

26. Juvenile status offenders are incarcerated more frequently for much less than adults, or even than juvenile felony offenders. It is not unusual for juveniles to receive a more severe punishment for a given crime than an adult. Gerald Gault faced up to a six-year term in a training school, whereas an adult could have received at most for the same offense a fine of $50 or two months in jail. See *In re Gault* 387 U.S. 1 (1967).

27. A. M. Platt, "The Triumph of Benevolence: The Origins of the Juvenile Justice System in the United States," in R. Quinney, ed., *Criminal Justice in America* (Boston: Little, Brown, 1974), 356-389.

28. See R. S. Cavan and T. N. Ferdinand, *Juvenile Delinquency* (Philadelphia: Lippincott, 1975) Chapter 18.

8

EIGHTEENTH CENTURY GAMING: IMPLICATIONS FOR MODERN CASINO CONTROL

DAVID MIERS

INTRODUCTION

In 1976 the Commission on the Review of the National Policy toward Gambling published its Final Report, "Gambling in America."[1] Among the many matters that it considered was the desirability of the extension of casino facilities to states other than Nevada and the Commonwealth of Puerto Rico. It concluded that it did "not believe that any clear benefits would derive from passage of legislation in the various States to establish casinos."[2] The report went on to say that if a state did decide to effect such legislation, it should introduce a style of casino regulation based upon the Nevadan legislation—but that in addition, it should introduce player protection controls, controls which the commission felt were conspicuously absent in the Nevadan gaming industry. Thus the commission urged that serious consideration be given to the implementation of stringent regulations over both the *opportunity* of individuals to engage in casino gaming (such as restricting the number and location of gaming machines and the ease of access to, and advertising of, casinos) and the subsequent *reinforcement* of that initial decision (such as restricting the availability of credit, of entertainment and refreshment, and of hours of play).

These proposals signify a quite radical shift in orientation toward the regulation of casino gaming in the United States. Historically, the primary objectives of such regulation have been to prevent the infiltration of criminal organizations into the gaming industry and to eliminate the illicit diversion of casino revenue. Influential writers now argue[3] that these objectives have in large measure been realized in Nevada by the complex regulatory mechanisms and supervisory controls established by the Gaming Control Act.[4] For the purposes of this article, I shall call the realization of these objectives the "casino control" model of gaming regulation. The administrative implementation of this model is characterized by the establishment of a bureaucracy which rigorously vets applicants for casino licences and which regulates the financial management of casinos through the use of sophisticated auditing techniques. However, I do not propose that these characteristics are unique to the casino control model; on the contrary, licensing control is a primary characteristic of the second model of casino regulation that I shall adopt for this article, namely, the "player protection" model. Its defining quality and what distinguishes it from casino control is that it aims to minimize the impact of gaming on the individual player. This, I shall argue, has been the paradigm of legal intervention in Britain, and it has resulted in the creation of a highly restrictive regime over recruitment to gaming. It is a regime which the commission finds appealing in a number of respects.[5]

Also I do not propose that these models be seen as alternatives: The pursuit of the objectives of casino control are not necessarily antithetical to the realization of player protection objectives. For example, a thorough vetting of applicants for casino licenses which eliminates members of criminal organizations may result in less manipulative entrepreneurs managing the industry, which in turn may lessen the financial impact of the "house edge" on the individual player, whether that edge is legally or illegally created. Rather, I use the two models to represent differing *emphases* on casino regulation and to suggest that whereas the primary emphasis in Britain has been on player protection—although there are clear casino control elements in the current legislation—in Nevada the latter is the only emphasis. Herein lies the significance of the commission's proposals: to shift the emphasis of casino regulation toward the objectives implicit in the player protection model.

The explanation for the differing emphases to be found in Great Britain and the United States is, I believe, largely historical. The substance of this article is to attempt to trace the history of legal control over gaming in England since the early eighteenth century and to set the implications of my analysis of these controls against the commission's desire to effect a change of emphasis in casino regulation in the United States. If I spend a smaller proportion of time on the history of gaming regulation in the United States, this is because it is, I believe, better documented[7] and its interpretation less debatable.[8]

A NOTE ON SOURCES

This last point introduces a difficulty with historical sources. In general, most of the literature on gaming in England during the eighteenth century and the Regency is anecdotal in nature. This is true both of contemporary accounts and of more recent biographical essays. Together these give a fascinating, if episodic and repetitive, account of the impact of gaming on particular individuals, and more generally give some background to the incidence of gaming in particular social groups, but they are of limited use of constructing historical explanations of the basis and efficacy of legislation introduced over a considerable period of time. The repetitive quality of these accounts had led to one or two instances of misinterpretation of events. One such is the reiteration[9] of the maintenance of English archery as the basis of the statute of 1541 which proscribed the playing of certain games except at Christmas.[10] A closer reading of the preamble to that statute shows that it was as much prompted by a complaint on the part of the makers of bows and arrows that their trace was in decline as a result of games playing, as a desire on Henry VIII's part to foster military preparedness.

The only significant exception to the anecdotal nature of the literature on gaming during this period is the monumental work of Radzinowicz.[11] Beyond the midnineteenth century, however, there is a relative paucity of literature of any sort, until more recent sociological studies of gambling practices.[12] In part this may be explicable by a decline in the incidence of gaming following the Gaming Act of 1845[13] and its substitution by other forms of gambling—notably off-track betting—which offered similar gambling characteristics. In addition, the second half of the nineteenth century saw a profound diversification of leisure pursuits, many of which involved a gambling element, together with discrete class-based preferences for particular gambling outlets, and so evidence of the incidence of gaming in Victorian England has to be sought in more general accounts of Victorian social life.[14]

DEFINITION OF "GAMING"

One further preliminary matter concerns the definition of gaming for the purpose of this article. The present English legislation does not define gaming as such, but instead specifies the places and financial conditions under which it may lawfully occur; I shall describe this style of control later. An old definition which is used in this article, and which still prevails in English law, is "the playing of a game for stakes hazarded by the players."[15] I have chosen not to define gaming in terms of the games played, partly because their names have changed with time and some have become obsolete; but it is useful to identify their structural characteristics.[16] The characteristics of casino games—typically roulette (American and French), craps and dice, machines, blackjack, baccarat and other card games of unequal change—and of their predecessors—ace of hearts, faro, basset (all card games), hazard (a dice game)—are high event frequency, rapid payout, a wide range of odds and stakes, and a high degree of player participation. These characteristics conduce to a high level of consumption, which is one of the factors in the player protection model of gaming regulation in Britain.

The article is divided into three unequal sections. First, I describe the social history of gaming in England until the midnineteenth century and give an account of the substance and impact of the legal controls enacted to regulate it. Second, I analyze the basis of these controls and the concerns which they reflected and endeavor to show that the paradigm of early legal intervention—player protection—survived to be one of the bases of the modern legislation. Third, I describe the present-day regulation of casinos in Britain and compare it with the salient features of the Nevadan legislation.

A SOCIAL AND LEGAL HISTORY OF GAMING UNTIL THE MIDNINETEENTH CENTURY

THE RESTORATION TO 1750

Although there is evidence of gaming as a social pastime dating back to the eleventh century,[17] it is convenient to take gaming during the Restoration as a starting point. This is so because, first, the intensity of gaming during this period—in particular the prevalence of "deep gaming"—set a pattern in social activity which lasted, with some fluctuation, throughout Georgian England and, second, the legislation introduced to curb the activity was, unlike the predecessors, not overtly political in design[18] but was, rather, directed to its social consequences.

Pepys noted in his diary in the early 1660s[19] the incidence of "deep-gaming"—that is, continuous gaming over a prolonged period for high stakes, either in cash or some acceptable substitute, usually a security on land. The likely impact on the English social structure of such uncontrolled exchanges of mortgages, bonds, conveyances, and other securities was not lost on the monarchy. In addition, such gaming encouraged widespread cheating—although this was by no means confined to the wealthy—and in 1664 Charles II sought to curb these excesses by law.[20] Unlike earlier statutes, this measure did not proscribe the playing of nominated games, but instead endeavored to minimize their impact on the individual player by giving the victim of fraud the right to recover three times any sum he lost from the winner who had cheated him, the sum to be divided between himself and the Crown, and by declaring all securities for gaming debts incurred "at any one time or meeting" in excess of £100 to be void.[21] However, gaming for high stakes continued to flourish, notably in London and Bath, where in the first decade of the eighteenth century, Beau Nash created the archetype of the modern casino, attracting professional gamblers from across Europe.[22]

At the other end of the social scale, gaming became the focus of attention of the numerous societies for the reformation of manners which were established at the end of the seventeenth century. Along with swearing, profaning the Sabbath, drunkenness, and frequenting bawdy houses, gaming was an instance of idleness and immorality of the poor which "came to be regarded as immediate causes of crime and therefore in themselves direct threats to social stability";[23] and for a while associations such as the Society for the Promotion of Christian Knowledge and the London Society for the Reformation of Manners vigorously pursued and prosecuted keepers of gaming houses, which had been made an offense in the statute of 1541.

Their concern to improve the morality of the lower classes was not, in the context of gaming at least, shared by Queen Anne, who was more exercised by the considerations which had prompted her uncle to enact the statute of 1664. Accordingly, because "the laws now in force for preventing the mischiefs which may happen by gaming have not been found sufficient for that purpose,"[24] Anne introduced more stringent controls along the lines of the 1664 act. The 1710 measure contained two principal provisions: first, that all securities for gaming debts were void and, second, that the loser could recover any losses over £10 from the winner within three months, and thereafter by a common informer who would receive three times the sum lost, to be divided between himself and the Crown. In addition, a person convicted of fraudulent gaming forfeited five times the sum won and increased powers were given to justices of the peace to enforce the legislation.

As this statute was to form a significant part of the legislative strategy to control gaming until the midnineteenth century, it is appropriate at this point to review the general legality of gaming and gaming contracts. Gaming, which was defined earlier as the playing of a game for stakes hazarded by the players, was per se not illegal at common law. What rendered it so were the conditions under which the gaming took place. This was the position created by the statute of 1541 which provided, first, that it was an offense to keep a house for the purpose of gaming[25] and, second, that it was an offense for certain specified persons (artificers, craftsmen, apprentices, laborers, and so on) to "play at the tables [the contemporary expression for backgammon, later excluded from this list][26] tennis, dice, cards, bowls . . . out of Christmas, under the pain of twenty shillings to be forfeit for every time."[27]

Put briefly, gaming was illegal when it took place in a house maintained for that purpose or when it was entered into by specified persons. Later, during the mideighteenth century, certain games were declared unlawful,[28] thus rendering the hazarding of stakes upon their outcome unlawful; but as with the former group, it should be emphasized that the gaming itself was not illegal, rather it was so in consequence of other proscriptions.

Neither were gaming contracts per se unlawful: Throughout this period—until 1845—gaming contracts could be sued upon by winner and loser alike[29] subject to the limitations on securities introduced by Charles II and extended by Anne, and the right of the loser to recover his losses where they exceeded £10.

Between them, the statutes of 1541 and 1710 set a pattern for gaming control which persisted, despite changes in particular legal techniques, until 1960. This pattern had essentially two strands. The older was to restrict gaming to a private, non-profit making and occasional activity by proscribing common gaming houses. The second strand represented the efforts of the oligarchy to protect their wealth from being freely negotiable across the gaming table—and beyond—whereas no such objection could be raised about "ready money" gaming, so long as it was not accompanied by fraudulent practices.

Cheating, which was relatively easy with dice, reached epidemic proportions by the 1730s. It was encouraged by the immense popularity of hazard—a dicing game—and by the success of various novel card games—ace of hearts, faro (or pharaoh), and bassett—which offered unduly favorable odds to their promoters. The incidence of fraud and excessive gaming prompted the enactment of the Gaming Act 1738[30] which provided that it was an offense to promote these four games. However, as with much prohibitory legislation which nominates particular activities to be outlawed rather than identifying them generically,[31] the affected population invented a new dicing game, called passage, which achieved instant popularity.[32] In the following year, passage was declared unlawful,[33] but other variations on existing games were invented—roly poly and even/odd (both kinds of roulette)—which prompted further prohibitory legislation in 1744.[34]

These three statutes represent the most concerted effort in the eighteenth century to control the incidence of gaming among the wealthy and to minimize its impact upon the individual's financial position, but there are accounts which indicate that within 10 years, gaming was being conducted at its previous levels, and with the familiar consequences.

THE INFLUENCE OF HENRY FIELDING

Although there was considerable Parliamentary concern with the impact of gaming on the stability and predictability of inherited wealth, this concern was equally matched, if not exceeded, by the sudden prominence of lower class gaming into the consciousness of the propertied classes during the late 1740s and early 1750s. This prominence was in large measure due to the judicial and extra-judicial pronouncements of the London magistrate Henry Fielding, in particular the publication in 1750 of his tract on crime and public order.[35] This was a subject about which the propertied classes were especially sensitive: Although the 1745 rebellion had been crushed, the experience left a profound and lasting impression.[36] The social instability of the country was nowhere more obvious than in the existence of an improverished, homeless, and generally inebriated population which was concentrated within certain areas of the metropolis.

The publication of Fielding's tract coincided with the appointment of a House of Commons Committee whose terms of reference were to revise the criminal law, later extended to include consideration of measures to enforce the law.[37] Both perceived the causes of the increase in crime as lying first in the maladministration of the law and, second, in the moral laxity of the poor, accompanied by extravagant and improvident habits. Radzinowicz[38] concludes that Fielding's contribution to the diagnosis of the causes of crime was "of unique importance" and that its "bearing upon the history of criminal legislation can hardly be overemphasised." This being so, the most significant judgment Fielding came to concerning gaming was that its incidence among the upper classes, while possibly immoral when carried to excess, was by no means as socially dangerous a habit as when practiced by "the inferior part of mankind."[39] This attitude which is to be found elsewhere in his Inquiry[40] and which was shared by contemporary moralists[41] may well be the explanation for the relative lack of Parliamentary concern with the gaming habits of the upper class—despite its extravagance—until well into the nineteenth century, as compared to the efforts directed against lower class gaming, as part of a concerted campaign against their other pursuits.

THE ZENITH OF GAMING IN GEORGIAN ENGLAND

During the last quarter of the eighteenth century and throughout the Prince of Wales's Regency and accession as George IV, gaming among the upper classes reached its peak. The activity was mostly conducted in their homes and in the many gaming houses frequented by the poorer population, but from the proliferation of coffee houses and dining clubs in London there emerged establishments solely devoted to gaming (Timbs, 1872). The four original gaming clubs—White's, Arthur's, Almack's (later Brooks'), and the Cocoa Tree offered banks of £5000 a night against the players, a figure which the gaming houses could never match. Nonetheless, the gaming houses offered alternative inducements—chiefly prostitution—which ensured their continuing popularity with all classes of gambler.

Under the patronage of the Prince of Wales, other gaming clubs were established during the first two decades of the nineteenth century, but the demand for gaming facilities was undiminished well into the 1830s, although there is at this time evidence of change. Unquestionably "the most celebrated gaming house in London"[42] was Crockford's, established in 1828. It offered its membership of just over 1000 the most sumptuous surroundings and cuisine of all the clubs and realized over £300,000 in its first two years. With its pretigious Managing Committee presided over by the Duke of Wellington, by far the most influential figure in London society, Crockford's set something of a more restrained tone to the gaming table, albeit the depth of play was still considerable.[43]

All these clubs—"gold and silver hells" in the vernacular—were, like the gaming houses preferred by the lower class, unlawful. That they were able to flourish openly without hindrance from law enforcement officials was due principally to two factors. The first, which has been indicated in the description above, was that they attracted the most influential individuals in the country—members of the government, of the aristocracy, and by no means least, of the monarchy. In their past, White's had been closely associated with the Tories, Brooks' with the Whigs, and these party preferences survived their emergence as gaming clubs. These allegiances probably ensured immunity from investigation as common gaming houses, and if there were any doubts on that score, the patronage of the Prince of Wales must have foreclosed any possibility of prosecution.

The second factor concerns the attitude to gaming which prevailed during this period, namely, that upper class gaming, while productive of some mischief, was not inherently disruptive of the polity, whereas lower class gaming was so perceived. This attitude was held and proselytized by the societies for the reformation of manners which were revived during the last two decades of the eighteenth century and the first decade of the nineteenth. Crucial in the formation of this attitude was Fielding's judgment, discussed above, that gaming among the lower class was one of the symptoms of the moral laxity which encouraged criminal behavior. The activities and significance of these societies are well documented[44] and I do not propose to rehearse them. One crucial factor concerning the enforcemnt of the law merits comment, however.

The legislation proscribing common gaming houses and providing for the recovery of losses in excess of £10 or of those induced by fraud employed a system of enforcement which "formed part of the deliberate and consistent policy of the legislature and pervaded the entire body of the criminal law,"[45] namely, prosecution on the evidence of common informers. Consequently it was possible for these societies to give expression to their attitudes to lower class gaming by employing agents to act as common informers. The "evangelical police"[46] pursued the keepers of common gaming houses, but they were well-known for their partiality. Relying on the wealthy to provide funds to support them, the societies could hardly lay information before a magistrate concerning gaming at one of the St. James' clubs frequented by their patrons; indeed there is no evidence of any such action. The onslaught on lower class gaming was, however, limited in its impact; there were far too many houses for their limited funds to investigate and their organization prevented easy acquisition of the information required by a magistrate. By no means least, the opportunities for corruption were legion.

By contrast with the directed efforts of the societies against gaming houses, the recovery of sums lost at the gaming table was haphazard and largely dictated by the avarice of common informers. They stood to divide with the Crown three times the sum lost if it exceeded £10 or five times whatever the sum if it were won by cheating, but were equally prepared to settle for a lesser sum to be paid by the winner in consideration for their dropping the *qui tam* action; or by the loser for not disclosing the extent of his losses to his family, or the fact of his nonpayment of gaming debts or other creditors and potential creditors.

Blackmail, extortion, and the compromise of suits of recovery were commonplace, and it is therefore unsurprising that gaming continued unaffected by the legislation, despite occasional prosecutions.[47] Nor did the gradual increase in the numbers and organisation of the police result in a substantial change in its prevalence. Ashton[48] noted that bribery of police officers was widespread; gaming houses expending between £250 and £1000 annually on bribes, depending on the nature of their custom. Nonetheless, tolerance among some sections of the public of these many abuses was perceptibly changing.

THE 1884 COMMONS COMMITTEE ON GAMING

Even as Crockford was winning "the whole of the ready money of the then existing generation"[49] over his gaming tables in the 1830s, the pressure to take decisive action against gaming houses was gathering momentum.

In the first place, the extent of corruption—both specifically connected with gaming houses and more generally associated with all forms of gambling—was by now too notorious to be dismissed as occasional deviance on the part of a few officers. The police were deeply implicated in the continued nonenforcement of the law.[50]

In addition, scandals associated with the state lotteries[51] and with horse racing [52] confirmed the view held by the burgeoning middle class, who were Victorian rather than Georgian in their attitude to work (the values of thrift and industry) and leisure (the irrationality of extravagance), that all types of gambling conduced to the perpetuation of beliefs which ran counter to the demands of economic progress and, worse, to social and political instability.

Other factors also (which cannot be discussed fully here) contributed to a shift in attitude to gambling. Briefly, the two most significant were the development of fiscal policy and taxation systems, and what Downes[53] describes as "the differentiation of gambling transactions from capitalist transactions." The latter was especially important: Respectability had to be acquired by a commercial world that had been too closely associated with the problems of gambling. One of the key developments was the reinforcement of the integrity of the law of contract to protect genuine capital transactions in the Gaming Act, 1845.[54]

In 1839 an attempt was made to suppress gaming houses in London by giving the police additional powers [55] but for a variety of reasons this was no more successful than its predecessors. When the impotence of the law was brought to judicial attention in *Smith v. Bond*,[56] the pressure for action became irresistable.

In 1844 the House of Commons appointed a committee "to inquire into the existing statutes against gaming of every kind, to ascertain to what extent these statutes are evaded, and to consider whether any and what amendment should be made in such statutes." [57] It heard evidence from magistrates, commissioners for making a digest of the criminal law, the two commissioners of police for the City of London and of the Metropolis, members of the horse-racing fraternity, and from Crockford, now 70 years of age. Chaired by Lord Palmerston, the committee must have been aware of the general extent of gaming in London, and its questions to the witnesses suggest that it was concerned, first, to elicit more detailed information about gaming and, second, to discover why the police had such a poor record of suppression of gaming houses.

As to the first, the committee received virtually no help from the magistrates, nor from Crockford, who, despite repeated offers of immunity refused to be drawn on any aspect of the management of his club. Reading his answers to the questions put to him, it is difficult to believe that he had any interest in the gaming tables at all. [58] The police evidence [59] was certainly more informative, especially of the *modus operandi* of the lower class gaming houses, but the committee was evidently less than satisfied with their record in suppressing them, despite the powers introduced in 1838.[60] There is no mention of police corruption as a contributory factor in the story of nonenforcement, save one isolated suggestion that an "occasional sovereign" may have changed hands,[61] and the committee appeared to have accepted the police's mistaken view of the law (that it required players to be caught red-handed as a condition precedent of a prosecution for keeping a common gaming house) as a genuine explanation. In the event, it recommended that the police be given additional powers of entry and search and that the offense of keeping a gaming house be easier to prove. Thus, the mere presence of "instruments of gaming" in a suspected house or in the possession of persons in such a house was prima facie evidence of the offense "although no play was actually going on in the presence of the superintendent or constable."[62] All of these recommendations were implemented in the Gaming Act in the following year.[63]

THE BASIS OF LEGAL
INTERVENTION IN GAMING REGULATION

THE ROLE OF LAW AS A TECHNIQUE OF CONTROL

Although most of the questions directed to the witnesses concerned gaming houses, the 1844 committee had very definite views on the sumptuary laws against excessive gaming. It had no doubt that they were both ineffectual and incompatible with current beliefs about the role of government. They were ineffectual because "if protection is the object of this law, does it not protect most those who from their station in life need protection the least, and leave comparatively unprotected those of an inferior class, who may be severe sufferers from apparently small losses?"[64] Following the influential philosophy of Adam Smith, the committee also took the view that even if it were possible to control closely the economic choices of individuals, such a legislative policy would be inconsistent with laissez-faire economics. Control over gaming expenditure was neither necessary nor desirable, and if that meant that where "private individuals choose to make wagers with each other, there seems no good reason why they should be prevented from doing so, or why they should be punished for so doing,"[65] then the corollary also held, that there does not "seem to be any sufficient reason why the valuable time of the courts of law should be consumed by adjudicating disputes which arise between individuals as a result of these wagers."[66] Cheating was to remain criminal, punishable as obtaining money by false pretences, but gaming itself, *so long as it was not conducted in a common gaming house*, remained untouched by the law—recognized neither as an offense nor as giving rise to enforceable claims.[67]

THE ARTICULATION OF THE PLAYER PROTECTION MODEL

The history described above supports the view that the paradigm of legal intervention throughout the period discussed was based on the player protection model of gaming regulation I outlined earlier. The players to be protected by the eighteenth century legislation fell into two groups, identified in 1769 by the eminent English jurist, Blackstone[68]:

> it [gaming] is an offence of the most alarming nature; tending by necessary consequence to promote public idleness, theft and debauchery among those of a lower class; and among persons of a superior rank, it has frequently been attended with the sudden ruin and desolation of ancient and opulent families, an abandoned prostitution of every principle of honour and virtue.

The latter group were intended to be protected by the sumptuary laws, mainly contained in the 1710 statute, which allowed recovery of losses, penalized cheating, and made securities for gaming debts unenforceable. In the words of the 1844 committee[69] they were designed "to prevent what the framers of those laws considered excessive gaming; and being thus destined to restrain private individuals wasting their substance by losing too much money on games and pastimes."

Unquestionably the motivating consideration behind these laws was the perpetuation of inherited wealth and the maintenance of the social order. The legislature, being composed of many who enjoyed gaming, chose not to proscribe, but to control the impact of the activity. Some games were declared unlawful in the mideighteenth century, as they were thought to conduce to deep gaming, but gaming itself remained lawful, provided it did not take place in a common gaming house. The fact that none of these laws prevented the wealthy from extravagant gaming is immaterial, for prevention was not their purpose.

Gaming among the lower class was regulated primarily through the most direct means of controlling its location. Clearly, losses in excess of

£10 and the transfer of securities for gaming debts would be unusual at this level of society, and without any kind of organized policing, legislation aimed at the premises on which gaming regularly took place must have been an obvious tactic. As was observed earlier, this legislation applied in theory to the gaming houses of all classes, but was generally invoked only against those frequented by the lower class. Designed to render gaming a domestic and non-profit-making pastime, the reinforcement of this legislation was prompted by two considerations. First, following Fielding's indictment of lower class immorality, the societies for the reformation of manners sought to improve the lower class by removing temptation. Later in the eighteenth century, their activities were additionally motivated by the desire to inculcate what they viewed as the proper attitudes to work and leisure. This was well-expressed by the Webbs,[70] "what the educated classes always had at heart was the reclamation of the lower orders to a life of regular and continuous work." Like the wealthy, the poor were to be protected against themselves.

THE IMPACT OF THE GAMING ACT, 1845

The Gaming Act 1845 declared all wagering contracts unenforceable at law and that "debts so contracted should be recovered by such means only as the usages and customs of society can enforce for its own protection."[71]

Ashton [72] notes that "for many years afterwards professional gaming houses were a tradition of the past," but it seems that any connection between the enactment of the Gaming Act and the decline in public gaming is coincidental, rather than causal. In short, the social and economic conditions which prevailed in Victorian England were simply not conducive to excessive gaming. In addition, there was a marked increase in the interest shown by the middle class in the leisure activities of the lower class, in what Bailey terms the pursuit of rational recreation. [73] This interest sought, not always successfully, to control the leisure outlets of that class and direct them to good use. More particularly, horse racing and betting had supplanted gaming as the principal gambling activity of all classes, and despite the prohibition of betting shops in 1853 [74] flourished throughout the nineteenth century.

Thus, the decline in gaming may have been hastened rather than prompted by the 1845 act. Evidently this decline was not fatal, for the legislature thought it necessary to pass further legislation in 1854[75] to counter the obstructionist moves taken by gaming house-keepers, and there is evidence[76] that lower class gaming continued in houses not dissimilar to the Georgian hells throughout the Victorian period. Nonetheless, there does appear to be a definite reduction in the frequency of gaming; but, as discussed earlier, it is difficult to give a precise account of this as there are few sources. Upper class gaming presumably continued more discreetly, and may have been transferred to the European casinos which were being established toward the end of the nineteenth century, and which were popularized by the Prince of Wales, later Edward VII. A House of Lords Select Committee on Betting in 1901 refers in passing[77] to the presence in London of a number of clubs in whose card-rooms orderly and well-conducted betting on whist was commonplace, and Ashton[78] refers obliquely, and without further detail, to gaming houses which abound, "thanks to the laxity of the law with regard to so-called clubs."

Nor is the documentation on the incidence of gaming in the first few decades of this century any more precise. In the debates on the Gaming Bill 1922,[79] which was inspired by a House of Lords decision on the recoverability of check payments to bookmakers, one Member of Parliament observed that "London is full of gaming houses at the present time."[80] However, the 1932-1933 royal commission on betting and lotteries made no reference at all to the number of gaming houses, let alone that they posed a problem, beyond the general statement that "The prohibition of gaming houses is of long standing and is accepted as necessary in the public interest."[81] The commission thought the law adequate, and its only recommendation was to consolidate the various pieces of legislation which stretched back to the 1541 act.

A similar picture emerges from the 1949-1951 royal commission,[82] although its recommendations, which are too numerous to discuss here, were of more substance than its predecessor. This commission holds a significant place in any account of the history of the legal regulation of gambling, for it is largely upon its recommendations that much of Britain's present-day gambling is based. Crucial to the thesis of this article, however, was its view on the conditions under which individuals should be permitted to gamble and, in particular, the conditions relating to gaming.

THE PLAYER PROTECTION MODEL IN THE 1949-1951 ROYAL COMMISSION

The commission concluded that gambling should be permitted provided that three general principles be observed. These were: "strict control over the provision on a commercial basis of all forms of gambling, including the licensing or registration of all those who provide such facilities";[83] equal treatment of all sections of the community; and the dissemination of information about gambling to the public. With reference to gaming, the commission acknowledged that it was the most tempting form of gambling, and that "the need for severe restrictions on commercially organised gaming has long been recognised."[84]

Evidence of a player protection model of casino regulation can be seen in a number of features of the report. First, in response to the suggestion by the Churches' Council on Gambling, that gambling was fundamentally immoral, the commission said, "Our concern with the ethical significance of gambling is confined to the effect which it may have on the character of the gambler as a member of society."[85] This concern with the impact of gambling on the individual is reflected also in the nature of the evidence considered, namely, the connection if any between excessive gambling and theft to sustain the habit. The commission was convinced that if there was a connection, it was coincidental and not causal. Conversely, there is little indication in the report of the concerns which would lead to the adoption of a casino control model. There is no mention at all of "organised crime."

Although the commission did not actively recommend the introduction of commercially managed casinos, but rather the method of control if such a decision were made, its conclusions were generally taken as signifying a fundamental shift in governmental attitudes to gambling, and specifically gaming. In 1960, the Betting and Gaming Act[86] introduced, with some modification, the commission's recommendations, thus permitting for the first time in Britain lawful gaming on premises designed for that purpose (hitherto such premises would have constituted a common gaming house). The modifications allowed gross exploitation of the market and, with inadequate enforcement mechanisms and a legal framework of considerable complexity, many casinos which were established during the 1960s became fronts for criminal organizations, or were in other ways connected with illegal activity. This situation was viewed with increasing disquiet, and in 1968 the Labour government introduced the Gaming Act[87] designed to "establish a strict but flexible system of control capable of containing all forms of gaming which were liable to be commercially exploited and abused."[88]

CONTEMPORARY CASINO REGULATION AND
THE INTRODUCTION OF PLAYER PROTECTION
CONTROLS IN THE UNITED STATES

CASINO REGULATION IN BRITAIN AND NEVEDA

The Gaming Act 1968 was the governmental response to the virtually uncontrolled gaming unintentionally permitted by the 1960 legislation. The principal deficiency of the 1960 act was the absence of any regulatory body to control the location and conduct of premises established for gaming and to enforce such regulations as were made as to their management. To remedy this, the 1968 act established the Gaming Board for Great Britain, which enjoys extremely wide powers over all matters concerning the management of commercial gaming.

As was observed earlier, the 1968 act contains no definition of gaming, but rather seeks to specify the locations and financial conditions under which it may lawfully take place. It does this by differentiating between types of gaming according to their potential for exploitation and abuse, and the greater they are, the closer the bureaucratic control. Thus gaming within the family setting or between friends is not subject to any control, so long as no charge is made for participation. Games of unequal chance may be played in such circumstances, but as they are confined to a domestic basis, they are not thought to conduce to exploitation. On the other hand, such games can only be played on a regular basis on premises licensed by the act, and here the control of the Gaming Board over casino gaming is at its most stringent. On premises not so licensed—typically social clubs—only games of equal chance may be played. Although most of this article has been concerned with casino gaming, it is confined to that activity in the following discussion.

Casino regulation in Britain is of two kinds. The first is based on the legacy of the legislation of the eighteenth century and conforms to the player protection model. Its object is to minimize the impact of gaming on the individual by restricting the opportunities for his recruitment and continued participation. In the words of the recent Royal Commission on Gambling "the underlying principle is that casino facilities in Britain should be sufficient, but no more than sufficient, to satisfy an unstimulated demand for gaming which might otherwise seek an illegal outlet."[89]

Of course there are difficulties with the notion of "unstimulated demand," but it gives clear expression in the objectives of a player protection model of regulation. The pursuit of this principle has resulted in a very restrictive regime over casino gaming, which I outline below.

The opportunities for recruitment of gaming are limited in four main ways: casinos may operate only in "permitted areas" which are designated by the Gaming Board; only members of the club (except bona fide guests) may take part, and on the first occasion only after 48 hours have elapsed since application for membership; only two jackpot machines (that is, gaming machines without financial limits on the amounts that can be won, save their physical capacity) to each licensed club; and no commercial advertising.

There are also four main techniques which are employed to restrict continued participation. These are: no gaming on credit (save the purchase of chips by check): hours of play 2 p.m. to 4 a.m. with restrictions on Sundays; no live entertainment; and no liquor served outside normal licensing hours, which generally end at 11 p.m. in London and 10:30 p.m. elsewhere.[90]

In 1976, the gross revenue before tax received by 121 casinos in operation that year was £100.5 million.[91] Using a dollar-sterling rate of 2:1, this is about a fifth of the amount generated in Nevada's casinos over a comparable period ($1,126,415,410 in 1975).[92] This suggests that the restrictions in Britain do indeed result in some limitation on expenditure, but there are a number of variables, for example the total population and origin of the players, and the availability in Britain of other legitimate gambling outlets, which make comparisons difficult.

The second strand in current casino regulations is based on the casino control model, designed to eliminate criminal enterprise from the commercial management of gaming. Whereas under the 1960 legislation, anyone could open a casino provided he observed certain formalities which were in fact easily evaded, the 1968 act was based upon the premise that "participation in commercial gaming was a privilege to be conceded only to those who satisfied the Gaming Board that they could be trusted to observe the letter and spirit of the law."[93] The Gaming Board has an unfettered discretion over the granting of certificates which permit individuals to be the proprietor of, or an employee in, a casino or to supply or sell gaming machines. In deciding whether to grant a consent certificate, the board is required to "have regard only to the question whether, in their opinion, the applicant is likely to be capable of, and diligent in, securing that the provisions of this Act . . . will be complied with."[94] The board is required to inform an applicant of the case against him and to give him an opportunity to rebut it, but it is not obliged to give any reasons for refusal to grant a certificate.

Moreover, mere possession of a certificate does not entitle an individual to open a casino; he must first obtain a gaming licence from the licensing magistrates in the area in question, and the Gaming Board is at liberty to object at this stage, for example on the grounds that demand has been met by existing establishments in that area. The board can also object to the renewal of a license, on the ground that the holder has not shown himself to be "fit and proper," as has occurred recently with Ladbroke's, a commercial gambling organization.

In short, the Gaming Board for Great Britain has powers very similar to those enjoyed by the Gaming Control Board of Nevada over the vetting of applicants. I think it is completely uncontroversial to observe that the Nevadan legislation, as amended, has been motivated almost exclusively by casino control considerations,[95] and although there are some differences between the two, for example, as to the limits of due process, the similarities in bureaucratic structure are striking.

On the other hand, player protection regulations are manifestly absent from the Nevada legislation, and this leads to the final question to be addressed, whether controls based upon that model could, as advised by the commission, be introduced in the United States.

PLAYER PROTECTION CONTROLS IN U.S. CASINO REGULATIONS

It is difficult to imagine controls as restrictive as those presently in force in Britain being acceptable in the United States, at least in existing gaming outlets in Nevada and New Jersey. Casino gaming in their resorts is simply a different quality to that to be found in Britain. Skolnick[96] says, "Tourists come to Las Vegas not only to gamble, but also to immerse themselves in a culture of gambling, which means a culture of entertainment, swimming pools, golf courses, food, booze, hookers—hedonism 24 hours a day." There are a number of reasons why the British regime is probably incompatible with the cultural expectations generated by gaming in the United States.

Prime among these is that gaming in Nevada and, more recently, New Jersey had been a conscious product of fiscal policy. Although the British government does derive revenue from all gambling outlets, this has never been a sole or even major reason behind the legalisation of gambling in Britain, which until the 1968 act has been based on the player protection model. This is not to say that player protection is incompatible with revenue raising, although the restrictions on opportunities for gaming must affect the market to the detriment of gross revenue receipts. On the other hand, there are many legitimate gambling outlets in Britain—horse-race betting, football pools, lotteries, and bingo—and so maximization of revenue from gaming is not essential to maximization of all gambling revenue, even if this were a conscious fiscal policy in Britain, which it is not. To the contrary, the government (of both complexions) has always taken the view that the primary concern is the facilitation of gambling within existing demand and the imposition of restrictions to discourage excess. If this provides revenue to subvent the costs of bureaucratic control and to stimulate the activities which provide the pretext for gambling (for example, subsidizing horse racing or improving football stadia), well and good, but it is not designed to maximize revenue as a technique of indirect taxation.

These considerations do not apply to the history of gaming control in the United States. Skolnick concludes that the recommendation to adopt British-style gaming control:[97]

> woefully underestimates the force of the economic motives and pressures associated with legal casino gaming where revenue is the reason for legalisation. For states other than Nevada or New Jersey which are considering legal casino gambling, the real question is not whether to adopt the major outlines of the English model, but whether in the American context, local governments can realistically contemplate such a choice.

> My conclusion is that the combination of revenue-producing motive, coupled with the power of already existing economic interests in the casino gambling industry, added to the cultural and legal constraints of American society will ensure that if ever casino gambling is adopted by an American state, the Nevada model—with its economic imperatives—will dominate.

An object lesson which underlines this conclusion is the nature of gaming control adopted in Atlantic City. Despite the commission's view[98] that casino gaming is unlikely to generate sufficient revenue to ease serious financial difficulty, it was introduced in Atlantic City for precisely that reason. Moreover, the original hearings for licenses, and those in 1979 to determine whether they should be extended, were to a considerable degree focused on the concerns of a casino control model of regulation. Even though limited player protection controls were introduced initially, these have since been considerably diluted.

Both New Jersey and Nevada are concerned with gambling as a fiscal alternative, but even for a state not so preoccupied, the likelihood of a significant shift toward player protection seems remote. Apart from Skolnick's general references to cultural factors, the commission's view that states should continue to be autonomous in gambling control, save for federal involvement in interstate gambling, is hardly likely to give force to its preference for the British model.

Another reason why I reach this conclusion is based upon the historical analysis presented in this article, namely, that the motivating considerations behind the British legislation have been productive of a primary emphasis on the player protection model. These considerations have been of marginal significance in the historical development of gaming legislation in the United States, and for this reason are unlikely to be seen as relevant considerations in choosing models for control for the present day.

NOTES

1. *Commission on the Review of the National Policy toward Gambling,* Final Report (Washington, DC: Government Printing Office, 1976); hereafter, *U.S. Final Report.*

2. *Ibid.*, 102.

3. J. Skolnick, *House of Cards: Legislation and Control of Casino Gaming* (Boston: Little, Brown, 1978); and *U.S. Final Report.*

4. Gaming Control Act, 1931, as amended; State of Nevada: Revised Statutes c.463.

5. *U.S. Final Report*, 100-104.

6. Gaming Act, 1968 c.65.

7. *U.S. Final Report;* and U.S. Department of Justice, *The Development of the Law of Gambling 1776-1976* (Washington, DC: Government Printing Office, 1977).

8. *Skolnick, op. cit.*

9. J. Eddy and L. Loewe, *The Gaming Act 1968* (London: Butterworth, 1969), 1; *Royal Commission on Betting and Lotteries* (London: Her Majesty's Stationery Office Cmd. 4341, 1932), 4; and U.S. Department of Justice, *op. cit.*, 6.

10. An act for maintenance of artillery and the debarring of unlawful games 1541, 33 Henry VIII c.9.

11. Sir L. Radzinowicz, *A History of English Criminal Law and Its Administration from 1750* (London: Stevens, Vol. 1, 1948; Vol. 2, 1956; Vol. 3, 1956).

12. D. Downes, *Gambling, Work and Leisure* (London: Routledge & Kegan Paul, 1976).

13. 8 & 9 Victoria c.109.

14. K. Chesney, *The Victorian Underworld* (Harmondsworth, England: Penguin, 1972); and P. Bailey, *Leisure and Class in Victorian Britain* (London: Routledge & Kegan Paul, 1978).

15. *Per* Hawkins J., *Jenks v. Turpin* (1884) 13 Q.B.D. 505; and *Halsbury's Laws of England* (London: Butterworth, 1974), Vol.4.

16. D. Cornish, *Gambling: A Review of the Literature* (London: Home Office Study 42, 1978).

17. J. Ashton, *The History of Gambling in Britain* (London: Duckworth, 1898); and U.S. Department of Justice, *op. cit.*

18. *Report from the Select Committee on Gaming* (London: House of Commons paper 297, 1844), iii.

19. Ashton, *op. cit.*, 42-45.

20. An act against deceitful, disorderly and excessive gaming, 1664, 16 Charles II c.7.

21. *Ibid.*, section 3.

22. W. Connely, *Beau Nash* (London: Werner Laurie, 1955), 19.

23. Radzinowicz, *op. cit.*, Vol. 2, 3.

24. Gaming Act, 1710, 9 Anne c.14.

25. *Op. cit.*, n.10, section 8.

26. Gaming Act, 1739, 13 George II c.19.

27. *Op. cit.*, n.10, section 11.

28. Gaming Act, 1738, 12 George II c.28; *op. cit.*, n.26; and Gaming Act, 1744, 18 George II c.34.

29. Such actions were rare; see U.S. Department of Justice, *op. cit.*, 19.

30. *Op. cit.*, n.28.

31. See *Royal Commission on Betting, Lotteries and Gaming 1949-51* (London: Her Majesty's Stationery Office, Cmd. 8190, 1952), 409.

32. Connely, *op. cit.*, 123-126.

33. *Op. cit.*, n.26.

34. *Op. cit.*, n.28.

35. "An inquiry into the Causes of the Late Increase of Robbers" in T. Roscoe, ed., *The Complete Works of Henry Fielding* (London: George Bell, 1889).

36. Radzinowicz, *op. cit.*, Vol. 1, 399.

37. *Journals of the House of Commons* (1750-1754), Vol. 23.

38. *Op. cit.*, Vol. 1, 401.

39. *Op. cit.*, n.35, 767.

40. *Op. cit.*, n.35, 763.

41. Radzinowicz, *op. cit.*, Vol. 1, 19.

42. Ashton, *op. cit.*, 118.

43. H. Blyth, *Hell and Hazard* (London: Weidenfeld and Nicolson, 1969) 117-130.

44. Radzinowicz, *op. cit.*, Vol. 3, 141-148; and E. Thompson, *The Making of the English Working Class* (Harmondsworth, England: Penguin, 1963).

45. Radzinowicz, *op. cit.*, Vol. 2, 146.

46. Radzinowicz, *op. cit.*, Vol. 1, 160.

47. Ashton, *op. cit.*, 75.

48. Ashton. *op. cit.*, 106.

49. Ashton, *op. cit.*, 127.

50. *Third Report on the State of the Police of the Metropolis* (London: Parliamentary Papers 423, 1811), Vol. 8; and Radzinowicz, *op. cit.*, Vol. 2, 296.

51. D. Miers and D. Dixon, "The National Bet: The Re-emergence of the Public Lottery" *Public Law*, 1979, 372-403.

52. Blyth, *op. cit.*, 67-71.

53. *Op. cit.*, 42.

54. *Op. cit.*, n.13.

55. Metropolitan Police Act, 1839, 2 & 3 Victoria c.47.

56. (1842) 152 *English Reports* 828.

57. *Op. cit.*, n.18, iii.

58. *Ibid.*, 172, 180; and Blyth, *op. cit.*, 164-166.

59. *Op. cit.*, n.18, 7, 15, 30-39.

60. *Ibid.*, vi.

61. *Ibid.*, 76.

62. Gaming Act, 1845, *op. cit.*, section 8.

63. *Id.*

64. *Op. cit.*, N.18.,v.

65. *Ibid.*, vi.

66. *Id.*

67. Gaming Act, 1845, *op. cit.*, section 18.

68. R. Kerr, ed., *W. Blackstone, Commentaries on the Laws of England* (London: John Murray, 1857), 171.

69. *Op. cit.*, iii.

70. S. Webb and B. Webb, *The History of Liquor Licensing* (London: F. Cass, 1903) English Local Government, Vol.11.

71. *The Three Reports from the Select Committee of the House of Lords on the Laws Respecting Gaming* (London: Her Majesty's Stationery Office, House of Lords papers 468, 544, and 604.

72. *Op. cit.*, 149.

73. *Op. cit.*, n.14.

74. Betting Act, 1853, 16 & 17 Victoria c.119.

75. Gaming Houses Act, 1854, 17 & 18 Victoria c.38.

76. Chesney, *op. cit.*, n.14, 123, 271; and Bailey, *op. cit.*, 113, 134.

77. *Report of the Select Committee of the House of Lords on Betting* (London: Her Majesty's Stationery Office, House of Lords papers 114 and 173; House of Commons paper 389).

78. *Op. cit.*, 149.

79. Gaming Act, 1922, c.19.

80. 155 *H.C. Debs.* col. 1550 (23 June 1922).

81. *Op. cit.*, n.9, para. 534.

82. *Op. cit.*, n.31.

83. *Ibid.* para 189.

84. *Ibid.*, para 406.

85. *Ibid.*, para 159.

86. Betting and Gaming Act, 1960, c.60.

87. *Op.cit.*, n.6.

88. *Royal Commission on Gambling* (London: Her Majesty's Stationery Office, Cmnd. 7200, 1978), para. 17.1.

89. *Ibid.*, para. 18.19.

90. The royal commission has recommended that this restriction be relaxed to permit casinos to serve liquor during normal licensing hours for clubs; *ibid.*, para. 18.72.

91. *Ibid.*, para. 1.3.

92. *U.S. Final Report*, 80.

93. *Op. cit.*, n.88, para. 19.3.

94. Gaming Act, 1968, *op. cit.*, schedule 2.

95. *U.S. Final Report*, 83-88; and Skolnick, *op. cit.*, *passim.*

96. Skolnick, *op. cit.*, 35.

97. *Ibid.*, 346.

98. *U.S. Final Report*, 101.

9

THE STATE AND PROSTITUTION: PROHIBITION, REGULATION, OR DECRIMINALIZATION?

MARY GIBSON

INTRODUCTION

Often called "the oldest profession," prostitution has posed a problem for states throughout history. A traditional belief in the universal nature of prostitution has often prevented researchers from looking more closely at this phenomenon in a certain society at a specific time.[1] As two sociologists, John Gagnon and William Simon, have written,

> Female prostitution is as much if not more vulnerable to the process of social and scientific simplification than are other kinds of sexual relationships.[2]

Such simplification arises at least partially from the tendency to view human sexuality, and male and female sex roles, as immutably rooted in biological imperatives. This reductionism not only makes the analysis of prostitution difficult but also affords little promise to those who wish to formulate new policies concerning this supposedly universal institution.

Those who make public policy should be aware of the multiple definitions of prostitution as well as the variety of responses developed in the past. An evaluation of the effectiveness of these responses should present lawmakers, administrators, and judges with guidelines for examining present regulations.

Unlike theft or homicide, prostitution does not constitute a rather clear-cut crime, but one that is especially susceptible to molding by the law. More than for other offenses, the law creates the crime of prostitution by the process of defining what constitutes that act. For example, in America today, most states, like Illinois, limit prosecution to those who commit sexual acts "for money."[3] But at least 16 states have at one time considered any promiscuous, extramarital sex on the part of women to constitute prostitution. In 1964, the Ohio law read that,

> the term "prostitution" shall be construed to include the offering or receiving of the body for sexual intercourse for hire, and shall also be construed to include the offering or receiving of the body for indiscriminate sexual intercourse without hire.[4]

Since legal descriptions are often ambiguous, police continue the process of definition by their selection of women arrested for prostitution. The Italian law of 1860, which designated as prostitutes "those women . . . who notoriously exercise the practice of prostitution," illustrates this vague, and sometimes circular, legal wording.[5] Since this law did not provide for court review of arrest, police were free to label any woman who was unemployed, homeless, or simply walking on the streets at night as a prostitute. Rather than making broad generalizations about prostitution, the researcher must be sensitive to differences in this "labelling" process across cultures and over time.

During the past 150 years, Western nations have employed three basic strategies to manage prostitution. Called "prohibition," "regulation," and "decriminalization," all three had supporters in nineteenth century Italy, the country with which I am most familiar and from which many of the examples in this article will be drawn.[6] While the social, economic, and political conditions of nineteenth century Europe certainly differ from those in contemporary America, the context of the debates about governmental policies to deal with prostitution have not. As Gagnon and Simon have pointed out,

> our attitudes toward prostitutes are based on the same origins as our current conventional vision of the natural order that should exist between women and men—i.e., the nineteenth-century English

models. Though the contours of most of our society have changed in the intervening century, the available legal, moral, and social scripts that exist for the act of prostitution are remarkably stable.[7]

In short, since the midnineteenth century, no Western state has been able to formulate a completely new policy to deal with prostitution. Therefore, the following sections will review the historical and geographical extent of the application of prohibition, regulation, and decriminalization. These policies will then be compared in three areas. Most fundamentally, was the act of prostitution considered a crime? Based on this judgment, what did proponents of each system believe should be the proper attitude of the state of prostitution? Finally, what have constituted the major practical problems in the enforcement of each policy?

PROHIBITION

Until the Enlightenment, with its revolution in legal theory and practice, most laws dealing with prostitution could be labelled as those of prohibition. The Catholic Church, later followed by the Protestant faiths after the Reformation, provided the religious basis for the moral crusades against prostitution. In the Middle Ages, when clerical courts had wide jurisdiction, the Church prosecuted prostitution as well as other sexual activities which it considered deviant.[8] With little separation of church and state in early modern Europe, religious prescriptions on morality permeated the law codes of both Catholic and Protestant countries. In a similar manner, the American colonists tried to suppress prostitution, and their Puritan values carried over into the legislation of the states of the early republic. With the secularization of the nineteenth century, most European states replaced prohibition with regulation or decriminalization. But the United States was one of the few nations to retain, and in fact strengthen, prohibition, which is still enshrined in the law codes of almost every state.[9]

At the basis of prohibitionist statutes was the assumption that extramarital sex was sinful, and therefore a crime. As Vern Bullough, a historian of sexuality, has written,

the Church Fathers regarded sex as at best something to be tolerated, an evil whose only good was in procreation. Western attitudes have been dominated by their concepts ever since.[10]

Significantly, most of these laws punished only the woman, and not her male client, for immorality.[11] As implied in the traditional phrase, "fallen woman," prohibitionists located the cause of prostitution in the moral failings of certain individual females. Because it was believed that some personal defect had caused their fall from grace, prostitutes themselves, rather than their social environment, bore the guilt for their fate. While incontinence of both sexes was officially deplored by church and state, moral lapses of male customers were generally tolerated and rarely proscribed by law.[12]

Prohibitionists devised a variety of punishments to counter female weakness, thought to be the cause of prostitution. Before the Enlightenment, European punishment was often harsh, ranging from requirements to wear distinctive clothing to "tortures, floggings, brandings, and banishment."[13] American variants in the colonies included the dunking stool, wearing a scarlet letter, and, later in the nineteenth century, forced sterilization. Generalization about punishment is difficult, since methods and severity varied according to the dictates of the ruler, rather than an abstract theory of justice.[14] Presently in the United States, sentencing is theoretically no longer harsh or arbitrary, being carried out in court according to laws which make the punishment equal to the crime, not the will of the executive. In most states, the maximum penalty for prostitution does not exceed one year and often is less than six months.[15]

The administration of prohibition statutes has encountered similar problems in both early modern Europe and contemporary America. At a very practical level, no government can easily afford the expense of effective enforcement. For example, one expert has estimated that in the United States today it costs the public about $1560 to arrest and process one streetwalker.[16] Speaking of all victimless crimes, including prostitution, the sociologist of crime, Edwin Schur, argues that,

> it is because of their transactional nature—and the evidentiary difficulties such situations present—that crime without victims are particularly costly to administer.[17]

Since a large section of society engages in an act which the law defines as criminal, the state would require an enormous "vice squad" to locate all offenders. Furthermore, as there is usually no complainant in such a case, police must use time-consuming and expensive techniques to obtain evidence.[18]

Not only is prohibition expensive but also it has historically proved to be ineffective. Before Italian unification, the popes, as the secular rulers of Rome, tried to suppress prostitution according to the dictates of Church doctrine. Yet throughout Italy, Rome was notorious as a center for sexual vice, with visitors claiming that prostitutes openly plied their trade in the shadows of the great cathedrals and government buildings. One of these travelers noted that, "prostitution had never ceased to exist in Rome in spite of the incarcerations, fines, torture, and harassments of every kind."[19] As for results in the United States, two researchers have concluded that, "it is apparent that under current conditions the attempt to suppress prostitution by present police methods is analogous to attempting to empty the ocean with a teacup."[20]

The attempt to enforce unpopular prohibition laws has tended to further corruption and lower morale among police officials. Because definitions of prostitution are ambiguous, and vice squads understaffed, police exercise wide discretionary powers in their choice of whom to arrest. Open to bribes and influence from powerful customers, police often overlook the violations of call girls or brothels catering to the wealthy. By ignoring these groups, police tend to redefine prostitution to encompass only the poor streetwalker. Furthermore, because of lack of complainants, police have to rely on methods which border on illegality; for example, the use of decoys to catch prostitutes in the act of solicitation often becomes entrapment, and thus a violation of the woman's civil rights.

REGULATION

In the early years of the nineteen century, Napoleon I introduced the policy of regulation as an answer to the failures of prohibition.[21] By midcentury, most states in continental Europe, including Italy, had copied the French regulation statutes with only slight modifications. Between 1864 and 1869, England passed a set of "Contagious Disease Acts" which established regulation in the major garrison and port towns. Although never as popular in the United States, regulation existed for a period in St. Louis, New Orleans, and several other cities.[22] Today regulation is relatively rare in Western nations, surviving only in a few Dutch and German municipalities as well as in some areas of Nevada. It survived until 1945 in France and 1958 in Italy, however, and in these countries there is still strong support for the former policy.

Although statutes resembling regulation had existed since medieval times in parts of Europe, the wave of nineteenth century legislation presupposed a secular and scientific point of view. Most often coming from the ranks of doctors and police, regulationists rejected moral crusades and pledged to treat prostitution rationally as an unpleasant, but eternal fact of life. What made prostitution "eternal," they suggested, was the nature of male sexuality which was strong and uncontrollable. For them, prostitution did not challenge the sanctity of marriage, as prohibitionists thought, but reinforced it by providing a safety valve for a male sex drive which might otherwise be directed toward "honest" women. Thus, while policies of prohibition theoretically rejected extramarital intercourse for both sexes, regulation explicitly acknowledged the double standard. Normal women were considered naturally passionless while excessive male sexuality was excused, or even applauded as healthy, on the grounds that it was determined by the male physiological and psychological constitution.

Believing prostitution to be necessary, and even in some ways desirable, to the proper functioning of society, regulationists rejected the prohibitionists' view of prostitution as a crime. As one Italian doctor concluded in 1882:

> Prostitution is not a crime and therefore cannot be prosecuted by the Penal Code; but it is a vice, morally and hygienically dangerous to Society. The practice of prostitution can therefore be considered from the same point of view as the practice of unhealthy industries, which Society submits with full right to special regulations and to special surveillance.[23]

If prostitution was not criminal, however, it often led to abuses of public health, order, and morality. Regulationists hoped to minimize these problems by legalizing prostitution and submitting it to police control. Legalization did not imply moral approval of the prostitute or acceptance of prostitution as a normal rather than deviant activity for a woman; it simply offered a more efficient strategy than prohibition for protecting society from these deviants.

In a regulation system, the state controls prostitution in three ways: It requires that all prostitutes register with police, undergo periodic health examinations, and report to a hospital if found infected. To safeguard public order and morality, police control the movements of prostitutes. Since police know the location of brothels, they can exercise special surveillance to prevent rowdiness, soliciting, or indecent exposure. Examination and hospitalization are intended to control the spread of venereal disease for which regulationists generally held prostitutes responsible. In fact, the desire to ensure a healthy population—especially that of the military—constituted the primary impetus for instituting regulation in many states including France and England. In Piedmont, the state which led Italian unification, Cavour established regulation specifically to prepare his troops for the war of liberation in 1859-1860.

Like the attempt to repress prostitution, problems arose in the administration of the system of regulation. Enforcement required the expertise of both police and health authorities, which in Italy constituted two distinct bureaucracies in the Ministry of the Interior. The problems of policing the regulation system resembled those of prohibiting prostitution: high expense, ineffectiveness, and corruption. Prostitutes seemed to resist registration with police almost as much as they had arrest. Thus Italian police chiefs constantly complained that they lacked sufficient personnel to locate "clandestine" prostitutes and make them comply with the law. Furthermore, the mobility of prostitutes frustrated attempts at surveillance. As one Italian authority complained in 1872,

> These unfortunates [prostitutes] exchange places, substitute for each other, recruit new members, and transfer from city to city, from province to province, and even from nation to nation. Surveillance for political and moral purposes is hardly possible unless the State has thousands of agents, all disciplined, all taking orders from the center, spread throughout the entire territory of the Kingdom, corresponding among themselves and ready to act at a moment's notice.[24]

The reality of Italian regulation did not match this vision of efficiency and total control. In 1897, the largest vice squads were those of Rome with 20 agents, Naples with 11, and Bologna with 7.[25] Yet the Minister of the Interior constantly bemoaned the expense of the system and ordered local police officials to prevent increases in their budgets.

Because of the resistance of prostitutes, only a portion were ever registered with police. Even supporters of regulation admitted that the majority of prostitutes escaped police supervision, while critics charged that only one-sixth to one-tenth of all prostitutes cooperated with the system.[26] While the total number of clandestine prostitutes was unknown, the fact that the figures for registered prostitutes dropped from about 10,500 in 1881 to 6,000 in 1908 tends to underline the ineffectiveness of regulation.[27] It is unlikely that the numbers of prostitutes decreased so drastically, especially during a period when population was increasing and cities expanding.

Finally, regulation, like prohibition, encouraged corruption. Brothels which catered to the upper classes were seldom submitted to police surveillance, although one critic charged that these fashionable houses were "notorious" and well known to police and citizens alike.[28] Even in the case of registered brothels, bribery and familiarity with madams and prostitutes often led to laxity in the enforcement of sections of the law which prohibited the prostitution of minors, soliciting, and the sale of food and drink in brothels. One newspaper, *Roma*, stated flatly that the morals police were delinquents and had nothing in common with ordinary, honest police.[29]

While the regulationist campaign to publicize the problem of venereal disease and the necessity of cure was very progressive, its methods were not totally successful. Most fundamentally, nineteenth century doctors had no reliable methods for diagnosing and curing venereal disease. Today, the development of the Wasserman test in 1907 and the discovery of penicillin and sulfa drugs in the 1930s and 1940s have largely resolved this problem. Yet debate continues on the effectiveness of the regulationist policy of examining and hospitalizing prostitutes by force. As noted earlier, the majority of prostitutes escape registration and, therefore, would not be submitted to periodic examinations. Furthermore, the focus on the prostitute as the carrier of venereal disease leaves the male client free to infect his girlfriend, wife, and, in the case of hereditary syphilis, his children. As extramarital contacts between men and nonprostitute women increase, the efficacy of applying health measures only to prostitutes diminishes.[30]

DECRIMINALIZATION

Like regulation, decriminalization developed in the nineteenth century as a progressive solution to the problem of the relationship of the state to prostitution. This movement opposed not only the traditional policy of prohibition but also more immediately the newly installed regulation laws. Calling themselves abolitionists, in a direct reference to American anti-slavery societies, early supporters of decriminalization campaigned to abolish regulation and what they viewed as its corollary, the white slave trade. The first abolitionist organization was founded in England in 1869 by a liberal and feminist, Josephine Butler. Butler and her followers successfully challenged the Contagious Disease Acts which were repealed in 1883. Abolitionists continued pressure in continental Europe, securing the endorsement of the League of Nations after World War I. Although the struggle often took decades, most European nations have now adopted abolition, most notably France in 1946 and Italy in 1958. Butler did establish a branch of her organization in the United States, but American opposition to regulation usually took the form of prohibition rather than abolition.

Like regulationists, abolitionists classified prostitution as a "private vice" rather than a crime and believed in attaching penalties only to its "objectionable manifestations."[31] They refused, however, to accept prostitution as natural and necessary to the functioning of society. As one abolitionist wrote, the two sides differed over the fundamental question of whether "the male instinct, to which the existence of prostitution is attributed, can or cannot be overcome."[32] While regulationists accepted a strong male sex drive as a scientific fact, abolitionists abhorred excessive sexuality as typical of the more primitive stages in the evolution of man. For them, the perfectibility of civilization depended on man's ability to overcome his lower, animal urges and submit them to spiritual control, as they believed women had. In short, they preached a single standard: chastity for all until marriage and sex only with one's spouse after marriage.

Although abolitionists, like prohibitionists, hoped eventually to get rid of prostitution, they rejected repression and moral crusades. Personally deploring prostitution, they insisted that prostitutes, as citizens, should be free to practice their profession as long as they observed existing laws concerning public order and decency. They denounced regulation systems for infringing on the civil rights of prostitutes and treating them like second-class citizens. For example, prostitutes had to carry special identification cards, get permission to change their residence, all of which were contrary to the principles of a liberal society. Furthermore, abolitionists charged both laws of prohibition and regulation with sexism, since they punished or controlled only the woman for an act performed by both sexes. While male customers retained their good standing in the community and were free from harassment and restrictions by police, women became outcasts who were submitted to constant surveillance, restraints, and insults. As Giuseppe Mazzini, an abolitionist and liberal leader of Italian unification, pointed out, legislation aimed only at the woman, and not her client, was not only unjust but also created disrespect for the law:

> If you punish the accomplice, leaving the sinner untouched, you destroy, by arousing the sense of injustice, every beneficial result of punishment.[33]

Yet, as Abraham Flexner, an early historian of prostitution, has argued, abolitionists did not preach a completely laissez-faire attitude toward prostitution:

> Abolition means only the abolition of regulation, not the abolition of prostitution; abolition does not require that prostitution be ignored, overlooked, tabooed, or treated in a spirit of prudery as nonexistent; it is entirely consistent with thorough inquiry into the whole phenomenon, and constructive social action aiming to deal with it.[34]

To curb the "objectionable manifestations" of prostitution, abolitionists supported laws against soliciting in public places which they felt infringed on the right of others not to be harassed or exposed to immorality. They were also eager to prosecute any third parties who made a profit from prostitution—that is, pimps, madams, and white slave traders. They blamed these figures for luring, tricking, and forcing women into a life which abolitionists believed to be naturally degrading. With the streets cleared of procurers they hoped that fewer women would "choose" to practice prostitution.

Abolitionists relied more on moral uplift than legal regulations to decrease prostitution. For example, the Italian Committee Against the White Slave Trade founded reformatories for those women who wanted to leave the profession.[35] Blaming prostitution on environmental conditions rather than individual immorality, the committee emphasized preventive measures. Its rehabilitation centers took in not only former prostitutes but also the "endangered": those girls who through poverty, loss of parents, or attempted seduction might subsequently turn to prostitution. A variety of organizations established dormitories, job-placement centers, and information offices in railway stations for female migrants. In Parliament, abolitionists supported legislation to ameliorate what they believed to be causes of prostitution—corruption of minors, abuse by parents, loss of family by young girls, and poverty among youth.

Abolitionists shocked Victorian society by their advocacy of sex education to fight prostitution, even though they emphasized the teaching of moral precepts rather than physiological information. Believing the fundamental cause of prostitution to be male demand, they preached a transformation of social values toward women. If men were taught to respect women as equal and intelligent beings, they would be ashamed to exploit them in the form of prostitution. Abolitionists also expected the state to foster the dignity of women by legislating equal civil and political rights for both sexes.

Several problems accompanied the establishment of abolition in European nations. Decriminalization has only been partial, legalizing the act of prostitution but not that of soliciting or maintaining a brothel. Since most prostitutes, especially the poor, must solicit to get business, streetwalkers have remained a target for arrest. Like the enforcement of prohibition and regulation, arrest for solicitation under an abolitionist system engenders the problem of high cost, ineffectiveness, and corruption of police. When public protest increases, police sweep the streets clean, only to have soliciting begin promptly after the release of the arrested prostitutes.

The transition from regulation to decriminalization also increases the exploitation of prostitutes by pimps.[36] According to regulationist laws, madams were expected to provide decent wages and living conditions in registered brothels. Although many madams defied the law by underpaying their employees and keeping them in debt, nevertheless prostitutes did not need pimps for protection. Pushed out of the legalized houses and into the street with the repeal of regulation, most prostitutes turned to pimps to seek safety from police and other male criminals.

Finally, some critics of decriminalization charge that rates of venereal disease increase when police do not repress or regulate prostitution. The charge is difficult to evaluate since both sides can produce statistics to prove its case, as was evidenced in nineteenth century Italy.[37] Certainly if a state decriminalizes prostitution, it can no longer subject women to medical examinations as in regulationist systems. In nineteenth century Italy, registered prostitutes seemed to have been in better health than the "clandestine" ones who escaped surveillance by health authorities.[38] But the percentage of prostitutes who registered with police was minimal.

CONCLUSION

How can the preceding historical overview of prohibition, regulation, and decriminalization aid those who must formulate present policy in the United States? The historian is probably most useful in pointing out the failure of previous experiments than in recommending detailed legislation for the future. In practical terms, prohibition and regulation have been notably unsuccessful in suppressing, or even controlling, the majority of prostitutes. Yet laws should be based not only on pragmatism but also on the political principles of a given society. In the United States, these principles are embodied in the Constitution which guarantees equality of all citizens before law and the protection of individual rights. I would argue that the present American policy of prohibition as well as the European systems of regulation have violated these fundamental principles.

Most basically, both prohibition and regulation deny the principle of equality for men and women. Both policies accept the traditional assumptions, disproved by scientific research, that male and female sexuality essentially differ.[39] Both prohibitionist and regulationist laws punish only the woman for promiscuity; they accept the same behavior in men as natural. As one critic of prohibition in the United States has written:

> Prostitution is really the only crime in the penal law where two people are doing a thing mutually agreed upon and yet only one, the female partner, is subject to arrest. And they never even take down the man's name. It's not his crime, but the woman's.[40]

Both prohibition and regulation deny equality to women by restricting the civil rights of prostitutes. Even when authorities do not really believe in the prohibition statutes which they are enforcing, prostitutes are subject to "a continuous intimidation and inconvenience . . . and a continual fleecing."[41] A legal aide has described the hypocrisy of the American system:

> The actual situation in the city is that prostitution is accepted by everyone—police, judges, clerks, and lawyers. Arrest and prosecution are purely gestures that have to be made to keep up the facade of public morality. The method of dealing with it is simply a form of harassment, not a form of prevention, abolition, or punishment. There is no conviction at any level that prostitution is a crime on anyone's part, only a total and satisfied acceptance of the double standard, excusing the male, accusing the female.[42]

Regulationists claim to replace repression with scientific and rational control. Once registered, however, prostitutes do not retain the freedoms granted other citizens. According to a study of the present regulation system in Elko, Nevada, "the prostitutes' behavior outside the brothel is severely circumscribed by law and custom."[43] Law defines not only what hours the women can go downtown but also how many times a week they can visit their children who are taken away from them. Although seemingly sympathetic to the system, the author of the study admits that "some of the restrictions on the prostitutes are so severe that they are repressive."[44]

Prohibitionist and regulationist laws compound the initial injustice of arrest or registration by creating permanent criminal or deviant identities for prostitutes. The ambiguities in the definition of prostitution point out the fact that the state of being a prostitute is more one of "labelling" by official authorities than a quality inherent in a certain act. For Schur, laws prohibiting victimless crimes simply compound the problems they are intended to solve:

> One of the major consequences of criminalizing mutually desired exchanges is the creation of much additional crime (that would not exist if consensual behavior were legal) and the proliferation of criminal self-conceptions among the "offending" individuals.[45]

By the process of what sociologists call "status degradation," the stigmatizing of prostitutes in prohibitionist states encourages the development of a deviant self-identity. For example, prostitutes become involved in the world of crime to seek protection from police. Furthermore, the criminalizing of prostitution, with the attendant guilt, shame, and isolation, makes reform, the supposed goal of prohibition, almost impossible. One ex-prostitute commented on this problem in the United States:

> I don't feel that I'm a whore now, but the social stigma attached to prostitution is a very powerful thing. It makes a kind of total state out of prostitution so that the whore is always a whore. It's as if—you did it once, you become it. This makes it very easy for people to get locked into it. It's very hard to get married.[46]

Although regulationists do not prosecute prostitution as a crime, they consider the individual prostitute to be sexually deviant. The state prevents contacts and identity with "normal" society by isolation in brothels and restrictions on her freedom of movement. A historian of prostitution, Judith Walkowitz, has described how the line between prostitute and nonprostitute women hardened in nineteenth century England after the implementation of the Contagious Disease Acts.[47] Regulation changed prostitution from a stage in the lives of many lower class women before marriage to a career for the stigmatized few.

Only decriminalization offers the possibility of equality, protection of civil rights, and freedom of choice to prostitutes. Yet, modern policy makers should modify nineteenth century abolition to minimize previous problems. The following suggestions should be considered and studied by experts. Decriminalization of soliciting might accompany that of prostitution so that the arrest of soliciters will not fall into the same abuses as that of prostitutes under the present system. Repeal of laws against renting to prostitutes might decrease the reliance of prostitutes on pimps. Finally, improved dissemination of information about the causes and cure of venereal disease to the entire population may improve health far better than relying on the repression or surveillance of prostitutes.

Rather than being discriminated against by special statutes, prostitutes should be protected by, and subject to, the same laws which apply to nonsexual activities. Benjamin and Masters have correctly identified two "fundamental precepts" for the reform of prostitution laws:

> (a) sexual acts or activities accomplished *without* violence, constraint, or fraud should find no place in our penal codes; (b) sexual acts or activities accomplished *with* violence, constraint or fraud should be punished according to the type of violence, constraint or fraud committed, and the *sexual* element should not be considered a relevant or aggravating circumstance.[48]

Decriminalization does not signify state approval of prostitution. Like many other relationships between men and women in our society, prostitution is characterized by an inequality of power and objectification of female sexuality which the government should not foster. Decriminalization does, however, allow the state to treat prostitutes with justice while working to indirectly ameliorate the causes of prostitution. Since history has documented the failure of prohibition and regulation, policy makers should direct their expertise to developing decriminalization laws which improve on the abolitionist experiments of Europe. Perhaps they can develop a fourth model which will overcome the limitations of the three employed by Western nations during the last two centuries.

NOTES

1. Most histories of prostitution survey many countries, often from the ancient world to the present. See, for example, Vern Bullough, *The History of Prostitution* (Hyde Park, NY: University Books, 1964); Gladys Mary Hall, *Prostitution in the Modern World* (London: Emerson, 1936); Fernando Henriques, *Prostitution and Society* (London: MacGibbon and Kee, 1962); Paul LaCroix, *History of Prostitution*

(New York: Covici and Friede, 1931); Ben L. Reitmen, *The Second Oldest Profession* (New York: Vanguard, 1931); George Ryley Scott, *The History of Prostitution* (New York: Greenberg, 1936); William J. Robinson, *The Oldest Profession in the World* (New York: Eugenics, 1929); William Sanger, *The History of Prostitution* (New York: Eugenics, 1939); Hermann Schreiber [Lujo Basserman], *The Oldest Profession* (London: Arthur Barker, 1967); Marcel Sicot, *La prostitution dans le monde* (Paris: Hachett, 1964). Recent historians, however, have begun to study prostitution in more specific historical contexts. See Judith Walkowitz and Daniel Walkowtitz, "We Are Not Beasts of the Field," in Mary S. Hartman and Lois Banner, eds., *Clio's Consciousness Raised* (New York: Harper Colophon, 1974); Richard Evans, "Prostitution, State, and Society in Imperial Germany," *Past and Present*, Vol. 70 (February 1976); Mary Elizabeth Perry, "'Lost women' in Early Modern Seville," *Feminist Studies*, Vol. 4 (February 1978); Robert D. Storch, "Police Control of Street Prostitution in Victorian England," in David H. Bayley, ed., *Police and Society* (Beverly Hills, CA: Sage, 1977).

2. John Gagnon and William Simon, *Sexual Conduct: The Social Sources of Human Sexuality* (Chicago: AVC, 1973), 218.

3. Harry Bejamin and R.E.L. Masters, *Prostitution and Morality* (New York: Julian, 1964), 381.

4. Benjamin and Masters, *Prostitution*, 25.

5. Tommasoli, *Prostitution et maladies vénériennes en Italie* (Brussels: H. Lamertin, 1899), Appendix.

6. The Italian evidence has been drawn from my study, "Urban Prostitution in Italy, 1860-1915" (Ph.D. dissertation, Indiana University, 1979).

7. Gagnon and Simon, *Sexual Conduct*, 219.

8. For the attitudes of the medieval Church toward prostitution, see James S. Brundage, "Prostitution in the Medieval Canon Law," *Signs*, Vol. 1 (1976).

9. Benjamin and Masters, *Prostitution*, 372.

10. Vern Bullough, *Sexual Variance in Society and History* (New York: Wiley, 1976), 196.

11. Edwin Schur, *Victimless Crimes* (Englewood Cliffs, NJ: Prentice Hall, 1974), 25; Kate Millett, *The Prostitution Papers* (New York: Ballantine Books, 1971), 137.

12. Although there are sanctions in the laws of a few states of America against customers of prostitutes, they are rarely enforced.

13. William Sanger, *The History of Prostitution*, 161.

14. For a discussion of punishment in early modern Europe, see Michel Foucault, *Discipline and Punish: The Birth of the Prison* (New York: Vintage, 1979), especially chapters 1 and 2.

15. Benjamin and Masters, *Prostitution*, 377.

16. Millett, *Prostitution Papers*, 12.

17. Schur, *Victimless Crimes*, 12.

18. Schur, *Victimless Crimes*, 12.

19. Giovanni Bolis, *La polizia e le classi pericolose della società* (Bologna: Zanichelli, 1871), 801.

20. Benjamin and Masters, *Prostitution*, 19.

21. For a history of French regulation, see Alain Corbin, *Les filles de noce: Misère sexuelle et prostitution* (Paris: Aubier Montaigne, 1978).

22. The period of regulation in St. Louis is described by John Burnham, "Medical inspection of prostitution in nineteenth-century America: The St. Louis Experiment and Its Sequel," *Bulletin of the History of Medicine*, Vol. 45 (May-June 1971).

23. Giuseppe Sormani, *Profilassi delle malattie veneree* (Milan: L. Bortolotti, 1882), 35.

24. Pietro Castiglione, *Sorveglianza sulla prostituzione* (Rome: G. Via, 1872), 54.

25. Archivio Centrale dello Stato(Rome), D.G. della Sanità, 1897, busta 562, fasc. 23000-6.

26. Arch. C.S.,D.G. della Sanità, 1899, b. 503, f. 21001-69; 1896, b. 598, f.2350.

27. Arch. C. S., D.G. della Sanità, 1908, b. 1011, f.23000-6.

28. Arch.C.S., D.G. Della Sanità, 1896, b.598, f.23511 and f.23525; b.599, f.23538 and f.23543.

29. *Roma*, August 13-14, 1894.

30. Alfred Kinsey, *Sexual Behavior in the Human Male* (Philadelphia: W.B. Saunders, 1948).

31. Abraham Flexner, *Prostitution in Europe* (New York: Century, 1914), 292.

32. Antonio Gramola, *Le prostitute e la legge* (no publisher, 1880), 20.

33. Josephine Butler, *Personal Reminiscences of a Great Crusade* (London: Horace Marshall, 1896), 25.

34. Flexner, *Prostitution in Europe*, 26.

35. The Comitato Italiano contro al Tratta delle Bianche issued a series of reports for 1902-1903, 1904-1905, 1906-1907, and 1910 which are located in the Arch.C.S., D.G. della Sanità, B.249, f. 10900.21.

36. Benjamin and Masters, *Prostitution*, 374.

37. For a review of this debate in Italy, see Tommasoli, *Prostitution*, 43.

38. All late nineteenth century statistics are questionable since the primitive state of medical knowledge did not allow complete accuracy in the diagnosis of venereal disease.

39. William Masters and Virginia Johnson, *Human Sexual Response* (Boston: Little, Brown, 1966).

40. Millett, *Prostitution Papers*, 137.

41. Millett, *Prostitution Papers*, 141.

42. Millett, *Prostitution Papers*, 134.

43. Lee H. Bowker, *Women, Crime, and the Criminal Justice System* (Lexington, MA: Lexington Books, 1978), 151.

44. Bowker, *Women*, 151.

45. Schur, *Victimless Crimes*, 25.

46. Millett, *Prostitution Papers*, 71.

47. Judith Walkowitz, "The Making of an Outcast Group," in Martha Vicinus, ed., *A Widening Sphere: Changing Roles of Victorian Women* (Bloomington: Indiana University Press, 1977).

48. Benjamin and Masters, *Prostitution*, 366.

HISTORICAL
ANALYSES
OF
LAW
ENFORCEMENT
AND
CORRECTIONS

10

POLICE IN AMERICA: FUNCTIONS AND CONTROL

JAMES F. RICHARDSON

Conferences of this sort pose an interesting problem for historians. Few of us would like to see history as a mode of inquiry excluded from gatherings devoted to consideration of current issues, yet many of us wonder about the extent to which history is, or can be made, a policy science. An article of faith among most historians is that appreciating how something came to be is a prerequisite to understanding what it is. Matters become stickier when one wants to move from the *is* to the *ought,* to what should be in some prescriptive fashion as well as a descriptive account of an existing situation. In most cases, however, even the most resolutely descriptive treatment rests upon some explicit or implicit sense of what would be desirable. Yet, it would be an unusual or a rash historian who would propose that a study of history could show us the way out of some current policy dilemma. Perhaps the best service a historian can render is to prevent the misuse of history, although the area of American police does not seem to be one where any serious person would be likely to argue that there was ever a golden age with all questions satisfactorily resolved. The historian is also aware of the phenomenon of unintended consequences of policy decisions which sometimes turn out to be more significant than the desired effects.

As in many other scholarly inquiries, historians' most important decisions often come at the beginning: "Are we asking the right question?" is a key issue. In the 1960s historians who studied police concentrated on administrative and political matters in the nineteenth century, employing an urbanization-social control model, perhaps because available sources lent themselves most readily to this kind of investigation and interpretation.[1] Recent years have seen a continuation of this trend; at the same time other scholars have broadened the inquiry into the twentieth century and employed other conceptual frameworks. Thus Wilbur Miller has contrasted the nature of police authority in New York and London between 1830 and 1870; Sidney Harring and Lorraine McMullin have provided a Marxist interpretation of Buffalo's police history in the late nineteenth century; and Robert Fogelson and Samuel Walker in separate studies have examined police reform from the 1890s on.[2] Other scholars have investigated the careers of particularly influential individuals in the field of police administration such as August Vollmer and O. W. Wilson.[3] There is also an increasingly rich literature on current police which is both informed by what historians have done and helps raise new questions for further inquiries into the past.[4]

By drawing upon these studies, it is possible to make some tentative generalizations about what policy makers, both within and without police departments, have thought about the police role in urban society and how those conceptions have changed over time. It is also possible to some extent to connect thought and behavior. Such an overview is useful, it seems to me, in providing a historical perspective for discussions of current policy issues and in reminding us that there are no panaceas for reconciling the diverse tasks police have traditionally been called upon to perform. In addition there is the central dilemma of the existence and the legitimacy of coercive authority in a polity that exalts, at least theoretically, the freedom and dignity of the individual.

The extremely broad, and sometimes contradictory, police mandate precedes the creation of police as organized bureaucratic agencies. Early in the nineteenth century the term *police* was used to refer to the general state of public order and public health of the city. Travelers considered the police of a city to be good if its streets were reasonably clean and there was a satisfactory state of public order.[5]

In the sense that we now use the term, police services in New York were provided by a number of different groups: a salaried night watch which kept a lookout for fires as well as disorderly youths; a small group of elected constables; and 100 marshals, appointed by the mayor. The constables and marshals were compensated on the basis of fee for service and much of their work involved civil processes. On the criminal side they acted only if engaged by the victim of a theft to seek to recover stolen property. To be successful in these attempts police officers cultivated the widest possible contacts among professional criminals and were often accused of compounding with thieves to recover stolen property, for a suitable reward of course.

The positive incentives for corruption in such arrangements and the unwillingness of police officers to spend any time on crimes where there were no prospects of rewards helped to bring into being police forces composed of salaried bureaucrats. The new police, modeled to a considerable extent upon the London Metropolitan Police force created in 1829, were designed to be a preventive force, that is, their presence and their activities would be a deterrent to the commission of crime.

This desire for a more effective and less corrupt crime fighting agency was only one of the impulses behind the establishment of a salaried police. The new department would also act to suppress and contain rioting. Urban riots have a long history in America and the more we study early American cities, the more we learn about the frequency of urban disorder. The riots of the 1830s and 1840s in Boston, New York, and Philadelphia did reach a new level of intensity with serious clashes between ethnic, religious, and political rivals. These riots aroused concern that cities could not rely either on the self-restraint of their inhabitants or on a militia which might favor one side in a conflict or refuse to act against a crowd composed of militiamen's friends and neighbors. The police would be a civilian body, yet under military discipline, able to act in a coordinated fashion against urban rioters. Later, in many jurisdictions, the police could be used to suppress labor "agitators" and help firms keep operating in the midst of strikes.

A third motive for the establishment of a salaried police involved the control and suppression of unseemly behavior in public places. Moralists on both sides of the Atlantic worried about the extent of alcoholic consumption, prostitution, and gambling. Recent research has earmarked the period from about 1790 to the 1830s as the high point of per capita consumption of alcohol in the United States.[6] In a perhaps predictable reaction, the latter decades of this period saw the emergence of an organized temperance movement which stressed the benefits to physical health and economic competence of restraint and eventually total abstinence from alcohol.[7] For example, Massachusetts law made alcohol more difficult and more expensive to obtain and stiffened the penalties for public intoxication. Prior to the establishment of bureaucratic police departments, sober citizens could do nothing about drunken ones except to avoid them or step over them. With such departments in being, citizens could demand that something be done about such nuisances as drunks or prostitutes who cruised in the wrong places.

Thus, from the beginning of their existence, American police departments had a broad mandate to prevent and detect crime, maintain public order, and suppress unseemly behavior in public places. These functions, broad as they are, do not encompass all that police were called upon to do. When the New York department was established in the 1840s, it took on the duties of street inspectors, health and fire wardens, dock masters, lamplighters, fire alarm bell ringers, Sunday officers, inspectors of pawn brokers and junk shops, inspectors of hacks and stages, and officers attending the polls at election. While some of these functions such as lamplighters were later taken away from the police, they acquired others such as providing temporary lodging to indigent vagrants, taking periodic censuses, inspecting steam boilers, enforcing the sanitary code, acting as truant officers, and, for about a decade, administering the city's street cleaning services. In addition, the police customarily did whatever chores could be considered public responsibilities and lacked a unit to perform them. The police telegraph in the 1850s carried more messages about lost children and stray horses than it did about criminal or disorderly behavior. Strangers in the city looked to the police to provide directions and in general serve as a bureau of public information.

Over time some of these police functions, by a process of bureaucratic diffusion and specialization, became the responsibilities of other, more specialized, agencies. For example, Jacob Ris and Theodore Roosevelt mounted a successful campaign in the 1890s for the creation of a municipal lodging house for indigents to relieve the police of the burden of providing such accommodations. In Boston there was a major debate in the 1870s about the police serving soup to unemployed transients—tramps in the vocabulary of that period.[8]

The above were the manifest functions of the police—those responsibilities openly acknowledged to be theirs on the basis of law or custom. In addition, there were important latent functions. Historian Robert Fogelson has recently argued that in the 1890s there was an informal consensus on these latent functions. The police were to serve as a source of good steady jobs for local working class young men; lower class lifestyles were morally acceptable in that the police would not attempt to enforce a uniform code of morality throughout the city; and police legitimacy rested upon local political control. The potentially dangerous power of the police, the unwarranted exercise of their coercive authority, could be held in check by their answering to locally elected officials.[9]

This conception of the police role and its attendant mode of controlling the police was consistent with a political system based upon partisan, district elections in which ethnic and class groups would be represented roughly in proportion to their voting populations. In such a system, maintenance of the party organization and recognition of diverse group interests took precedence over efficiency and uniformity of service delivery. The way in which such public services as schools and police functioned varied with the class and ethnic makeup of a particular locality. In many cities local boards controlled the schools in a given ward and the precinct commander in effect determined police policy for the area. In order to survive, his conception of police work had to coincide with that of local political leaders.

From the late nineteenth century into the 1920s, reformers of various persuasions systematically sought to undermine this locally oriented, partisan system and to replace it with more centralized, nonpartisan, and efficient forms of local government. Police scandals, such as that associated with the revelations of the Lexow Committee in New York in 1894, provided useful occasions for reformers to launch assaults not just against the police but against prevailing patterns of local government generally.

The structural reform of urban government reached its culminating point in the city manager movement of the 1910s and 1920s. The plan called for a small council elected on a nonpartisan, at-large basis—thus ensuring disproportionate representation of large-scale businessmen and professionals. The council was supposed to set policy and the manager and his aides to administer that policy. Ideally there should be complete separation of these spheres with no attempts on the part of councilmen to influence administrative matters such as police assignments and promotions—common occurrences in a partisan, district system. Such a system was most likely to be adopted in small homogeneous communities without large class and ethnic minorities. Under the city manager system, there should be no doubt about police functions: to provide services for the respectable and to enforce the law against the deviant.[10]

Furthermore, as Fogelson indicates, substantial changes occurred in police administration even in those cities which did not adopt the city manager plan. Police reformers, whether elite outsiders or would-be professionals within police work, pushed for clearer lines of authority and freedom from political interference for the chief administrator, whose job it was to mold the department into an impartial, efficient organization.[11]

Increasingly, efficiency came to be defined as effectiveness in combatting crime. To be effective in the war against crime, police departments had to recruit the best possible material without reference to ethnic background, geographical origin, or political connections. Promotions should be based on competence and leadership qualities, not on whether one was a Catholic or a Mason or a member of the right political clubs. Police departments should be equipped with the latest and best technology in communications, transport, and record keeping to give them the best possible chance of catching and convicting criminals.

In the 1920s local crime commissions pushed for such changes, to be joined in the 1930s by the highly media conscious FBI under J. Edgar Hoover. Specialists in police administration downgraded the noncriminal functions of the police as distractions from the essential business of fighting crime. For particulars, let us look at the work of August Vollmer who built a national reputation as chief of the Berkeley, California, department and later as a professor at Berkeley and consultant to departments around the country. In the 1910s and early 1920s, Vollmer was interested in an ameliorative preventive intervention approach to crime control. If a juvenile showed signs of antisocial or criminal behavior, the police should intervene in an attempt to straighten the boy out before he engaged in serious misconduct.[12] Later, Vollmer's writings move away from this sort of preventive intervention to a more restrictive crime-attack model, based upon the latest technology, of police performance.[13] In his 1936 volume, *The Police in Modern Society,* Vollmer devotes only one paragraph to police response to calls on domestic disputes. Everyone now knows that such calls are among the most frequent, and most dangerous, that police receive. Also there is increasing current concern about the extent of intrafamilial violence and what public agencies, including the police, might legitimately do to limit such violence. Vollmer says only that such calls may impinge seriously upon the time available to the police.[14]

By the 1930s then, a model of the police as professional crime fighters dominated the literature. A particular department was a professional one to the extent that it was free from political interference, had stable long-term leadership, employed the latest technology, and emphasized its crime-fighting capabilities. Certainly not all cities followed this model, but it was the goal toward which all departments should aspire.[15] The development of the Uniform Crime Reports (UCR) and the National Police Academy under FBI auspices further strengthened this model. The UCR with its major crime index and clearance ratio gave citizens and specialists in police administration a measure of how well police departments were doing relative to others. The UCR also provided strong incentives for departments to fudge the figures. Attendance at the National Police Academy became a useful ticket-punching service for ambitious police administrators and would-be administrators, and Director Hoover could reward his disciples and punish his rivals by extending or withholding invitations to the academy.[16] The view of the police as primarily crime-fighters was so strong that it took a generation for scholars to realize that the bulk of active police duty time is spent on noncriminal matters. Police officers themselves often considered their noncriminal functions as not real police work. For both citizens and police officers, it was the detective who was doing real police work, who held the position of highest prestige.[17]

At the same time that the professional crime control model advocated sloughing off as many noncriminally related functions as possible, the police acquired a major new responsibility in the regulation of automobile and truck traffic and parking. By the mid-1920s, about 15% of Cleveland's police were assigned to traffic duties. Traditionally the police exercised their coercive authority upon people below them on the social scale. When middle and upper class people came in contact with the police it was as service providers, public servants. Enforcement of traffic and parking regulations now had police officers imposing sanctions upon people sometimes far above them on the social scale. In some jurisdictions the ability to fix a ticket became the dividing line between those with clout and the powerless.[18]

The inability or unwillingness of drivers to observe all traffic and parking regulations eroded any clear distinction between the law abiding and the law breaking and presented police departments with delicate problems in building and maintaining a favorable public image. So, too, did demands that police enforce sumptuary legislation, laws restricting behavior that many people thought perfectly legitimate such as drinking after midnight or playing baseball on Sunday.

Conflicts over the legitimacy and level of enforcement of such legislation had been endemic in cities with large lower class and ethnic populations since the beginning of organized police forces. By the late nineteenth century, a rough consensus had been reached which kept saloons and brothels out of respectable areas but permitted them to flourish in semi-official red-light districts. One of the latent functions of the police was to regulate illegal enterprise so that only those acceptable to local leadership would engage in such businesses. As Mark Haller has noted, the gamblers were not simply connected to the politicians; the gamblers were the politicians. William F. Whyte's famous participant-observation study of Boston's North End in the late 1930s showed patterned relationships among the police, politicians, and racketeers which allowed each group to perform its functions without undue difficulty. For the police this meant periodic bursts of activity against numbers operations to satisfy reformers, a fact of life which the gamblers accepted as long as the crusades were short-lived.[19]

In general the police received little scholarly attention during the 1940s and 1950s. William Westley's famous 1951 dissertation, *Violence and the Police,* was not published in full until 1970.[20] Most concern among citizens and scholars revolved around the degree to which particular departments fit the model of impartial, efficient crime control. Political interference was considered inherently vicious and almost guaranteed an inadequate and biased level of law enforcement. Political scientists could use the reputation and quality of a city's police department as a measure of whether it was a "reformed" one. An unreformed city almost by definition had a poor police department and high incidence and visibility of illegal enterprise.[21]

As in so many other areas of American life, the 1960s were a decade of profound change in American public and scholarly perception of the police. From a position of relatively low scholarly visibility, the police became one of the most written about institutions in the society. The riots of the mid-1960s, virtually all of which began with an encounter between a police officer and black citizens, raised disturbing questions about the police role and the police image in inner city areas. Prestigious groups such as the Kerner Commission and the United States Civil Rights Commission singled out the state of police-community relations as one of the most serious grievances of black urbanites.[22] Students of public administration presented portraits of American police departments as insulated, tradition-directed bureaucracies more intent on maintaining customary practices and privileges than in serving the public.[23] The once-vaunted freedom from political interference to allow proper police performance now looked like abdication of responsibility for police behavior by elected officials and corresponding autonomy for police officials to conduct their operations without accountability.[24] According to some scholars, comparing American with English and European police, we had arrived at the worst of both worlds in the absence of the careful administrative controls characteristic of English and European police and the decay of the tradition of control of the police by elected officials.[25] Police reform no longer meant exclusively the creation of nonpolitical, efficient crime-fighting units. Now sympathetic observers lamented the difficulties mayors like New York's John Lindsay had in gaining control over the city's police department which could appeal to the shibboleth of no political interference to resist outside pressures for change.

As part of this sweeping inquiry into policing, scholars learned what cops knew all the time, that as an occupation policing abounds with paradoxes. Police departments are authoritarian, often semimilitary, hierarchic institutions in which the lowest level, the patrolmen, exercises enormous discretion. The bosses may control many aspects of a police officer's life, but often they leave him on his own with respect to the most sensitive and difficult aspects of his job. For example, before the 1960s, few law departments provided much guidance about the circumstances under which an officer could use his gun. The police officer is expected to be both a coercive authority figure and a supportive service provider, often having to switch from one role to the other within the same encounter. The technological innovations that enabled the police to respond more readily to calls for service—the telephone, the automobile, and the radio— also vastly increased the number of calls for service. Investigations of these calls showed that only a minority dealt with criminal matters and more with aided cases, victims of accidents and heart attacks, and disputes and disturbances. Police officers have been quick to point out that many of the latter involve at least the potential of law breaking and must be approached accordingly. Still, only a relatively small portion of active police duty time is spent on criminal matters.[26]

Moreover, as sociologist Albert Reiss pointed out, despite the fact that organized police have the legal authority to intervene in citizen's affairs on their own initiative, most of their work requires citizen mobilization. In Reiss's terminology, the bulk of police activity is reactive, responding to a citizen's call for service, rather than proactive, taken on the officer's own initiative. Officers realize that citizens are more likely to accept their presence as legitimate if they are responding to a call rather than asserting their authority independently. Thus, the creation of bureaucratic police has not eliminated citizen involvement in criminal justice matters; if no one calls them, the police are not likely to become involved.[27]

On the specific question of functions, recent studies have emphasized that the police should not be looked upon solely as part of the criminal justice system; rather, the police are a municipal agency with a wide variety of tasks, many of them of a social service nature. The range and complexity of police functions is such that it is virtually impossible to give them all equal time and attention. Also, concentration on one such as law enforcement may weaken or contradict another such as order maintenance. Techniques of aggressive preventive patrol replete with street stops could help generate the kind of hostility expressed in the riots of the mid-1960s.[28]

The variations in police conceptions of their primary purpose led James Q. Wilson to make his famous distinctions among police styles: the watchman, the legalistic, and the service. The watchman style, common in unreformed cities with larger lower class populations, stressed order maintenance and did not worry unduly about enforcing vice laws. Reformed cities tended to have either legalistic or service-oriented departments. In the former, the better elements took pride in a police force committed to honest and efficient law enforcement; in the latter, the police functioned primarily as a service agency for a predominantly middle and upper class population.[29]

Wilson's case studies consisted of communities with small or moderate populations. Larger cities might show considerable internal variation depending upon the ethnic and class character of the area being policed. There is a superb book on a contemporary big city police department, Jonathan Rubinstein's, *City Police.*[30] After earning a Ph.D. in history, Rubinstein worked as a police reporter in Philadelphia, attended the police academy, and rode as the number two man in police cars, nonuniformed, but armed. He functioned as a working partner, not just an observer. In so doing, he learned, and makes vivid to his readers, the nature of police work and the physical, and especially the moral, problems of the job. The police officer must impose his authority on resentful and often resistant citizens and must be prepared to use force, if necessary. His colleagues will neither trust nor accept him if he is not so willing to use his stick or as a last resort, his gun, when needed to overcome resistance or direct threats. At the same time, they do not want to work with hotheads or the fearful too prone to unsnap the holster. As one instructor said, "If you need security, carry a blanket."

Vice laws cause the most serious dilemmas. Not only are there the obvious temptations to accept or extort money from illegal entrepreneurs but also it is impossible to make arrests, generate vice activity, without breaking the law. Philadelphia is not now thought of as a reformed city, and there is a generally tolerant attitude toward gambling. Still, the police are under pressure to make a show of enforcing vice laws, and no man can satisfy his superiors and advance in his platoon without vice activity. Thus, all policemen must break the law and everyone knows it. It also means that policemen must keep secret from each other sources of information and possible vice pinches. Rubinstein does not propose any solutions, but his account makes clear the costs associated with the vice laws and any attempts to enforce them, no matter how ineffective.

Rubinstein's focus is on the work itself and how the men on the street do it (there are no policewomen cited in the book). He is very good on the nature of the reciprocal obligations and expectations of patrolmen and their first-level supervisors, the sergeants. He is not concerned with senior administrators or policy makers, nor does he say much about variations in expectation between one district and another.

In cities large or small, an identifiable style of policing presupposes either an acceptable tradition or a set of policy choices about where to put resources and how to exercise discretion. Police histories showed that at least in cities like New York there had been repeated controversies over how police should deal with sumptuary legislation and that some traditions were best eliminated. Students of contemporary police administrators often discerned a reluctance to establish priorities and set policies on the exercise of discretion for fear of arousing political opposition. Administrators found it simpler to maintain the fiction of giving all functions equal attention and to refuse to structure discretion because any policy formulation would threaten or slight the interests of some members of the community. Any announcement that some laws and ordinances would receive less attention than others opened the police to charges of attempting to be lawmakers instead of law enforcers.

The unwillingness formally to set priorities and issue guidelines has left discretionary situations either to some nebulous tradition or informal understanding based upon the values and orientations of particular police officers. Recently, William Ker Muir, Jr., has produced a superb study of the influence of world view upon individual police behavior. His case studies consisted of 28 officers of and 800-member department, free—at least at the time of his study—from the effects of political interference and corruption. He listened to them talk and watched them do their jobs. In each instance, the way in which an officer looked at the world corresponded with the way he performed.[31]

Muir found four distinct world views among his subjects. The *professionals* realized that all people were likely to err and had compassion for the human condition. At the same time, they were ready to use fear and coercion when necessary. The *reciprocators* wanted all transactions to be exchanges and could not deal effectively with people too irrational or dispossessed to perceive the consequences of their actions. The *enforcers* divided people into the good and bad and took an aggressively legalistic stand toward their work; they were the quickest to apply sanctions. The last group were the *avoiders* who constantly narrowed their conception of their job and avoided any situation that was at all troublesome or ambiguous. Muir argues convincingly that the successful police officer's main stock-in-trade is "bullshitting," the exercise of verbal skill to get people to do what he wants them to do, whether it is to cool a family fight, break up a crowd, or submit to a traffic citation. So, no matter what his world view, the policeman is a craftsman in human relations who must often operate in a climate of animosity and hostility. The ends he seeks and the means he uses in dealing with citizens are influenced in varying degrees by the law, the political climate of a given community, departmental tradition and policy, the wishes of his immediate superiors, and his own conception of the world and his role within it.

The varying mix produced by the interaction of these factors means that any generalizations about American police functions must be limited and cautious. We can discern broad trends of thought in the past but must be careful not to assume that everyone behaved according to the dictates of current thinking. If, as William Bopp argues, "The movement to professionalize the police is in large measure a search for identity," much of our confusion about police professionalism relates to hazy or internally contradictory thinking about the nature of the police role in society.[32] The crime control model achieved clarity at the expense of ignoring too many other social needs and the ways in which police officers actually spend their time. We now have some empirical evidence on what police officers actually do, but these observations do not constitute the basis for any theory of police performance. Questions of police functions involve fundamental moral and political questions, which must always be asked and reasked in an ongoing democratic society.

NOTES

1. Roger Lane, *Policing the City: Boston, 1822-1885* (Cambridge, MA: Harvard University Press, 1967); James F. Richardson, *The New York Police: Colonial Times to 1901* (New York: Oxford University Press, 1970).

2. Wilbur R. Miller, *Cops and Bobbies: Police Authority in New York and London, 1830-1870* (Chicago: University of Chicago Press, 1977); Sidney L. Harring and Lorraine M. McMullin, "The Buffalo Police 1872-1900: Labor Unrest, Political Power and the Creation of the Police Institution," *Crime and Social Justice, 4*

(Fall-Winter 1975), 5-14; Robert M. Fogelson, *Big-City Police* (Cambridge, MA: Harvard University Press, 1977); Samuel Walker, *A Critical History of Police Reform: The Emergence of Professionalism* (Lexington, MA: Lexington Books, 1977).

3. Gene E. Carte and Eloise H. Carte, *Police Reform in the United States: The Era of August Vollmer, 1905-1932* (Berkeley and Los Angeles: University of California Press, 1975); Nathan Douthit, "August Vollmer, Berkeley's First Chief of Police, and the Emergence of Police professionalism," *California Historical Quarterly,* 54 (Summer 1975), 100-124; William J. Bopp, *"O.W.": O.W. Wilson and the Search for a Police Profession* (Port Washington, NY: Kennikat, 1977).

4. Herman Goldstein, *Policing a Free Society* (Cambridge, MA: Ballinger, 1977).

5. The next several paragraphs are based upon James F. Richardson, *Urban Police in the United States* (Port Washington, NY: Kennikat, 1974).

6. W. J. Rorabaugh, *The Alcoholic Republic: An American Tradition* (New York: Oxford University Press, 1979).

7. Joseph R. Gusfield, *Symbolic Crusade: Status Politics and the American Temperance Movement* (Urbana: University of Illinois Press, 1963); Norman H. Clark, *Deliver Us from Evil: An Interpretation of American Prohibition* (New York: Norton, 1976).

8. Richardson, *New York Police*; Lane, *Policing the City.*

9. Fogelson, *Big-City Police.*

10. On the transformation of urban government generally, see Martin J. Schiesl, *The Politics of Efficiency: Municipal Administration and Reform in America, 1880-1920* (Berkeley and Los Angeles: University of California Press, 1977).

11. Fogelson, *Big-City Police.*

12. The policewoman's movement of the same time period was based upon similar premises. Policewomen's bureaus would function as social workers in helping families avoid crime and delinquency among their members. Women's bureaus became less popular in the late 1920s and 1930s.

13. Walker, *Police Reform* is especially good on the role of the crime commissions and the FBI and the changes in Vollmer's thinking.

14. August Vollmer, *The Police and Modern Society* (Berkeley: University of California Press, 1936).

15. Bruce Smith, *Police Systems in the United States* (New York: Harper & Row, 1940); Nathan Douthit, "Police Professionalism and the War Against Crime in the United States, 1920s-30s," in George L. Mosse, ed., *Police Forces in History* (Beverly Hills, CA: Sage, 1975).

16. Bopp, *O.W. Wilson*; Patrick V. Murphy and Thomas Plate, *Commissioner: A View from the Top of American Law Enforcement* (New York: Simon and Schuster, 1977).

17. This conclusion draws upon a number of conversations with police officers and media coverage of police activities.

18. Richardson, *Urban Police*; John A. Gardiner, "Police Enforcement of Traffic Laws: A Comparative Analysis," in James Q. Wilson, ed., *City Politics and Public Policy* (New York: Wiley, 1968).

19. Fogelson, *Big-City Police*; Mark H. Haller, "Urban Crime and Criminal Justice: The Chicago Case," *Journal of American History,* 57 (December 1970), 619-635; William F. Whyte, *Street Corner Society* (Chicago: University of Chicago Press, 1955).

20. William A. Westley, *Violence and the Police: A Sociological Study of Law, Custom, and Morality* (Cambridge: MIT Press, 1970).

21. Bruce Smith, Jr., *Police Systems in the United States* (New York: Harper & Row, 1960); Edward C. Banfield and James Q. Wilson, *City Politics* (New York: Vintage Books, 1966).

22. National Advisory Commission on Civil Disorders [Kerner Commission], *Report* (New York: E.P. Dutton, 1968); President's Commission on Law Enforcement and the Administration of Justice, *The Challenge of Crime in a Free Society* (New York: Avon Books, 1968) and *Task Force Report: The Police* (Washington, DC: Government Printing Office, 1967).

23. Wallace Sayre and Herbert Kaufman, *Governing New York City* (New York: Russell Sage Foundation, 1960).

24. Cyril D. Robinson, "The Mayor and the Police–the Political Role of the Police in Society," in George L. Mosse, ed., *Police Forces in History* (Beverly Hills, CA: Sage, 1975).

25. George E. Berkley, *The Democratic Policemen* (Boston: Beacon Press, 1969).

26. Goldstein, *Policing a Free Society* is an informed discussion of current trends.

27. Albert J. Reiss, Jr., *The Police and the Public* (New Haven, CT: Yale University Press, 1971).

28. Goldstein, *Policing a Free Society*; Richardson, *Urban Police in the United States.*

29. James Q. Wilson, *Varieties of Police Behavior: The Management of Law and Order in Eight Communities* (Cambridge, MA: Harvard University Press, 1968).

30. Jonathan Rubinstein, *City Police* (New York: Farrar, Straus and Giroux, 1973).

31. William Ker Muir, Jr., *Police: Streetcorner Politicians* (Chicago: University of Chicago Press, 1977).

32. Bopp, *O. W. Wilson.*

11

JONATHAN WILD
AND THE
MODERN STING

CARL B. KLOCKARS

In all things *police* and *criminal,* Jonathan Wild, master fence of the first quarter of the eighteenth century, occupies a unique position. At once, to quote his best biographer, Gerald Howson, "the 'first' modern gangster" and "the 'father' of the C.I.D.,"[1] Wild's history reveals with bolder and more dramatic strokes than any other before or since the intimacies between both occupations and their limits in seeking to move from the source from which they both sprung more than two and one half centuries ago. Elsewhere I have used Wild's history to suggest a series of continuities in the business of dealing in stolen property: most important, the requirement that a successful professional fence play the role of police informant, but also that he learn to employ and enjoy police assistance in regulating his clientele, managing his employees, and sustaining his criminal reputation.[2] In order to insure the safety of my active key informant, these suggestions had to be kept oblique.[3]

AUTHOR'S NOTE: This research was supported in part by DHEW Grant No. 1 R01 DA 01827 from the Division of Research, National Institute on Drug Abuse.

Here, I should like to turn the lessons of the history of Wild toward the inspection of a similar institution: not "real" fences who manage to conceal that they are "really" police agents, but "real" police agents who manage to appear to be "real" fences. I refer, of course, to those dramatic varieties of modern proactive policing known as "sting operations" or "stings," which, in the past few years have swept the country. Unfortunately, save one *ex post facto* journalistic account,[4] a naive but not uncritical police training manual,[5] and police public relations releases,[6] almost nothing else is known, outside of police circles, about the methods, control, consequences, and uses of these modern stings. Moreover, if the Law Enforcement Assistance Administration (LEAA) continues to impose upon evaluation studies of these operations the types of restrictions which limited the first,[7] the immediate probability that anyone outside of those who fund and work such operations (and upon whose "successes" careers and reputations often rest) will know more appears to be rather dim.

This essay, then, like its predecessor on the other side of the fence, must also approach the target of its inquiry obliquely, using Wild to make points, suggest continuities, and raise questions which research bargains and restraints on access currently prevent revealing or exploring directly. Such is one of the most important uses of history: the discovery and identification of long-standing issues and problems and the restatement of them in a way which obliges modern practitioners to account for the differences between them and their dangerous predecessors in whose traditions they appear to work.

JONATHAN WILD

In 1712 Jonathan Wild reached the age of 30 with no achievement which would even hint at his future importance. Born in a small Staffordshire town, apprenticed to a bucklemaker by his father at age 15, Wild gave up his trade in 1710, came to London to make his fortune, and promptly found himself imprisoned for bad debts within the year. In prison he worked his way up to a position as "trusty" and was released in December of 1712 upon passage of an act which freed debtors who appeared unlikely to ever be able to repay their debts (10 Anne c.29).

While in prison Wild reports that he "was, in some measure, let into the secrets of the criminals there under confinement."[8] Among the "secrets" was a racket known as the "buttock and twang" which, after his release he practiced with his prostitute mistress, Mary Millner, a woman he had met while in prison. Pringle offers the following somewhat flip description of Wild's postrelease employment:

[A]t first Mary was the main breadwinner, [But] it would perhaps be misleading to say that he lived on her immoral earnings, for the normal rate was only a sixpence for a short time and there was no premium in that. Besides, Wild did his bit. Like many of her colleagues on the game, she was, in the crooks slang of that time, a buttock-and-file. The first word meant whore and the second pick-pocket and the reason for the hyphens is that she did both jobs at the same time. Most whores did their business standing in the street, and a girl with a light touch was in a good position to pick her customer's pockets when he was likely to be somewhat off his guard. The main danger was that he would discover the theft before she had time to get away, so most girl's liked to have a boy-friend lurking in the shadows. He was called a twang. When he was not making buckles Wild went out as Mary's twang.[9]

By disposing of the watches, pocketbooks, snuff boxes, and other small articles his buttock-and-file had stolen, Wild managed, in less than a year, to amass enough capital to open a small brandy shop from which he was able to expand his fencing operations from merely peddling what Mary had lifted to dealing in the goods offered to him by the thieves who frequented his shop.

WILD'S APPRENTICESHIP

Although Wild's stay in prison, his work as a prison trusty, his associa-tion with Mary, her friend's and victims, and his small-scale dealing gave Wild a street savvy he would unlikely have been able to gain otherwise, an equally important part of his education came in the form of an apprentice-ship to a man named Charles Hitchen, Under-City Marshal (the second most powerful law enforcement officer in London) and the City's largest dealer in stolen property. It is unclear whether Hitchen was attracted to Wild as a promising young fence or whether Wild conducted his business in stolen property in such a way as to intentionally attract Hitchen, but in order to understand what Hitchen's offer of an apprenticeship meant to

Wild it is necessary to describe some features of the police system of the early eighteenth century.

At the time of the first meeting between Wild and Hitchen, June of 1713, four features of the English Police system marked it for distinction. The first was the extent to which it was *decentralized*. Each ward within the City of London and each parish outside the City had its own police force consisting of an appointed constable and perhaps one or more unpaid or poorly paid deputies. The authority of these constables stopped at the boundaries of their wards or parishes, limits which enterprising thieves were aware of and exploited to their own advantage. But while there was no organized, central police force, the two chief posts of Upper and Under-City Marshal gave to those who held them powers of arrest throughout the city.

The second distinguishing feature of the English Police system of the early eighteenth century was the extent to which they were creatures, if not creations of the *private sector*. The parish constables, for example, were appointed to one-year terms and the position rotated throughout the parish membership. Anyone refusing to serve as a parish constable or failing to hire a stand-in or obtain an exemption in other ways could be fined and jailed. Likewise, Hitchen, who occupied one of the few central police posts in London, had bought his post at auction for £700 (a sum roughly equivalent to $35,000 in modern money).

The motive parish constables were given for doing their work was the avoidance of punishments intendant upon their failure to do it. The reason Hitchen saw fit to pay £700 for the position of Under-City Marshal was that he expected to be able to exploit the powers of the post in ways that would allow him to recover his investment and, of course, make a profit, too. The cornerstone of Hitchen's enterprise was dealing in stolen property. A form letter of the type Hitchen sent to recent victims of theft is found in a pamphlet published by Wild:[10]

To Mr. A - Merchant,

Sir,
I am inform'd that you have lately had the misfortune to be Depriv'd of your Pocket-Book. It is not long since I labour'd under the same Calamity, and perhaps to a greater Degree than you, I having Notes for very considerable Sums enclos'd in the same; but upon applying myself to Mr. C-s H-n, in St. Paul's Church-Yard, whom I was inform'd was the greatest Proficient in the business of Thief-Taking in England, he took care to serve me effectually. There

is no doubt but he will serve you likewise to the Extent of his Abilities, and I can assure you he has universal Aquaintance with, and Influence over all Persons in the Town Employ'd in Thefts of this Nature. But I must give you this Caution, that you go to him with your Pockets well lin'd, or He'll have nothing to say to you.

I am, tho' unknown,
Your Friend Etc.
A.B.

The reason it is appropriate to speak of Hitchen's trade in stolen property as the cornerstone of his business is that it supported a wide and diverse array of criminal activities which were complemented and sustained by it. For example, though Hitchen was charged with the duty to apprehend felons, he found it profitable to extort stolen property from productive thieves under the threat of arrest rather than actually arresting them. It was the less productive, occasional theives whom Hitchen found it profitable to prosecute for the £40 rewards he could collect upon their conviction. Likewise, he learned that innocent and not so innocent alike were ripe targets for blackmail when they lost their wallets, watches, account books, and other personal property to a buttock-and-file. It was these lessons in the arts of perjury, extortion, selective enforcement, and entrapment which Wild's apprenticeship to Hitchen allowed.

In all, Wild spent about a year as Hitchen's man. The two quarrelled and Wild left Hitchen to embark upon an independent career as fence/policeman, an undertaking made possible by a third main feature of the Police system of the early eighteenth century, this being the extent to which it relied upon, rewarded, and legitimated the work of *criminal informer policemen.* This occupation was brought into being officially by three provisions of the Highwayman's Act of 1692 (4&5 William and Mary c. 8, 7, 6) The first offered a reward of £40 (roughly equivalent to $2000 today) to anyone who captured a thief and provided evidence that led to his conviction. The second permitted the thief-taker to keep the thief's horse, guns, money, and just about any other property he had which was not stolen. But it was the third provision of the Highwayman's Act which opened thief-taking as a career to criminal informers. It gave a Royal pardon and a £40 reward, and the right to keep thieves' property, to anyone except a convicted felon who informed on at least *two* other thieves and secured their convictions. The strategy of the law was clear: by allowing one thief to go free and rewarding him for the conviction of two others, the State was getting a bargain. Unfortunately, however, the State got a great deal more than it had bargained for: entrapment, perjury, false witness, blackmail, extortion, and a trade in stolen goods in the vicious combination that was thief-taking.

The thief-takers, created by the £40 rewards and Royal Pardons, might have proven a tolerable abuse in the first quarter of the eighteenth century had they managed to control crime rather than increase it. But the thief-takers soon learned that a £40 reward was not worth risking one's life or wasting one's energy over in pursuit of the many armed, vicious, and dangerous gangs which roamed London at the time, when the same rewards could be obtained by enticing young children and newcomers into theft and taking them. Likewise, perfectly innocent victims, fearful of the costs, corruption, and loss of reputation defending a false charge, were easy targets for blackmail and extortion. Although thief-taking was not abolished until well into the nineteenth century and gained at least a temporary respect when organized under John and Henry Fielding, few occupations in English history have been regarded with such uniform and thoroughgoing contempt. And at least part of the contempt is owed to Wild, who for more than a decade managed to sustain the impression that he was different.

JONATHAN WILD'S SYSTEM

It was in this milieu of bribery, corruption, theft, extortion, blackmail, police impotence, and inefficiency that Wild gave birth to a series of solutions to the twin problems of policing and fencing. The power of Wild's system is confirmed by the fact that within a decade of his leaving Hitchen, Wild used it to destroy most of the major criminal gangs of London, sent more than 100 felons to the gallows, organized a nationwide investigative police force, and earned wide popular acclaim. At the same time, he built a gigantic business in stolen property, employed, according to Defoe, some 7,000 thieves, and bought a cargo ship which made regular runs to Europe to sell stolen property Wild could not sell in England.

Wild managed these achievements in the formidable environment of the early eighteenth century by fashioning a system which solved certain problems of crime and policing *elegantly,* in the way mathematicians and logicians use that term. What we wish to suggest is that the solutions devised by Wild are so powerful, so simple, and so direct, in short so *elegant,* that subsequent systems contain an inherent tendency to develop and resolve themselves in similar ways. This is the case we will make presently for the properties of the modern sting, but first it is necessary to return to Wild and the system he worked to dominate policing in the first quarter of the eighteenth century.

While Hitchen understood policing and fencing as protection rackets, Wild understood them as businesses. However understood, the motive in both is profit, but the difference between them is that a protection racket depends upon keeping one's customers scared while a business relies upon keeping them satisfied. Wild changed the face of policing and crime in eighteenth century London by presenting an image of himself which attracted thieves, customers, and the public alike. Thus, it is best to see Wild's system in embryonic form as a mix of simple images joined and sustained by one another, the first of which is most visible in a contemporary account of a presentation Wild made to thieves shortly after he left Hitchen:

> "You know, my Bloods" (*quoth he*), "that as *Trade* goes at present, you stand but a *queer* Chance; for when you have made taken anything, if you carry it to the *Fencing-Culls* and *Flash Pawn-brokers,* these unconscionable dealers in *contraband* goods will hardly tip ye a quarter of what it is worth; and if ye offer it to a Stranger, it't ten to one but you are *hobbled* [arrested]. So that there's no such Thing as a Man's living by his Labour; for, if he don't like to be half starved, he must run the Hazard of being *scragg'd* [hanged]—which, let me tell ye, is a damn'd hard Case! Now, if you'll take my Advice, I'll put ye in a Way to remedy all this. When you have been upon any *Lay,* and spoke to some Purpose stolen something worth while let me know all the Particulars; and I'll engage to *pay-back* the Goods to the *Cull* that owns them, and raise ye more *Cole* cash upon that account, than you can expect from the rascally *Fencers.* And at the same Time take Care that you shall all be Bowmen [successful thieves]."[11]

To thieves Wild presented an image of himself as one of them. He spoke their language and by his presence and manner conveyed his understanding of the hard times a thief was dealt by men like Hitchen, the *rascally Fencers,* and free-lance thief-takers. What is more, he offered to pay them more than they could get from other dealers. In fact, if a thief were skeptical of Wild's proposition, Wild could point out that he did not even want to take possession of the goods until they were sold. He only wanted a description of them and details of when and where they were taken in order to find the victim with whom he might negotiate for their return. If

Wild could not make good on his promise of better prices, the thief could take his stolen goods to fence elsewhere.

Wild was, though, able to keep his promise of better prices by promoting his enterprise through presentations of a quite different face to victims whom he approached upon thieves' particulars:

> I happened to hear that you have lately been robbed, and a friend of mine, an honest broker, having stopped a parcel of goods upon suspicion, I thought I could do no less than give you notice of it, as not knowing but some of them might be yours; if it proves so (as I wish it may), you may have them again, provided that nobody is brought into trouble, and the broker has something in consideration of his care.[12]

On occasion, a victim approached with a presentation of this type would question Wild about his association with thieves, perhaps suggesting that he was their confederate or, still worse, nothing but a common fence. In response Wild would feign outrage and take his leave, indignant at the suggestion:

> Sir. . . . I come only to serve you, and if you think otherwise, I must let you know you are mistaken. I have told you that some Goods being offered to pawn by a suspect Person, the Broker had the Honesty to stop them; and therefore, Sir, if you question me about Thieves, I have nothing more to say to you; but that I can give you a good Account of myself, my Name is Wild, I live in Cock Alley by Cripplegate, where you may find me any Day of the Week; and so, Sir, your Humble Servant.[13]

Standing before an honest man, Jonathan Wild was the reflection of an honest citizen: a permanent resident, the friend of an honest broker wanting no trouble, a man who went out of his way to help another honest man recover his stolen property. In the face of thieves he was a thief, in the face of gentlemen a gentleman. Like mirrors back to back these two images were the central elements of Wild's system. As long as he sustained them his control and power over the eighteenth century London underworld and his popularity in the London upperworld continued to grow.

Reflections are, of course, only a part of reality and no system, criminal or police, could survive for long without a legal and economic infrastructure to support it. Economically, Wild was able to pay more than the "rascally Fencers" by dealing in hard-to-fence items (highly identifiable property whose value depended upon unique workmanship), items of sentimental value to their owners (for which they would be willing to pay more than any other buyer), and items of special value to victims and no one else (account books, documents, and so on). Legally, Wild's images also left him most secure. The thieves kept possession of the stolen property until it was sold. Wild did not receive it, he received only descriptions of it. Undoubtedly, Wild also learned of thieves' hiding places in the course of dealing with them. Most important of all, the information thieves gave to Wild was enough, should Wild wish to use it against them, to have them hanged. In brief, the thieves took all the legal risks.

Likewise, as Wild stood before honest citizens and victims he could not be forced to return their property or charged with possession of it as he did not have it. Not an accessory to theft but a friend of an "honest broker," he was doing his friend and the true owner-victims a "favor." Most victims, understandably, wanted to be helped. Bracketed by thieves' legal risks and victims' self-interests, Wild, standing between the two images he fashioned for himself, was nowhere to be seen.

ENLARGING AND ELABORATING THE IMAGES

Although the core of Wild's system was these two images, the growth of Wild's system depended upon his development of them in proportion to the volume of business he would do. Clearly, as the number of transactions Wild handled multiplied, he could not plausably maintain that each emerged from "honest broker" friends nor could he make a personal visit to every victim's home pretending to be just "Jonathan Wild of Cock Alley near Cripplegate," a public-spirited, respectable citizen. Recognizing the need for better, more efficient organization and an identity with a capacity to grow, Wild opened up the "Lost Property Office" in 1715.

Located in the shadow of London's criminal courts and drawing respectability and an official air from the Old Bailey address, the Lost Property Office was a place where recent victims of theft were able to go to consult with Wild, give him information about their victimization, ask his opinion on what amount of reward to offer, or what to pay for the recovery and repurchase of the goods which had been stolen from them. This information, of course, placed Wild in an exceptional bargaining position:

When they came [to the Lost Property Office] according to appointment, and desired to know what success he had met with? why [sic] indeed says Jonathan, I have heard something of your goods, but the person I sent to inquire tells me that the rogues pretend they can pawn them for more than you offer, and therefore, if they make restitution, it must be upon better terms. However, if I can but once come to the speech of the rascals, I don't question but I shall bring them to reason.[14]

The front of the consultation appointment (for which Wild charged a shilling), the taking of careful notes on the crime, and the fictional negotiation with thieves who believed they could get more from pawning the victims' property than what the victim offered for its return placed Wild in a negotiating position in which he could not lose. If the victim offered more, Wild made more. If the victim refused a greater offer, it was the thieves' avarice to blame. If Wild "persuaded" the greedy thieves to return the property for the victim's firm price, was that not testimony to Wild's skill, integrity, and ability?

As Wild's business grew it required trustworthy assistants, people who Wild could employ in the Lost Property Office, within the City of London, and outside of it to manage Wild's affairs. Finding such people, giving them access to information which could mean one's demise and finding ways to control them once they were given it has meant the downfall of more than one criminal enterprise. Wild's solution was made possible by the Transportation Acts (4 George 1 c.11 and 6 George I c.23).

The Acts provided for the transportation of felons to the Colonies and added that should they return before their time they could be summarily retransported for twice as long or hanged. Many felons did return from the servitude of the Colonies and their vulnerability to retransportation or capital punishment fit them perfectly to Wild's needs. If they became difficult or disobedient, Wild needed only to identify them to authorities to have them retransported or disposed of. Moreover, as convicted felons they were not able to take advantage of the provisions of the Highwayman's Act to avail themselves of a Royal Pardon for their own crimes by turning evidence against other criminals.

THIEF-TAKER GENERAL

Although Wild had found a suitable and flexible identity as head of the Lost Property Office, affected a presence pleasing to the victims who consulted with him, solved the problem of dependable (i.e., disposable) assistants, and offered prices to thieves which caused them to flock to him, Wild was still vulnerable to the charge that he was a promoter rather than a preventer of crime. Although the charge was true, it was not likely to come from thieves, for obvious reasons, nor from victims, who were most appreciative of Wild's help in recovering their stolen property. (To blandish an anachronism, Wild understood that dealing in stolen property had all the necessary sociological features of a "crime without victims.") More likely it would arise from "the public" whose outrage would be mobilized by the media, social critics, pamphleteers, politicians, and other molders of public opinion.

To defend against the charge that one is too intimate with criminals, their agent, or their confederate at the same time one works in their presence, a single role recommends itself most strongly: policeman. And for Wild whose intimacy with thieves was broadcast far and wide and obvious to everyone, no "mere" policeman's role would suffice. To sustain his legitimate face Wild appointed himself "Thief-Taker General of Ireland and Great Britain," took to carrying a silver staff as the symbol of his authority, and proceeded in dramatic fashion to earn the puffed-up title he had bestowed upon himself:

> in a short time he began to give himself out for a person who made it his business to procure stolen goods to their right owners. When he first did this he acted with so much art and cunning that he aquired a very great reputation as an honest man, not only from those who dealt with him to procure what they had lost, but even from people of higher station, who observing the industry with which he prosecuted certain malefactors, took him for a friend of Justice, and as such afforded him countenance and encouragement . . . *And so sensible was Jonathan of the necessity there was for him to act in this manner, that he constantly hung up two or three of his clients [thieves] in a twelve-month period that he might keep up the character he had attained.* [Italics added] [15]

As Hitchen and others had done before him, Wild used police powers to control thieves in his employ, using the provisions of the Highwayman's Act. But Wild did not find it necessary, as his predecessors had, to use the threat of police powers to force thieves to trade with him. His better prices insured their business. He *did* use those powers to control those thieves who would not submit to his organization, restrict their theft to certain areas, or obey the commands of his assistants. Perhaps even more important, Wild recognized that it was not the prosecution of small-time thieves that would curry the image he desired but the apprehension and prosecution of violent criminals, particularly those against whom public outrage had been focused.

At the hub of an intelligence network fed on one side by victims of theft and robbery and on the other by the thieves and robbers who victimized them, and backed by an organization of assistants skilled in underworld dealings and trustworthy to the man who could have them transported or hanged, no one in England was in a better position to take on notorious criminal gangs, discover perpetrators of heinous crimes, and manage the prosecution of offenders who were newsworthy. In 1716, Wild captured an especially brutal gang of murderers, for which he "was universally and justly praised"[16] and from that time on the papers, journals, and pamphlets of the time carried frequent accounts of Wild's courageous and daring acts of thief-taking.

Wild had destroyed most of the major criminal gangs of London by 1720, the same year he was consulted by the Privvy Council for his advice on controlling crime. In 1723, he petitioned the Lord Mayor of London to award him the honor of a Freedom of the City, a petition which was not granted but which in the making had a public relations value of its own.

THE DEMYSTIFICATION

In 1725, Jonathan Wild was arrested, tried, convicted, and hanged before a crowd which stoned him as he rode to the gallows. Wild attempted suicide on the eve of execution by drinking laudanum, a mixture of opium and alcohol. Even by the standards of the times, his final hours were particularly brutal:

> He went to execution in a cart, and instead of expressing any kind of pity or compassion for him, the people continued to throw stones and dirt all along the way, reviling and cursing him to the last, and plainly showed by their behavior how much the blackness and notoriety of his crimes had made him abhorred, and how little tenderness the enemies of mankind meet with, when overtaken by the hand of Justice.

> When he arrived at Tyburn, having by then gathered a little strength (nature recovering from the convulsions in which the laudanum had thrown him), the executioner told him he might take what time he pleased to prepare his death. He, therefore, sat down in the cart for some small time, during which the people were so uneasy that they called out to the executioner to dispatch him, and at last threatened

to tear him to pieces if he did not tie him up immediately. Such a furious spirit was hardly ever discovered to the populace upon such an occasion. They generally look on blood with tenderness, and behold even the stroke of Justice with tears; but so far were they from it in this case that had a reprieve really come, 'tis highly questionable whether the prisoner could have been brought back with safety, it being far more likely that as they wounded him in the head in his passage to Tyburn, they would have knocked him on the head outright, if any had attempted to have brought him back.[17]

To understand how Wild fell from the position of enormous power and prestige he had attained to the level of contempt and outrage visited on him in his final hours, it is necessary to see how each of the images he labored to sustain, fence and policeman, benefactor of thief and victim, failed him before the audiences he most needed to impress.

In June of 1724, William Kneebone's drapery shop was robbed. Kneebone immediately suspected a former employee, Jack Sheppard, who had recently begun to distinguish himself as a thief. Kneebone advertised for the return of the stolen goods and Wild approached Kneebone with an offer of assistance. Kneebone agreed and Wild contacted William Field, a known associate of Sheppard, a thief in Wild's employ, and a man indebted to Wild for once saving him from the gallows.

Field, it seems, had been approached by Sheppard and a thief named "Blueskin" Blake to fence the goods and knew where Blake and Sheppard had hid them, Wild and Field decided to act on this information, recover the goods, "take" Blake and Sheppard, and secure the £40 reward for their convictions. The prosecutions were successful, but Wild suffered greatly from them.

Wild's difficulties began with Blueskin, who had worked as a thief for Wild for many years and trusted him. Wild came to Blueskin's trial. On the steps of the Old Bailey court, the two met and Blake pleaded with Wild to use his influence to get him off. Wild taunted him. Whereupon Blake pulled out a knife he had concealed under his coat and slit Wild's throat.

To the surprise of everyone who witnessed the assault, Wild survived, but only to run into a wholly different and ultimately more damaging attack from Sheppard. At the time of his capture, Sheppard enjoyed a small folkhero's reputation. He had once broken into a prison to rescue his mistress, the kind of exploit the press of the early eighteenth century appreciated. And while awaiting trial on the charge of the drapery shop robbery, he escaped from Newgate twice. The first brought press attention to Sheppard, allowing the retelling of his earlier escape, it also brought attention to Blueskin who had not yet been hanged. The second, after Blueskin's death, made Sheppard nothing less than a national hero.

It was a truly spectacular escape. Embarrassed by the first escape and not wanting further bad press from a second, the keepers of Newgate loaded Sheppard down with dozens of restraints, leg irons, and hand cuffs and bolted him to the floor in one of the deepest chambers of the prison. Somehow Sheppard managed to free himself and after doing so worked his way through at least six iron reinforced doors that stood between him and freedom. For 10 days Sheppard roamed the streets of London before he was rearrested.

When Sheppard was returned to Newgate, hundreds of visitors came to see him in his cell. Defoe took his life story and the press faithfully reported what he had said. A great deal of it had to do with Jonathan Wild and his system, the hundreds of thieves in his employ, the way he treated Blueskin Blake, and the perjury of William Field, Wild's accomplice in receiving and theft. Almost overnight, Wild's public image withered. The anger that people typically felt for common thieves was turned on Wild as their sponsor and creator. In all the poems and ballads sung to celebrate the exploits of the dashing and romantic Jack Sheppard, Wild played the role of perfect villain.

Wild might have been able to withstand the deterioration of his image in the songs of the London masses and the popular press which fed and was fed by them had his system not developed an internal flaw which eroded his reputation with a more influential audience. In August of 1724 one of Wild's most trusted thieves had stolen a very large amount of valuable jewelry from a group of London's most influential citizens. They enlisted the help of Wild and, anxious to preserve their good graces, Wild agreed to recover it for them. Johnson, however, discovered that by stringing out the return of the jewelry over many months and returning it piece by piece, Wild was willing to pay more for it as his customers became impatient (and willing to pay more for fear that it might not be returned). So while the London masses were reading and singing of the exploits of Jack Sheppard, stories and songs always ending with the vile acts of Wild, some of the most influential citizens in London began to suspect that they, too, were being had.

The events of Wild's arrest and trial are extremely complicated and cannot be recounted here in the detail which would do them justice. Suffice it to say that the case against Wild was extremely shaky. He was arrested on one charge, detained in prison on yet others, found innocent of those and convicted on yet another. The act under which he was finally convicted, passed nine years earlier as a section of the Transportation Acts, had acquired the nickname "Jonathan Wild's Act" because it was so clearly an attempt to stop Wild early in his career. Its author, Sir William Thompson, sat as chief judge at Wild's trial. Had it been anyone but Wild, the Wild who had successfully eluded the provisions of Jonathan Wild's Act for nearly a decade by maintaining the images which now failed him, there is little doubt but what the prosecution would have failed to secure a conviction.

Howson says of Wild's demise, "Just and necessary though it might have been, Wild's death taught no lessons, brought no reforms, and alleviated no suffering."[18] Thief-taking continued for another century, for a time people found it difficult to recover their lost property, but new entrepreneurs, though none so dramatic in their successes as Wild, emerged to take his place. The resistance to the lessons of Wild, both those of his life and death, are grounded in many sources: the myopia of victims willing to recover what they have lost "No Questions Asked"; the urgency and emotion with which demands are made that "something" be done about crime; the attractions of police images which boldly promise to do it.

THE LESSONS OF THE CAREER OF
JONATHAN WILD FOR FENCE-POLICEMEN

The single most important lesson of the career of Jonathan Wild for fence-policemen flows from the two images which sustained his career. For fences, at least large-scale generalist fences like Wild was, the central lesson is: "Be a policeman." For policemen, at least large-scale investigative policemen like Wild was, the central lesson is: "Be a fence." Throughout history there is evidence that successful fences have learned Wild's lesson and sought to realize his advice by acting as police informers.[19] Only recently, however, have policemen begun to realize Wild's lesson by posing as fences.[20]

Wild's career suggests that working as a fence, at least as long as one can sustain that role successfully, is a more powerful method of detective policing than any other which existed in the eighteenth century. Are things different today? Are modern methods of investigative policing powerful enough to make sting operations and the risks and dangers inherent in them unnecessary? The most comprehensive study of detective policing currently available suggests that for all the mystery, science, and myth our culture has attached to the detective role, that by and large unless a victim supplies the name of the perpetrator, he will not be subsequently identified.[21] But while Wild's career suggests that sting operations have the potential to produce more impressive results than conventional methods, are the risks and dangers worth the benefits? Can those risks and dangers be controlled?

Wild's career, the prototype for all fence-policemen, suggests that the answer to both questions should be offered carefully. For at least a decade Wild succeeded in keeping outsiders from penetrating the costs of his system and carefully engineered the celebrations and appreciations of its benefits, a pattern which the architects and employers of modern sting operations have also followed.

In using the case of Wild to probe for costs and dangers inherent in police-fence operations, we propose an analytical strategy similar to the one we used to dissect the career of Wild. What must be seen, we suggest, is that the sting depends upon the maintenance of two images: one the image of a fence maintained during the period of the undercover operation; the other the image of a policeman during the period which follows it. And as was true of Wild, both images must be bigger and better, stronger and more compelling than their conventional counterparts. A sting cannot be "just another fence" anymore than Wild could. Likewise a sting operation must be better than conventional investigative policing, just as Wild understood his need to become "Thief Taker General of Ireland and Great Britain."

THE COSTS AND DANGERS OF MAINTAINING AN IMAGE AS A FENCE

Unlike conventional detective policing, running a sting operation requires a considerable investment in equipment and materials to create an environment in which the image of a fence can be sustained. In addition to the rental of a location which will serve as the front, videotape equipment to record transactions, storage space for purchased goods where they can be kept secure and out of sight, merchandise supporting the impression that the front also carries on legitimate business, cars, trucks, and vans which undercover personnel can operate full-time, and money for field expenses, "flash," and buys, a considerable investment is required to install monitoring equipment, build bulletproof walls and counters, wire alarms and install silent triggering devices, and fit them to the architecture of the rented front in ways that will not arouse suspicion at the same time they will insure the safety of the officers who work the counter. All of this work which must be done before a sting front opens its doors incurs costs which are typically hidden in two ways. First, most of the work is done by policemen from the agency running the sting operation. During the time these policemen are searching for an appropriate location, doing the carpentry, electrical, and construction work necessary to turn it into a working front, purchasing materials to outfit it as a business, finding undercover vehicles, and leasing or purchasing the other equipment necessary to sustain their image, they are not employed at other police duties; however no accounting is made of the loss of their manpower while they are employed, sometimes for months, in preparations. Second, these preliminary image sustaining and generating costs, most of which cannot be recovered after the sting goes public, are also not included, either as capital expenditures or salaries, in the typical police public relations accountings offered for public consumption, where, if any cost-benefit information is provided at all, it consists of reporting buy money expended in relation to the value of property recovered.[22]

An allied problem associated with meeting and accounting for the costs involved in generating a fence image involves securing the money for such expenditures while preserving the proposed operation. In dealings with LEAA this means that obtaining a grant for a sting operation cannot be handled through the same funding channels or reviewed by the same accounting procedures as can conventional, nonclandestine grants. We have reason to believe that in order to maintain the clandestine image of sting operations, some of them have been funded in advance of ever submitting a written request for funds.

Aside from the hidden economic costs and dangerous accounting practices involved in generating an image of a fence, the career of Wild suggests a variety of costs and risks associated with maintaining and managing that image which are not easily measured in economic terms. A first set of such difficulties is associated with making the fence image attractive enough to entice thieves to trade with it. Wild, we know, managed this problem by offering thieves better prices than his competitors were paying. This strategy is available to sting operations but, should the price offered become "too high" or too far out of line with the prevailing market for the stolen goods in question, the authenticity of the fence image will be

endangered. There is an analogous problem in undercover narcotics policing where drug dealers are sensitive to the fact that narcs are typically
willing to pay more for drugs than "genuine" users.

Whether or not a sting fence is willing to pay prices at or above the
going rate, the problem of getting that message out to prospective customers remains. With considerable street experience and a sufficiently
disreputable identity to back him up, Wild could approach thieves directly
with his offer of better prices. Sting operations seem to approach this
problem of advertising their disreputability in two rather different ways.
The first seems to involve the creation of some preposterous story. The
Washington Sting operation advertised themselves as a group of Mafiosi
come to town to take over the stolen property business in the nation's
capital.[23] Promoting employees with names like "Rico Rigatoni" and
"Angelo Lasagna" the Washington sting demonstrates the level of subtlety
such stories need to attain to secure the confidence of thieves of the level
of sophistication they dealt with.

A second strategy which sting operations sometimes employ to secure a
more plausible image of illegitimacy involves the purchase of a genuine
criminal reputation or at least someone with some real experience in
playing the role of a bad actor. In four sting operations of which we have
inside knowledge, this second strategy was employed by hiring a professional criminal. In one of the cases the criminal was a fence who had been
arrested and given a plea bargain deal wherein the charges against him
would be dropped if he allowed his real fencing operation to be used as a
sting for a period of nine months (Buffalo, NY, 1976). In the other three
(the names of which cannot be revealed because doing so would compromise my informants), a three-time loser was given the option of going
to jail for the rest of his natural life under a habitual criminal prosecution
or joining the staff of a local sting (a use of the habitual criminal statute
which recalls Wild's use of the Transportation Acts). After working one
such operation and finding the work to his liking, the man became a
professional informant and was salaried by sting operations in two other
states.

Whether the fence image of the sting operations is enhanced by imaginative policemen spinning stories to explain its presence or by employing
former criminals under coercive plea bargains, the object of these tactics is
to bring thieves into the fence front where their sale of stolen property can
be taped and recorded. The focus on this front stage scene in the sting
drama has a tendency to divert attention from the fact that unless the
sting's reputation for paying higher than normal prices spreads through the

subculture of theft and attacts thieves on that basis alone, the real work in generating, cultivating, and maintaining an enticing image of the fence is done by those undercover operatives who work the street and bring thieves to the counter where their transactions are recorded.

This type of work—which is never photographed, hard to describe in the saturated detail which makes it sensible, and, when challenged, becomes an issue of whether one believes the account of the undercover officer, professional informant, or the thief—is highly varied. In our experience it begins by frequenting places where bad actors congregate and staging performances likely to impress them with the illegitimacy and connections of the undercover operatives. This may mean hanging in certain bars, pool rooms, coffee shops, and luncheonettes, getting in on gambling games, horse parlors, and bookie joints, offering stolen property for sale in these places, picking up hitchhikers late at night and telling stories to them about one's own criminal exploits, attending parties, after hours clubs, and other establishments frequented by people "in the life" and so forth. Once such activities succeed in sponsoring the impression that the undercover operatives are thieves themselves, "street reps" for a good fence whom they have dealt with themselves, or traffickers in other kinds of criminal endeavor, it is not unusual in our experience for them to be asked to participate in the commission of thefts and burglaries, taking more active roles than mere receivers or connections for stolen property.

Sometimes, it is possible to arrange for the arrest of thieves and burglars in the act, but often there is not time to set such a trap and the undercover operative must become a participant in the crime. He could, of course, reveal his identity as an undercover agent and make an arrest at the scene of the crime himself, but doing so would run a substantial risk of destroying the fence image, which may well have required months of work and many tens of thousands of dollars to generate. Of course, the danger in such participation, necessary though it might be to preserve the image of the fence, is that in addition to such preservation it may also promote crimes which would not have occurred without the undercover operative's image preserving participation in them.

A final series of risks and costs associated with generating and maintaining the fence image which are not usually calculated in the evaluation of sting operations involves the toll that the work requires upon those who do it. Here again, the burden does not fall most heavily upon the officers who work the counter and whose work is usually the evidentiary core against the thief but those operatives who work the street, build the fence's image in the eyes of thieves, and entice them into the front to make a transaction which can be recorded. It is hard to imagine a more morally corrosive environment than that of the working world of the "ropers," as they were called on one sting operation with which we were familiar. The seductions of the undercover life, the drugs, the drinking, and the sex, present one sort of problem, while the exposure to people whom one can grow to like, who do favors for one, and whom one eventually will betray, presents to the best of undercover policemen a problem of quite a different sort. In this connection Wild provides a character model for the kind of person ideally suited to such intimate predation:

> What were his personal requisites? Wild had no sensitivity, probably little creative imagination and, morally, he was an oaf. But he did have an abundance of what the eighteenth century called 'Genius'— that is, ingenuity, cunning, resource, energy, and that mysterious power we sometimes call 'personal magnetism'. He was able to manipulate thieves for so long because, I suspect, they felt he was really on their side, no matter how murderous his behavior.[24]

THE COSTS AND DANGERS OF MAINTAINING
AN EXEMPLARY POLICE IMAGE

Because sting operations involve risks which are far greater than that of conventional detective policing and are constantly in danger of being overwhelmed by the disguises and deceptions sting work requires, the precarious adoption of the role of fence demands, at some point, that it be counterbalanced with a police image of even larger and more dramatic proportions. Stings, like the thief-taking efforts of Wild, make good press—they need to do so.

However, the demands of producing and maintaining an exemplary police image tend to encourage practices, procedures, ways of working, and manipulations which puff the image beyond proportions, lay it open to dramatic deflation, and encourage doctoring and cover-ups which further complicate an already complex scene. In part, of course, sting operations engage in these practices as part of the syndrome which has beset many "exemplary" projects drawing federal funds: a granting agency spends enormous sums of money and is hungry for some successes to legitimate its spending grants money to an agency which promises to do so. To keep its promise the receiving agency produces an evaluation of its work designed to emphasize its successes, findings which the funders, not about to argue that they made a poor investment, are not likely to dispute with, unless the puffing is conspicuous or transparent.

Although this syndrome has marked many federal projects, most which were "great successes" which folded after the federal moneys for their support disappeared, it takes on some special properties, some of which are rather risky and potentially dangerous, when added to the already deceptive and clandestine operation of a sting. The first set of such problems can be discerned from a careful reading of the two documents which currently summarize the "successes" of some 62 sting operations in 39 American cities since 1974: *Taking the Offensive*[25] and *What Happened.*[26] The latter volume is the more systematic and comprehensive volume and is subtitled "A Special Report to the Commissioner." Its summary, printed in boldface type, seeks to establish the exemplary character of sting operations with the following review of findings:

1. Subjects who sell stolen property to undercover operatives in anti-fencing operations are considerably older than individuals arrested nationally for property crimes.
2. Nearly one in five of the subjects apprehended and/or identified in anti-fencing operations have been classified as a fence.
3. Most subjects have a prior arrest record and many have lengthy criminal histories, while some had long escaped police attention because of their cautious approach to criminal activities.
4. Prosecutors enjoy a very high conviction rate for subjects arrested in anti-fencing operations.
5. The anti-fencing projects examined showed decreases in property crime at the termination of their operations.
6. Further analysis focusing on the impact on incidence of the individual types of property crime is strongly indicated.
7. The assumption that the impact is maximized at termination may be questionnable, since education and sentencing often take place over an extended period of time.
8. Undercover personnel have paid a very small percentage of fair market value for the stolen property recovered.
9. The recovered property usually has been returned to the victim or insurance company.
10. The property recovered in anti-fencing operations has ranged from small auto parts to Rembrandt paintings.[27]

TABLE I   Age Distributions of Sting Arrestees and Burglary, Larceny,
and Auto Theft Arrestees Nationally, 1977 (percent of Total)

ARRESTEES	17 and Under	18-20	21-25	26-30	31+
Stings	3%	13%	30%	25%	29%
			(21-24)	(25-29)	(30+)
UCR Burglary	51.5%	19.8%	12.7%	7.9%	9.1%
UCR Larceny-Theft	42.9%	16.8%	13.0%	9.7%	17.6%
UCR Auto Theft	53.0%	18.5%	11.9%	7.6%	9.0%

As this summary includes many but not all of the dimensions along which architects and advocates of sting operations seek to construct an exemplary police image, each of the claims, the evidence, and the work necessary to support it deserves careful attention.

1. *Subjects who sell stolen property to undercover operatives in antifencing operations are considerably older than individuals arrested nationally for property crimes.*

The premier finding of the *What Happened* summary is supported by data gathered on 20 sting operations which produced 1693 arrested subjects. The age distribution of sting arrestees is compared with the 1977 national arrest data which we have compiled from the 1977 Uniform Crime Reports (UCR) in Table 1.[28]

If we assume that for the three varieties of property crime above the UCR arrest data accurately reflects the age distribution of perpetrators of those crimes, we are presented with a rather curious finding: sting operations manage to arrest most people from age categories least responsible for property crimes. In fact, the age group most responsible is rarely (3%) stung at all. In order to understand this finding and the policy it mirrors, we must ask ourselves how it would look and what it would do for the sting's exemplary police image to report that half the people brought into the front, enticed there by undercover policemen and informants, and subsequently arrested were juveniles. Hardly the kind of heroic thief-taking results sufficient to warrant the deceptions, illusions, efforts, and expenditures which stings necessitate.

Consequently, it is our experience, based upon inside knowledge of four separate sting operations and the inference we are obliged to draw from the data above, that most sting operations avoid arresting juveniles even though they are most likely responsible for nearly half of all property crime. This is not to say that the informants and undercover agents whose job it is to bring thieves into the front do not meet these young thieves or are not approached with offers of stolen property by them, but rather, when they are approached with such offers, by and large, they pass them up in order to forestall possible hostile public opinion.

2. *Nearly one in five of the subjects apprehended and/or identified in anti-fencing operations have been classified as a fence.*

If the premier finding of *What Happened* must be understood as masking a policy of ignoring juvenile property crime, the second seeks to sponsor the impression that the targets of sting operations, while less common than juvenile perpetrators, are more important, more serious, and more professional criminals than their juvenile counterparts. Some rather unusual stretching and shaping is required to make this point.

First, if we take the statement above at face value, it asks us to consider sting operations as *anti-fencing operations* on the basis that *nearly* one in five subjects *apprehended or identified* in them has been classified as a fence. Even if this statement were faultless, it would be hard to defend understanding sting operations as anti-fencing operations on the basis of the fact that fewer than 20% of the people involved in them has been classified as a fence. Sting operations are not *anti-fencing* operations. They are *anti-thief* operations.

Second, were we to take the second major finding of *What Happened* at face value we would miss at least three face-making manipulations which rest beneath the surface and support the second finding above. The first is that the only data in *What Happened* dealing with the proportion of fences encountered in sting operations[29] establishes that 16%, *one in six, not one in five*, subjects were classified as fences. Second, decisions to classify such subjects as fences were "subjective judgments made by operational personnel,"[30] "personnel," we might add, employed in "anti-fencing operations." Finally, it must be emphasized that both the one in six figure above and the "subjective classification" refer to subjects who were "arrested or identified" or merely "encountered" in sting operations. No data is given in *What Happened* solely on the arrest of fences, subjectively or objectively classified as such.

3. *Most subjects have a prior arrest record and many have lengthy criminal histories, while some had long escaped police attention because of their cautious approach to criminal activities.*

As was the case with the second major finding of *What Happened*, the third major finding also seeks to establish that it is the more serious, experienced, and professional criminal that the sting operation manages to

TABLE 2   Prior Arrest Records of Subjects
          Encountered in 19 Operations

Prior Arrest Groups	*(Sample = 1620 Subjects)* Percent
No Prior Arrests	16
1 to 5 Prior Arrests	52
6 to 10 Prior Arrests	17
Over 10 Prior Arrests	15

"encounter" (i.e., arrest *or* identify). Again, *What Happened* provides no data which differentiates between arrests and identifications of subjects encountered. It does, however, support its third major finding with Table 2.

The problem with Table 2, as any first semester statistics student should be able to explain, is that the intervals chosen mask the distribution they should be designed to express. With more than half the cases in the "1 to 5 Prior Arrests" category, it is impossible to know, absent measures of central tendency or dispersion (which are absent in *What Happened*), what the distribution of prior arrest records of encountered subjects really was.

As if the problem of deciphering the concept of "encountered" subjects combined with a choice of intervals patently designed to hide the distribution of the prior arrests were not enough, *What Happened* adds, "it was not possible to distinguish between felony and misdemeanor arrests. However, a cursory examination of the charges reveals that the subjects encountered with previous records had been arrested for serious crimes, not petty or traffic offenses."[31] If a cursory examination of the charges can reveal that the subjects had serious prior arrest records, one wonders why a sample, even a small one, could not have been drawn as evidence in support of this revelation.

4. *Prosecutors enjoy a very high conviction rate for subjects arrested in anti-fencing operations.*

The construction of an exemplary police image for the sting requires not only that it avoid the reputation of targeting juvenile offenders and concentrate its attentions on serious, professional criminals but also that it do so successfully or at least more successfully than conventional police methods. In support of this aspect of an exemplary policy image one would think that stings, armed with videotaped records to support their charges, would easily surpass the success of conventional prosecutions based upon less exotic evidence. On the basis of the data presented in *What Happened,* which we have composed and included in Table 3 along with certain comparable national data, it would appear that stings do in fact produce higher conviction rates than conventional methods, but this statement requires some quite important qualifications.

The most important of which is that the claim in *What Happened* of a "very high conviction rate" (91%) is based on 750 completed cases, 609 of which were settled early by guilty pleas. Of the 197 cases which went to trial, 76 (38%) ended in convictions, 27 (14%) were acquitted or dismissed, and 94 (48%) remain pending. It may well turn out that all 338 pending cases (those not included in the above conviction rates) will end in convictions, in which case the 17 sting operations on whose cases finding four is based will have achieved a 94% conviction rate. But should only half of the pending cases result in convictions, the stings will have achieved a conviction rate no better than the national average for larceny-theft and only slightly (8%) better than the national rate for burglary.

5. *The anti-fencing projects examined showed decreases in property crime at the termination of their operations.*

6. *Further analysis focusing on the impact on incidence of individual types of property crime is strongly indicated.*

7. *The assumption that the impact is maximized at termination may be questionable since ajudication and sentencing often take place over an extended period of time.*

With the fifth, sixth, and seventh findings above, *What Happened* seeks to establish what is to the general public perhaps the most important aspect of an exemplary police effort—that in the long run or even the short run it serves to lessen the chance of victimization and makes our person or property more secure; brief, that it makes a difference that justifies the risks, dangers, deceptions, and expenditures it necessitates. In fact, so strong is the need to demonstrate this effect that *What Happened* seeks to do it and implies it has, at least in finding five above, in the face of almost overwhelming odds against it. Who could believe that a single sting operation or even a series of them, netting an average of 80 subjects, could show an appreciable decrease in property crime rates in any city or county of sizable proportions?

In order to test this hard-to-believe finding, the authors of *What Happened* perform a time series analysis of property crime rates at three project sites: an unidentified western city of population 385,000, a second

TABLE 3   The Disposition of 1,088 Subjects Arrested in 17 Sting Operations as Compared with National Rates for Selected Property Crimes.[32]

	Persons Arrested	Cases Pending	Guilty Pleas	Guilty (Trial)	Guilty (Total)	Referred to Juvenile Court
Sting Operations	1088	338 (31%)	609 (56%)	76 (7%)	685 (63%)	Less than 3%
TOTAL						
UCR Burglary	26,821				30.9%	57%
UCR Larceny-Theft	161,450				49.1%	37.7%
UCR Auto Theft	17,726				23.5%	64.8%
ADULT						
UCR Burglary	11,534				71.8%	—
UCR Larceny-Theft	100,583				78.8%	—
UCR Auto Theft	6,240				66.7%	—

western city of population 331,000, and a third "midwestern jurisdiction" of population 746,000. The lags were computed from monthly UCR reports submitted between January 1974 and September 1978. True to the letter of finding five above, analysis of the property crime rate at the first western city site showed a decrease after the third sting operation in that city. However, the decrease was not statistically significant.

The second site examined, the midwestern city of population 331,000, also enjoyed the benefits of three sting operations. There the analysis showed no statistically significant reduction in the property crime rate after the first operation; an increase, but not a statistically significant one, after the second; and a statistically significant decrease ($p < .05$, one tail) after the third. The third site examined, the jurisdiction of 746,000 people, showed a decrease in the property crime rate which was marginally significant ($p < .1$) after the termination of one sting which resulted in the arrest of "more than 100 subjects . . . including 27 fences."[33]

While one cannot fault finding six, which calls for further study (except to say that it is not a finding), and it is hard to argue with the logic of finding seven (which asserts that an "assumption," which is by definition questionable "may be" and is also not a finding), finding five, asserting that "anti-fencing projects examined showed decreases in property crime at their termination" seems to be based on the also questionable assumption that readers of *What Happened* would not read further. For within *What Happened* they would find that of the seven sting operations conducted in three cities and which were subject to analysis, one was followed by a statistically insignificant *increase* in property crime rates, five were followed by statistically insignificant decreases ($p < .05$), and one was followed by a statistically significant decrease. On the basis of those results, finding five ought to have read: *no evidence exists to show that sting operations produce declines in the rate of property crime, either at their termination or at any time in the future.*

8. *Undercover personnel have paid a very small percentage of the fair market value for stolen property recovered.*

The key to Wild's system, from its embryonic beginnings to its brutal final hours, was the maintenance of two images, one satisfying thieves and the other pleasing victims. When joined and kept in proportion to one another, Wild's business grew, his competition suffered, and Wild's reputation made him invulnerable to criticism. By the same token, when his images failed him, when thieves understood his manipulation of them, when the public understood him as a promoter of theft, and when his victims realized that they were not getting the bargains he had promised them, his system fell apart, the images he had to keep joined, separated, and he was tried in an atmosphere of scorn and contempt which insured his conviction and execution.

The eighth finding above addresses two facets of the exemplary police image which stings in the likeness of Wild seek to maintain. The first facet is defensive and aspires to deflect the charge of entrapment. Wild understood that his image of Thief-Taker General would not be enhanced if he were seen as leading the impressionable into theft in order to collect the reward money for their prosecution. Similarly the modern stings must demonstrate that their willingness to buy stoken property does not encourage people to steal in response to the encouragement of the market they create.

The second facet of the exemplary image finding five seeks to support is the reading of sting operations, by victims of theft and the public alike, as economically responsible. Just as Wild was sensitive in his dealings at the Lost Property Office to give off the impression that he was a hard bargainer with thieves and worked very hard to secure the return of property from them at the lowest possible price, so, too, do modern stings need to demonstrate their bargain rates.

We have composed the data on sting bargaining offered in *What Happened* into Table 4. But before we analyze its image making and defending properties, some notes on the figures which compose it are in order. First, the data range in their precision from figures correct to the nearest hundred thousand or million (#'s 8, 15, 16), through figures correct to the nearest thousand (# 1, 4, 9), to those which appear accurate to the final dollar. This variability is understandable in estimation of the value of property purchased, but surprising for the six projects (#'s 4, 7, 8, 14, 15, 16) which apparently could not account for buy money with any more precision than the closest thousand.

Second, the inclusion of stings 15 and 16 skews the table (and were excluded from the tabular presentations in *What Happened*) but the reason for their skewing and exclusion reveals some further problems in accounting. According to *What Happened* sting 15 was excluded because it managed the purchase of $4 million worth of heroin, a product not identifiable as stolen and classed as "contraband." Likewise, *What Happened* says of sting 16:

Approximately $42 million of stolen [sic] property was recovered in Operation 16 of which $23 million proved to be stolen. Again much of the remainder apparently was contraband.[34]

TABLE 4 Value of Property Purchased, Property Identified as Stolen, Property Not Identified as Stolen, Buy Money Expended, and Buy Money Expended per Dollar of Property Purchased in 16 Sting Operations.

Sting #	Value of Property Purchased	Value of Property Identified as Stolen	Value of Property Not Identified as Stolen	Buy Money expended	Buy Money Per Dollar of Property Purchased
1	$ 3,335,000	$ 3,335,000	$ 0	$ 155,929	.05
2	1,488,760	1,449,210	39,550	73,604	.05
3	1,049,983	1,047,215	2,768	75,283	.07
4	1,020,000	1,008,000	16,000	41,000	.04
5	897,794	841,576	56,218	91,812	.10
6	1,244,022	1,217,974	26,048	74,289	.06
7	502,019	425,000	77,019	67,000	.13
8	1,500,000	1,300,000	200,000	137,000	.09
9	989,000	985,000	4,000	74,745	.07
10	264,835	221,320	43,515	47,421	.18
11	1,000,293	989,548	10,745	59,516	.06
12	747,791	746,318	1,473	18,533	.02
13	947,682	903,700	43,982	60,717	.06
14	890,153	849,041	41,112	115,000	.13
15	6,300,000	2,200,000	4,100,000	99,000	.02
16	42,000,000	23,000,000	19,000,000	504,000	.01
Totals (1-16)	$ 63,175,332	$ 40,518,902	23,662,430	$1,694,849	.03
Totals (1-14)	$ 15,875,332	$ 15,318,902	$ 562,000	$1,091,849	.07

SOURCE: Roger Lane, *Violent Death in the City: Suicide, Accident and Murder in Nineteenth Century Philadelphia.* Copyright 1979 Harvard University Press. Reprinted by permission.

These comments indicate some difficulty in evaluating the data reported on the 14 other sting operations. For example, it would appear that sting #1 either purchased no drugs or contraband (e.g., illegal destructive devices made from legitimate materials) or failed to exclude them from property classified as "stolen." The same appears likely to be true of sting #3 and possibly 9 and 12 as well in that they report an unusually large percentage of property purchased identifiable as stolen.

The third qualification which must be registered before we subject the data to analysis is that the appraisal of the value of property was, to quote *What Happened,* a "subjective" process. It was, however, likely to be influenced by a policy endorsed by LEAA instructing stings to strive to pay less than 10% of the fair market value of goods they purchased. The extent to which this directive influenced sting bargaining policies is difficult to separate from the extent to which it influenced "subjective" evaluations of the fair market value of purchased goods.

These deficiencies in the data from *What Happened* notwithstanding, it is on the basis of the 7% of the value of the stolen property figure which the image of an exemplary policeman, careful not to entrap and efficient in his use of moneys, that sting operations need to defend and maintain. Let us first consider what seven cents on the dollar means on the purchase price of some commonly stolen property. It means that one can buy a $5 carton of cigarettes for 35¢, $100 stolen suit for $7, a $50 Timex quartz crystal watch for $3.50, a $90 case of decent scotch whiskey for $6.30, and a new $150 stolen Schwinn ten speed bicycle for $10.50. Any two-bit thief in any city in the United States on any day of the week can do better than that.

He can because there are large and ready markets for such goods and most thieves like most people are smart enough to know it and steal accordingly. Some, of course, are not smart enough to understand this and others steal whatever is available when the opportunity presents itself and come up with some quite unusual things for which finding a buyer is no small problem. Consider the predicament of the thief who steals three 1977 Ford Pinto carburetors. He is unlikely to know three people who own such vehicles, much less three who own such vehicles and are having or anticipate carburetor problems. Even so, tracking them down, showing them his wares, and getting any sort of decent price for his efforts, even if it was "good luck" that gave him the opportunity for theft, is simply not worth the effort. That, I suggest, is one kind of product and one kind of thief from whom one is going to be able to buy at 7¢ on the dollar.

There are, though, others. Consider the thief who steals a truck, a car, or a van. Although there is a large legitimate market for such items, few people are willing to buy a stolen car because they have no idea how to go about dealing with title and registration problems, altering serial numbers, and so on. So while the streets are filled with vehicles in the $8,000 to $10,000 range, and many costing more, most of which are simple to steal, the vast majority of them which are stolen are found abandoned. However, should a budding young car thief find a fence who is foolish enough to pay 7¢ or even 3¢ on the dollar for stolen cars, trucks, or vans, he can, in short order, make his fortune. Two $8,000 cars a night, easily within the range of even a lazy thief, will bring $1,120 a night at 7% and $480 a night at 3%.

Third, one can appear, in the final accounting, to buy at 7% of the fair market value of stolen property in one other situation which deserves emphasis. On those occasions when an undercover operative (policeman or informant) accompanies a thief at his work and splits the profits (with him) on the sale of the goods to the sting fence, it is possible to buy at 14¢ on the dollar and, assuming an equal divvy and the subsequent return of half, end up showing a buy ratio of 7%.

Do we show with these examples that stings seduce certain types of thieves and encourage them to theft in an effort to comply with the directive which instructs them to strive for a 10¢-on-the-dollar buy rate? Do we show that in their desire to appear as economically efficient, exemplary policemen, sting operatives are obliged to operate in ways which more modest aspirations might have prevented? The possibility exists that such practices are beneath the surface of the image of the accounting which the stings have offered of themselves. But in point of fact the accounting itself is so poor that it makes access to what happened highly speculative at best. If, however, stings did manage to buy property at an average rate of 7¢ on the dollar, our experience suggests that they and those who fund them have some serious accounting to do.

9. *The recovered property usually has been returned to the victim or insurance company.*

There is, as the model of Wild suggests, one group of people who are least disposed to demand an accounting of the costs, social or economic, of fence policemen. We refer, of course, to victims who, if the price is right, are inclined to welcome the recovery of their stolen property, "No Questions Asked." Along this dimension stings have the capacity to offer bargains in the recovery of stolen property the likes of which Wild only imagined. Howson writes of Wild's scheme, proposed in the autumn of 1721, for the creation of a theft insurance company:

> While I have impugned Wild's reputation for originality in some fields, perhaps he should be given credit in this, as a pioneer in, if not the inventor of, what is now one of the most universal types of insurance in existence. 'HD' one of Wild's contemporary biographers, says that he even went so far as to pretend 'to settle a sufficient Fund, and give good security for the Performance of Articles: sometimes showing a manuscript Paper of Proposals, and consulting People whom he supposed to have any Understanding in those Affairs, extolling the great Use and advantage this Project wou'd be to the Publick; not doubting, he said, but that all Trading People, as well as Gentlemen and Noblemen, who kept great Quantities of Plate in their Houses, wou'd for their own sakes encourage so useful an Undertaking . . . but the Thing was usually receiv'd as a Banter, or a Piece of Mr. *Wild's* wit.[35]

Had he been able to bring it into being, Wild's scheme for theft insurance would have suited his image-building needs perfectly. With it he could have reduced his victims' concern for recovery of stolen property, directed thieves in his employ to steal from those who refused to buy his policies, or recover the cost of returning property by raising rates and paying for his "loss" over the term of the policy; all of which would have made his public image more secure by making the harmful consequences of his system even more indirect.

Unfortunately, there is no evidence in *What Happened* to support finding eight above, other than the line which reads:

> A cursory examination of the disposition of the recovered stolen property reveals that the overwhelming majority of it was returned to the owner (or appropriate insurer) in a timely fashion.[36]

While maintenance of an exemplary police image requires only the demonstration that one has recovered stolen property and made its return possible, nothing can be said on the basis of the evidence of "cursory examination" except that for *What Happened* it is true to form. It would, though, have been most interesting to know what proportion of the victims refused to accept their recovered stolen property and preferred to keep their insurance money, what proportion took it back and neglected to inform their insurer, what proportion of insurers refused the trouble of taking it back and trying to get rid of it, and what proportion of insurers got it back, recovered their "loss," made a profit at taxpayer's expense, and raised their clients' rates anyway.

10. *The property recovered in anti-fencing operations has ranged from small auto parts to Rembrandt paintings.*

The immediate inclination of the reader to this last of *What Happened's* major findings might well be "So What?" regarding it as but another failure of *What Happened* to disclose detail which would make knowing what happened possible. While *What Happened* gives no information whatsoever on the distribution of type of property purchased, it would, I think, be incorrect to see this last major finding as merely a vague, defensive claim. Rather, I think it is intended to sponsor the impression of the egalitarian impact of sting policing. It seems to claim that stings succeed in serving everybody, rich and poor, recovering both small auto parts and priceless Rembrandts.

Both types of owners deserve to be served, of course. But it is possible that stings tend to work on behalf of one group more than another, and one interpretation of the data in *What Happened* may suggest that it does. *What Happened* reports that 18 sting operations made a total of 4791 transactions in which stolen property or contraband was purchased. They do not report the total amount of buy money expended in all 18 operations, but we do have a total figure for 16 operations from the data in Table 4. If we assume that the average number of transactions in these two additional sting operations were not grossly different from those in Table 4, we can arrive at a rough approximation of mean amount paid by stings per transaction. Using all 16 operations from Table 4, we arrive at a figure of $398 by dividing the total amount of buy money expended in those 16 operations by sixteen-eighteenths of 4791 transactions. Following the same procedure, but excluding operations 15 and 16 which tend to skew the table, our calculations yield an average of $293 in buy money per transaction. Using the lower figure and taking sting policemen at their word in spending an average of 7¢ on the dollar for property purchased, we estimate that the average sting purchase was for property valued in excess of $4000 ($4186). That is quite a few small auto parts.

We must, however, remember that the $293 and $4000 figures are only means and give no indication of the distribution of transactions which compose them. It may be that the median transaction is at or near that level and most buys are for that amount and recover that much stolen property. It may also be that while most transactions are for much smaller amounts, a few big purchases raise the mean substantially and take up an inordinate share of the buy money. If the latter distribution proves to be the case, it might suggest that those who have the most to lose, owners of large quantities of merchandise and single items of great value who now enjoy the benefit of having them bought back for them at public expense, should be the major source of funding for stings in the future. But before they offer their support they would, we think, do well to consider the virtues of holding back their funds—and perhaps the funds of others—in order to force the market for their special kinds of stolen goods still lower than its present 7%.

"You know, my Bloods" (quoth he), that as *Trade* goes at present, you stand but a *queer* Chance; for, when you have made (taken) anything, if you carry it to the *Fencing-Culls* and *Flash Pawnbrokers*, these unconscionable dealers will hardly tip ye a QUARTER OF WHAT ITS WORTH; and if ye offer it to a Stranger its ten to one but you are *hobbled* (arrested). So there's no such Thing as a Man's living by his Labour."

NOTES

1. Gerald Howson, *Thief-Taker General* (London: Hutchison & Company, 1970), 7.

2. Carl Klockars, *The Professional Fence* (New York: The Free Press, 1974).

3. See Carl Klockars, "Field Ethics for the Life History," in Robert Weppner, ed., *Street Ethnography* (Beverly Hills: Sage, 1977).

4. Ron Shaffer, Kevin Klose and Alfred E. Lewis, *Surprise! Surprise!* (New York: Viking, 1977).

5. Marilyn Walsh, *Strategies for Combating the Criminal Receiver of Stolen Goods* (Washington, DC: Government Printing Office, 1976).

6. U.S. Department of Justice, Criminal Conspiracies Division, *Taking the Offensive* (Washington, DC, 1978); and U.S. Department of Justice, Criminal Conspiracies Division, *What Happened* (Washington, DC, 1979).

7. The original R.F.P. for evaluation of sting operations specified that researchers would not be allowed access to projects until six months after they were terminated.

8. The quotation is from a pamphlet which Wild had published in 1718. It was probably the work of a ghost writer and was entitled: *An Answer to a Late Insolent LIBEL, entitled, A Discovery of the Conduct of Receivers and Thief-Takers, in and about the City of LONDON: presumptuously Dedicated to the Lord Mayor, Aldermen and Common Council. Written by C-----s H-----n. Wherein is prov'd in many particular Instances, who is originally the GRAND Thief Taker: that a certain Author is Guilty of more flagrant Crimes, than any Thief Taker [sic] mention'd in his Nonsensical Treatise and that he has highly reflected on the Magistracy of the City, in the said Scandalous Pamphlet. Set forth in several entertaining Stories, Comical Intrigues, merry Adventures, particularly of the M----------l and his Man the Buckle Maker. With a Diverting Scene of a Sodomitish Academy.*

9. Patrick Pringle, *The Thief-Takers* (London: Museum Press, 1958), 21.

10. Jonathan Wild, *An Answer to a Late Insolent Libel* . . . (London: Printed by T. Warner, 1718).

11. The quotation appears in Gerald Howson, *op. cit.,* 1970:67, and is taken from *Select Trials at the Session House in Old Bailey* 1742 ed.

12. Quote taken from George Borrow, *Celebrated Trials* (New York: Payson and Clarke) 519

13. *Ibid,* 519-520.

14. *Ibid.,* 512.

15. Taken from Arthur Hayward, ed., *Lives of the Most Remarkable Criminals* (London: George Routledge and Sons, 1927), 251.

16. See Patrick Pringle, *Hew and Cry* (Great Britain: William Morrow and Co., no date), 34.

17. Hayward, *op. cit.,* 1927: 271-272.

18. Howson, *op. cit.,* 1970: 283.

19. My work has included research in intimating (Klockars, *op. cit.,* 1974) and exposing (Klockars, op. cit., 1977) the fence-informer solution. The following also give evidence in support of the long-standing intimacy between the two occupations: Danny Ahern, *How to Commit a Murder* (New York: Ives Washburn, 1930), 62; John Bowers, "Big City Thieves" in *Harpers Magazine,* Feb., 1967: 50-54; Kellow Chesney, *The Anti-Society: An Account of the Victorian Underworld.* (Boston: Gambit, 1970), 187-189; Charles L. Clark, *Lockstep and Corridor* (Cincinnati: University of Cincinnati Press, 1927), 17-19; Patrick Colquhoun (A Magistrate), *A Treatise on the Police of the Metropolis* (London: Printed for H. Fry for C. Dilley in the Poultry, 1796), 211; Clayton Ettinger, *The Problem of Crime* (New York: Ray Long and Richard R. Smith, Inc., 1923), 33; Jerome Hall, *Theft, Law, and Society,* 2nd Edition (Indianapolis: Bobbs-Merrill, 1952), 199-204; John Bartlow Martin, *My Life in Crime* (New York: Harper and Bros., 1952), 67.

20. Charles Edward Merriam (1929) cites the following report of an experiment with a sting-type operation conducted in connection with the work of the Chicago Crime Commission in the twenties:

At one time during a crime investigation we undertook to study fences or receivers of stolen goods; and among the other devices we set up a shop with various kinds of goods which we undertook to sell to purchasers who understood the goods had been stolen. The investigators came back with a smile of triumph, showing a long list of prospective purchasers and seeming to think they had clinched the case. I laughed and said, "Boys, you have proved too much." Too many were willing to buy. We encountered something nearly approaching a custom.

21. See Peter W. Greenwood et al., *The Criminal Investigation Process* (Santa Monica: The Rand Corporation, 1975), 3 Volumes, viii.

22. See U.S. Department of Justice, Criminal Conspiracies Division, *op. cit.*, 1979: 4-1, 4-4.

23. See Shaffer, Klose, and Lewis, *op. cit.,* 1977.

24. Taken from Howson, *op. cit.,* 1970: 286.

25. U.S. Department of Justice, Criminal Conspiracies Division, *op. cit.,* 1978.

26. U.S. Department of Justice, Criminal Conspiracies Division, *op. cit.,* 1979.

27. *Ibid.,* iii-iv.

28. Statistics taken from William Webster, *Uniform Crime Reports for the United States* (Washington, DC: Federal Bureau of Investigation, 1979), 180-191.

29. U.S. Department of Justice, Criminal Conspiracies Division, *op. cit.,* 1979: 2-12.

30. *Ibid.*

31. *Ibid.,* 2-10.

32. Webster, *op. cit.,* 1977: 216.

33. U.S. Department of Justice, Criminal Conspiracies Division, *op. cit.,* 1979: 3-8.

34. *Ibid.,* 2-4

35. Howson, *op. cit.,* 1970: 127.

36. U.S. Department of Justice, Criminal Conspiracies Division, *op. cit.,* 1979: 4-5.

12

MATRONS AND MOLLS: THE STUDY OF
WOMEN'S PRISON HISTORY

NICOLAS FISCHER HAHN

The recent renaissance of the women's movement has stimulated interest in female deviance—conceptions of it and reactions to it. More specifically, criminal justice researchers and feminist historians are turning attention to the incarceration of women: the creation of institutions designated for females, the kinds of treatment they have provided, and the effects of these institutions on both those institutionalized and the larger society. Over the next 10 years we will probably see the production of a number of studies dealing with the origins and early development of the women's prison system.

In what follows, I attempt to forecast some of the directions which will probably be taken in the study of women's prison history over the next decade and to predict ways in which such studies will prove useful to those concerned with reform of our present system. I begin by reviewing relevant literature in the fields of, first, criminal justice and, second, women's studies. On the basis of these reviews, I then project ways in which we may expect studies in women's prison history to illuminate key current issues in female corrections and, indeed, in corrections as a whole.

THE CRIMINAL JUSTICE LITERATURE

Until quite recently the incarcerated female offender was all but
ignored by criminal justice researchers and commentators—historical penologists, researchers of contemporary penal problems, and legal theorists
alike. Critics of this neglect point out, for example, that "the presumably
comprehensive study of crime and corrections in the United States published in 1967 by the President's Commission on Law Enforcement and
Administration of Justice included no information whatsoever on
women."[1] These critics often trace the origins of this neglect to the
correctional system itself, contending that "the system has been run by
men, primarily for men."[2] This explanation is not entirely satisfactory, for
women's prisons appear to have assumed leading roles in our correctional
system from time to time. But whatever the explanation, it seems undeni-
able that the incarceration of women has been neglected by criminal
justice specialists.

Historians of the penal system, for example, have paid scant attention
to prisons for women. Most histories of our prisons have either ignored
women's institutions or treated them as mere imitators of methods developed in institutions for men.[3] As a result, when information is given on
women's prisons, it is frequently inaccurate. According to the American
Correctional Association, for instance, New York's Bedford Hills Correctional Facility opened in 1933.[4] Now it is true that a new *unit* was
established at Bedford Hills in 1933. But in point of fact this prison for
women, historically one of the most influential prisons in the country,
actually opened in 1901. Similarly, a recent book titled *Women in Prison*
states, "As we know, women's prisons were created as a reform measure in
the 1920's";[5] in fact, at least 15 women's prisons were established before
the 1920s, the first women's reformatory opening in 1873. Rita Simon's
otherwise impressive study, *The Contemporary Woman and Crime*, states
that "Separate prisons were established for women, beginning in the
1880's"; Freda Adler's *Sisters in Crime* has them starting at several
different dates.[6] It is not an exaggeration to say that women in prisons and
prisons for women have almost no history: Little is known about when
such institutions were established; who founded them and under what
circumstances; how they have developed; and how they have affected
other aspects of American penology.

This neglect appears to be unwarranted even if we use traditional
standards for historical importance like leadership and influence: There is

a good deal of evidence to suggest that women's institutions directed by women have frequently been on the cutting edge of correctional reform. The Elmira, New York, men's reformatory is usually cited as the first reformatory for adults. The Indiana Reform Institute for Women opened in 1873, however, four years before Elmira; the Massachusetts Reformatory for Women opened contemporaneously with Elmira in 1877; and one of the earliest proposals for indeterminate sentencing and reformatory treatment was made in 1848 by the matron of the women's division at Sing Sing.[7] During the Progressive era, the most innovative and politically powerful prison administrator in the country was Katherine B. Davis, first superintendent at Bedford Hills and later Commissioner of Correction for New York City. The list of management techniques and reformatory programs first developed in female institutions evidently includes classification according to behavioral criteria, progressive grading, rehabilitative education, and work release. Important aspects of modern corrections, then, appear to have been pioneered in prisons for women, frequently under the direction of women.

Thus the traditional neglect of the history of women's prisons has led to both misinformation about and disparagement of the historical contribution made by these institutions. Another result has been the literature's failure to raise issues which might force us to rethink some of our assumptions about the incarceration process. Examples of such issues are provided, significantly enough, by some of the few studies which have taken a historical approach.

In "Women's Prisons: Laboratories for Penal Reform," Helen E. Gibson "present[s] historical data to show how women's institutions have helped lead the way to penal reform."[8] Gibson's study raises the issue of whether women's prisons have in fact been backwaters, as most of the prison literature assumes. Her data, in combination with other information on women's prisons such as that mentioned above, suggest that these institutions may have sometimes functioned as a testing ground for major innovations in social control which were only later applied in prisons for men. This hypothesis, if confirmed by further research, might significantly alter our understanding of the development of the prison system as a whole.[9]

A second example of the way historical study of the incarceration of women can bring important issues to the surface is provided by W. David Lewis's "The Female Criminal and the Prisons of New York, 1825-1845." Lewis demonstrates that response to the female felon "was heavily influenced by the 'double standard' which nineteenth century Americans used in judging the relative seriousness of moral lapses, depending upon the sex of the offender, and thus illustrates the consequences of an important social attitude."[10] Lewis here raises the issue of whether assumptions about "women's nature" (such as those embodied in the "double standard") may not rather directly affect treatment of incarcerated women.

This leads to a third issue which a women's prison history could help settle: that of sentencing disparities. Have women traditionally received lighter sentences than men, as the criminal justice literature commonly finds?[11] Or has the situation been more complicated, with female property offenders receiving relatively light sentences while female sex offenders were punished with disproportionate harshness? (Some of the recent literature makes this claim.[12]) If in fact there have been patterns of sentencing disparity (between sexes, between types of female offenders, or both), have these affected time actually served? Development of a historical data base on imprisoned women can help us answer such questions as well as stimulate the formation of entirely new hypotheses.

Just as historical penologists have tended to neglect the incarceration of women, so, too, have researchers concerned with "contemporary" problems (regardless of the period to which "contemporary" is applied). *Penology in the United States,* Louis Robinson's classic of 1921, devoted only three pages to women's institutions.[13] Until recently the major work on women's penal institutions was one published in 1931 in Holland— Eugenia C. Lekkerkerker's *Reformatories for Women in the United States.*[14] Studies which *have* dealt with incarcerated women have usually been more interested in discovering the sources of female criminality than the sources of our *assumptions* about female criminality and their effects on treatment.[15]

Recent work has, fortunately, begun to right this imbalance. I have already mentioned Gibson's article of 1973 on the Wisconsin prison for women. A far more substantial contribution will probably soon be made by Claudine Schweber, a professor of criminal justice at State University College at Buffalo who is engaged in long-term research on the first federal prison for women, that established at Alderson, West Virginia, in 1927. To date, Schweber has reported her findings only at conferences, but she has located the inmate records, is studying sentencing patterns as well as demographics, and is formulating and testing some very interesting hypotheses.[16] For example, from the inmate records she is gathering data which permit testing of the old assumption that women are relatively passive criminals, led astray by their more aggressive male partners-in-crime.[17] Schweber's Alderson study, in short, promises to be one of the first to test such assumptions about female criminality and their effects on prison treatment.[18]

Histories of our women's prisons, then, will probably correct misconceptions, challenge old assumptions, help us generate new hypotheses, and provide a better understanding of the origins of contemporary problems. Although the field of criminal justice is only beginning to show an interest in women's prison history, researchers in the area of women's studies have been more alacritous and are already filling gaps in our knowledge. The section which follows reviews some of their work.

THE WOMEN'S STUDIES LITERATURE

Some of the most important research on female deviance is being done by a handful of scholars concerned with women's studies. Their output has been small, but for the most part it is of high quality, usually taking the form of close, methodologically sophisticated studies of specific institutions or localized social control movements. These women's historians have been developing detailed data on particular reform efforts and working from there toward theory; their theory, however, is kept closely tied to the specific historical situation under consideration.

Although some of these studies have focused on juvenile rather than adult female deviance, these, too, are relevant to the history of women's prisons. Brenzel's "Lancaster [Massachusetts] Industrial School for Girls: A Social Portrait of a Nineteenth Century Reform School for Girls," the first full-length study of a female institution, provides a useful model for work of this type.[19] Broader in scope is "The Crime of Precocious Sexuality: Female Juvenile Delinquency in the Progressive Era" by Schlossman and Wallach. This article observes that "during the Progressive era female juvenile delinquents often received more severe punishments than males, even though boys usually were charged with more serious crimes,"[20] and it explains this relatively harsh treatment in terms of social ideologies which also affected adult female prisoners: Progressives' preoccupation with eugenic solutions to social problems and their "social purity" movement.

One recent history of female deviance does deal with women's prisons— a doctoral dissertation by Estelle B. Freedman, "Their Sister's Keepers: The Origins of Female Corrections in America."[21] Covering the period from midnineteenth century to World War I, Freedman concentrates on the founding of the first entirely independent institutions for women, in Indiana, Massachusetts, and New York. She concludes that:

> Although the separate prisons did not succeed in converting the fallen or in rehabilitating criminals for productive roles, they did provide a base for the emancipation of the keepers. The reformers had defied the norms of female behavior by gaining control over their own institutions and carving out a new professional realm for their sex. Such was the mixed record of women's prison reform: for the fallen, retraining as traditional females; for the keepers, transcendance [sic] of women's roles and entry into public and professional careers.[22]

As this conclusion shows, Freedman's treatment includes study of the effects of the first women's prisons on the broader society, particularly their effects on the social roles of women of different classes.

A more general source of relevant information is the work being done by women's historians on conceptions of "woman's nature": studies such as Welter's "The Cult of True Womanhood: 1820-1860" and Rosenberg's "In Search of Woman's Nature, 1850-1920."[23] These provide highly useful background material for research on the incarceration of women by analyzing the intellectual and social contexts in which specific theories of female criminality and its treatment were generated. These studies, in other words, are establishing the norms against which deviation was measured. Similar studies are coming out of the deviance section of the annual meetings of the Berkshire Conference on the History of Women. Few of the "woman's nature" studies, however, bridge the gap between concepts of female deviance and actual punishment practices; they emphasize intellectual and social history at the expense of institutional history which might inform us about the impact of theory on treatment.[24]

Historians concerned with female deviance are making significant forays into hitherto unexplored territory. Much of their material will contribute to the study of the roots and development of the women's prison system as a whole. Historians of women's prisons, in turn, will probably aid some of these scholars by establishing a general context for their studies of particular social control movements; they may aid others by exploring links between theory of female deviance and its treatment.

RESOURCES: THE UNTAPPED POTENTIAL

Primary resources for the study of women's prison history are extensive and very nearly untapped. Among the most important are the reports produced annually or biennially by the institutions and usually printed in the states' public document series. Almost as valuable are the official reports of supervisory bodies such as prison commissions or boards of charity. Official reports, of course, cannot be trusted to tell the whole truth or even to provide accurate counts of prisoners. There are, however, ways to test and supplement them. Serious disturbances within a prison, for example, sometimes led to appointment of investigating committees, bodies which reported independently. Prisoner records can be used to confirm or correct statistics given in official reports. Court documents and the papers of private prison reform groups such as the Prison Association of New York also provide tools for probing the accuracy of official reports.

As for those most intimately associated with women's prisons—the matrons and their charges—documents remain by which we may, in many cases, learn about them as individuals and in interaction with each other. Many of these materials can be found in state archives and in the historical records retained by departments of correction. Others are autobiographical and biographical, and in a wealth of instances, the prison matrons themselves published works on crime, its treatment, and prison administration.[25]

Over the next decade, I expect, researchers will explore these resources with some thoroughness. Their studies of women's prison history will establish an empirical foundation for theory about the punishment of women. These studies will also clarify the role played by female institutions in the development of our prison system as a whole. Finally, by uncovering roots of the current correctional system, these studies in women's prison history should lead us to a better understanding of, and perhaps more intelligent solutions to, problems faced by the women's prison system today.

NOTES

1. Linda R. Singer, "Women and the Correctional Process," *American Criminal Law Review* 11 (Winter 1973), 295.

2. Ibid. Singer reviews the literature and states the argument in full, pp. 295-296. Also see Marlene C. McGuirl, " 'The Forgotten Population': Women in Prison," *U.S. Library of Congress Quarterly Journal* 32(4), (1975), 338-345, and Ray R. Price, "The Forgotten Female Offender," *Crime & Delinquency* 23 (2), (April 1977), 101-108.

3. See, for example, Blake McKelvey, *American Prisons: A Study in American Social History Prior to 1915* (Chicago: University of Chicago Press, 1936).

4. American Correctional Association, *Directory,* 1975-1976 Edition (College Park, MD: Author, no date), 77.

5. Kathryn Watterson Burkhart, *Women in Prison* (Garden City, NY: Doubleday, 1973), 366.

6. Rita James Simon, *The Contemporary Woman and Crime* (Rockville, MD: National Institute of Mental Health, 1975), 69; Freda Adler, *Sisters in Crime: The Rise of the New Female Criminal* (New York: McGraw-Hill, 1975), 174, 231.

7. New York Inspectors of State Prisons, *Annual Report, 1848* (Sen. Doc. No. 30, 1849), 240.

8. Helen E. Gibson, "Women's Prisons: Laboratories for Penal Reform," in Laura Crites, ed., *The Female Offender* (Lexington, MA: Lexington Books, 1976), 93.

9. Juvenile institutions seem also to have been a locus for experimentation; evidently children and women were viewed as more malleable than men and thus more susceptible to reformatory treatments.

10. W. David Lewis, "The Female Criminal and the Prisons of New York, 1825-1845," *New York History* 42(3), (1961), 215.

11. See, for example, Ruth M. Glick and Virginia V. Neto, *National Study of Women's Correctional Programs* (Washington, DC: National Institute of Law Enforcement and Criminal Justice, LEAA, 1977), 141 (finding that violent female offenders receive more lenient sentences than violent male offenders) and W. David Lewis, *From Newgate to Dannemora: The Rise of the Penitentiary in New York, 1796-1848* (Ithaca, NY: Cornell University Press, 1965), 158-159 (on more lenient sentencing of females in the early nineteenth century).

12. Dorie Klein, "The Etiology of Female Crime: A Review of the Literature," in Laura Crites, ed., *The Female Offender* (Lexington, MA: Lexington Books, 1976), 5-31; Meda Chesney-Lind, "Judicial Enforcement of the Female Sex-Role: The Family Court and the Female Delinquent," *Issues in Criminology* 8 (Fall 1973),

51-69; Meda Chesney-Lind, "Judicial Paternalism and the Female Status Offender: Training Women To Know Their Place," *Crime & Delinquency* 23(2), (April 1977), 121-130.

13. Louis N. Robinson, *Penology in the United States* (Philadelphia: John C. Winston, 1921).

14. Eugenia Cornelia Lekkerkerker, *Reformatories for Women in the United States* (Batavia, Holland: Bij J.B. Wolters' Uitgevers-Maatschappij, 1931).

15. See, for example, Mabel Ruth Fernald, Mary H.S. Hayes, and Almena Dawley, *A Study of Women Delinquents in New York State* (New York: Century Co., 1920); Sheldon Glueck and Eleanor T. Glueck, *Five Hundred Delinquent Women* (New York: Knopf, 1934); Cesare Lombroso and William Ferrero, *Female Offender* (New York: Philosophical Library, 1958); Edith R. Spaulding, *An Experimental Study of Psychopathic Delinquent Women* (New York: Bureau of Social Hygiene, 1923).

16. Claudine Schweber, "Pioneers in Prison: Inmates and Administrators during the Founding Years of the Federal Reformatory for Women at Alderson, West Virginia, 1925-1930," presented at the American Historical Association, San Francisco, December 1978, and "Women and Federal Crime in the Early Twentieth Century," paper submitted to National Archives for publication in *The Law and American Society: New Historical Perspectives and Resources*, 1978.

17. So far, Schweber has found that about one-third of the early Alderson inmates had male codefendants; however, she also finds that the women could not have been unaware of the illegality of their own behavior.

18. For another effort to trace the effects of assumptions about female criminality on the punishment of women, see Nicolas F. Hahn, "Too Dumb To Know Better: Cacogenic Family Studies and the Criminology of Women," *Criminology* 18 (May 1980), 3-25.

19. Barbara Brenzel, "Lancaster Industrial School for Girls: A Social Portrait of a Nineteenth Century Reform School for Girls," *Feminist Studies* 3 (Fall 1975), 40-53.

20. Steven Schlossman and Stephanie Wallach, "The Crime of Precocious Sexuality: Female Juvenile Delinquency in the Progressive Era," *Harvard Education Review* 48(1), (February 1978), 65.

21. Estelle B. Freedman, "Their Sisters' Keepers: The Origins of Female Corrections in America" (Ph.D. dissertation, Columbia University, 1976; forthcoming, University of Michigan Press).

22. Freedman, "Their Sisters' Keepers," 3.

23. Barbara Welter, "The Cult of True Womanhood: 1820-1860," *American Quarterly* 18 (Summer 1966), 150-164; Rosalind Rosenberg, "In Search of Woman's Nature, 1850-1920," *Feminist Studies* 3 (1&2), (Fall 1975), 141-154. Also see Rosalind Rosenberg, "The Dissent From Darwin, 1890-1930: The New View of Woman Among American Social Scientists" (Ph.D. dissertation, Stanford University, 1974).

24. Some recent works on the punishment of women which have appeared outside the women's studies area also suffer from this problem; see, for example, "Punishing Women," Chapter 23 in G.J. Barker-Benfield, *The Horrors of the Half-Known Life: Male Attitudes Toward Women and Sexuality in Nineteenth-Century America* (New York; Harper & Row, 1976), and "Punishment and Obedience: Punishing Women, Children, Slaves, and Soldiers," Chapter 4 in Graeme Newman, *The Punishment Response* (New York: J.B. Lippincott Company, 1978).

25. For example, Katherine Bement Davis, "Treatment of the Female Offender," New York State Board of Charities, *Annual Report 1906*, 785-790; Eliza W. Farnham, Notes and Illustrations to Marmaduke B. Sampson, *Rationale of Crime and Its Appropriate Treatment* (New York: D. Appleton & Company, 1846); Ellen C. Johnson, "Discipline in Female Prisons," National Prison Association, *Proceedings 1891*, 137-143.

13

FOR THE GOOD OF ALL: THE PROGRESSIVE
TRADITION IN PRISON REFORM

DAVID J. ROTHMAN

In criminal justice, as in so many other areas of American life, the Progressive era marked a major dividing point. Reformers in the opening decades of the twentieth century not only broke with inhereited traditions but also set out an agenda for social and economic change that would dominate through the 1950s. They established both the means and the ends for a liberal social policy, the tactics and the goals that enlightened and benevolent-minded citizens were to pursue. Hence, this period has a particular fascination for the historian of criminal justice as well as for social policy analysts. To the historian, Progressivism represents a critical moment in modernization, when the nineteenth century gave way to the twentieth in substantive terms. To the policy analysts, it stands for the origins of all that we are in revolt against today. From prisons to mental hospitals to schools, the Progressive platform is under current attack. Critics may be less certain of where to move, but they do agree on what they wish to avoid.

Nowhere do these generalizations hold more force than in criminal justice. It was the Progressives, for example, that enacted probation and parole statutes; they invented the juvenile court and offered a new model for prisons and juvenile reformatories. Looking at their programs from the perspective of the nineteenth century, the Progressives were the successors to the Jacksonians, in the sense that they created the second grand design for the criminal justice system. Looking back at them from a contemporary vantage point, it is obvious that every one of their innovations is now highly controversial. Parole is under sustained attack and has been or is about to be abolished in several jurisdictions. The juvenile court has lost most of its appeal, so that for constitutional reasons and for reasons of fairness its traditional authority has been restricted. And in ways that this essay will attempt to clarify, the prison, too, has lost the legitimacy that Progressives gave it. In terms of sentencing practices and internal routine, dissatisfaction with Progressive models is widespread.

PROGRESSIVE PLATFORM FOR PRISON REFORM

The Progressive platform for prison reform can be summarized rather succinctly. First, these reformers were convinced that prisons could fulfill both a custodial and a rehabilitative function. There was no intrinsic conflict between guarding men securely and making them better men, between incapacitation and reformation. The guard and the inmate had an identity of interests. As one Progressive prison warden put it: "The basis of our whole social philosophy here must be that the staff and the inmates will cooperate for the good of all. I cannot see even a small wedge driven between the two if we are to build and educate men in the right social attitudes."[1]

All the Progressive innovation in the field of criminal justice expressed this judgment. Probation and parole presupposed that surveillance and assistance could join together, that the roles of counselor and police officer were identical. Let the probation officer always bear in mind," one of the program's leading advocates told his colleagues, "that he is not only a social worker, but that he is also an officer of the court and the state." The therapeutic and police functions, however, were not in opposition. "He need not worry, he will still help the prisoner. . . . For the great social discovery of these days . . . is just this: The interest of the prisoner and the interest of the state are, in fact, identical; the best service to one is also the best service to the other."[2]

This premise was equally relevant to the juvenile court. "Its great discovery," in the words of another reformer, was that "individual welfare coincided with the well-being of the state. Humanitarian and social considerations thus recommend one and the same procedure." The court could simultaneously and without contradiction promote "sympathy, justice and even the self interest of society."[3] And the judge who decided that a delinquent should be sentenced to a training school was not elevating the safety of the community over the welfare of the child. To incarcerate the young, as the most important decision upholding the constitutionality of the juvenile court ruled, was not to deprive them of their liberty but to exercise "the wholesome restraint which a parent exercises over his child. . . . No constitutional right is violated but one of the most important duties which organized society owes to its helpless members is performed."[4]

Following upon this principle, it seemed necessary and right to expand the discretionary authority of the principal actors in criminal justice. As the favorite slogan of Progressive reformers put it: "Treat the criminal, not the crime"; and that phrase contained not only a special view of the deviant but also a special perspective on the authority of criminal justice officials. The system had to be responsive not to the act of the criminal (the traditional, Jacksonian orientation) but to the criminal himself, his state of being, his motivation, his personality. As Progressives explained, the criminal act was merely symptomatic of some more fundamental and underlying problem and it was the task of the criminal justice system to get to the root of the cause, that is, to the character of the criminal himself. Progressives, it is true, did not agree on where to look in order to understand that character. To some, particularly in the pre-1920 period, the origins of deviant behavior were located in a faulty environment, more specifically, in the disorganization of slum life; to others, whose views became increasingly popular after 1910 and dominated after 1920, the sources of deviant behavior were to be found in the psychological make-up of the deviant; he was, in a word, maladjusted, and it was the duty of criminal justice to adapt him to his society. Still, whatever the interpretation, environmental or psychological, both schools agreed wholeheartedly on the need to explore in depth the state of the criminal himself, not just to examine what he had actually done. Accordingly, criminal justice officials required vast discretionary authority. Only by giving them wide latitude would it be possible to move from punishing the criminal to treating and rehabilitating him.[5]

To Progressives, this formulation seemed so much superior to inherited practices (or, more accurately, what they defined as inherited practices) that they were remarkably confident of the wisdom of their program. From their perspective, the alternative to treatment was vengeance, a motive which might have been acceptable in more primitive societies but certainly had no place in their own. Moreover, when justice represented nothing more than the infliction of punishment, the offender would inevitably repeat his crime; he was likely to come out of prison embittered and ready to seek his retribution. A treatment orientation, on the other hand, was far more humane and effective. To make this point, Progressives delighted in using a rhetoric of medical treatment, offering analogies drawn from medicine. In criminal justice, as with disease, the purpose of intervention should be to cure; and just as doctors enjoyed wide discretion in treating and releasing patients, so, too, criminal justice officials should enjoy similar prerogatives with the deviant.

From these postulates, Progressives proceeded to draw up a novel design for the prison system. Although they were eager to treat some offenders in a community setting (through probation), they did not doubt for a moment that prisons would remain integral, even central, to criminal justice. And this belief did not disturb them. To the contrary, they were convinced that they could alter the prisons in keeping with Progressive principles; they could turn the prison into a reformatory. They would simultaneously hold men against their will and cure them.

This confidence reflected Progressives' faith in two new models that they believed would fundamentally change the character of the prison. These two models were not necessarily consistent, but Progressives did not dally with this point. Rather, each of the models stood in opposition to Jacksonian routines and promised to fulfill the Progressive aims. First, Progressives were certain of the desirability and possibility of having the community serve as a model for the prison—a reversal, if you will, of the Jacksonian notion that the prison ought to serve as a model for the society. The prison routine, according to Progressives, was to be as close as possible to that of the normal society, and in this way its organization would prepare inmates for life in the normal society. It was absurd to force men to live in silence or to march in lock step when the ultimate purpose of prison life should be to prepare them for reentry into the community. It was ridiculous to cut them off from intercourse with the outside community when the point was to be training them to become lawful members of society. No Progressive spokesman made the case for this position more forcefully than Thomas Osborne, and his eagerness to bring sports, exercise, social occasions, movies, and even self-rule inside the prisons represented the goal of all Progressive reformers.[6]

At the same time, another design attracted the Progressives, a model of the prison as hospital. Those who were convinced of the psychological (as opposed to environmental) causes of deviancy felt especially comfortable with this scheme. For them, the prison was to institute classification schemes, employ psychologists and psychiatrists to diagnose and treat the various types of criminals, and establish the individual programs that would be rehabilitative for each of them. Reformers devoted enormous attention to devising taxonomies for criminals. They distinguished between "socially adaptable" and "socially unadaptable" offenders or between "situational cases" ("the man whose circumstances and situation are at the bottom of his difficulties") and "asocial cases" ("the men who believed in belonging to the gang who are going to get theirs by hook or crook").[7] Ostensibly, by adhering to such a classification scheme, the prison would respond to each criminal in a particular and relevant fashion and thus promote rehabilitation.

To the Progressives, both models justified a sentencing system that was open-ended and indeterminate. By making the prison into a community, officials would have at hand a predictable index as to how the inmate would behave after release. The good prisoner would be the good citizen; the inmate who obeyed prison rules would obey community rules. By the same token, the prison as hospital meant that highly skilled professionals would be able to predict with some degree of confidence how an inmate would behave upon release. Just as the doctor knew when the sick patient was cured and thus ready to be discharged, so the psychologist would know when the sick criminal was cured and ready to go free. Accordingly, sentences that did not specify the moment of release, a change from flat time to indeterminate time, seemed more appropriate. Ideally, the judge should sentence an offender to a term of "one day to life"; that failing, sentences that, for example, set terms between 2 and 10 years were appropriate—with administrators (here the parole board) deciding the precise moment of release. Thus, whatever else may be said of it, the Progressive agenda for prison reform was internally consistent, each of its pieces fitting well together. One moved logically and inevitably from premise to program with a sure sense of the possibilities for improving the prison system, and even more, the possibility of controlling if not eradicating crime.[8]

LIMITATIONS OF THE PROGRESSIVE PLATFORM

However attractive the model in its formulation, actuality was far different. No sooner does one move to examine the realities of prison life from 1900 through the 1950s than one discovers the incredible gap that separated rhetoric from performance. Yes, the Progressive principles did have some bearing on the daily prison routine. Over these years, prison bands, commissaries, freedom of the yard, movies, radios, and abolition of rules of silence and lock step were all implemented in one or another jurisdiction; and many prisons did institute classification systems and hire psychologists for their staffs. But nowhere—and this sweeping generalization is valid—were prisons able to become normal communities or hospitals. There is no need to belabor the point here; all of the failings of prisons need not be recited. Suffice it to say that substituting baggy grey pants for stripes did not make for a normal community; nor did placing one psychologist on a staff to serve 3000 inmates constitute meaningful treatment. Instead, it is more important to examine the causes of failure, to understand the dynamics that undercut the reform effort.

The list of problems is certainly a long one. The disparity between rhetoric and reality is so great that there is no shortage of places to heap blame. It is clear that part of the difficulty in implementing the reform program had to do with stingy legislatures: They were unwilling to give prisons appropriations large enough to hire personnel; so too, prison personnel were woefully undertrained to undertake anything as complicated as rehabilitation—and one can point either to shortages of funds or shortages of available personnel to account for the failure. It is also clear that social science theory and psychological theory could not keep up with ideological ambitions. It was one thing to be eager to cure the criminal, quite another to have at hand a medicine with which to carry out the task. The classification systems were generally no more than descriptive categories. These labels did not manage to provide guidelines for treatment, let alone clues as to how prison officials might begin to cope with the deviant.[9] But the matter goes even deeper, reflecting not just upon administrative failure of one sort or another but also casting doubt upon the very premises of Progressive reform. Indeed, to the degree that observers can now analyze and agree upon the causes of failures, current policies in criminal justice will have some significant lessons to learn.

The critical issue involves the Progressives' first principle: the commitment to guard and help, to incapacitate and rehabilitate. As we shall immediately see, a historical analysis that pursues this matter poses an even more fundamental question. Is it possible to guard in a humane way? Can a prison *system* step short of cruel and unusual punishment? The answer to both these queries may well be no. Let us address first the easier of the two issues. With some confidence the historian can conclude that among the most important failures of the Progressive design was the fact that the needs of custody again and again undercut the reform program. The Progressive attempt to make prisons into places of treatment, into normal settings, ran up against the need to hold men securely, to administer a system that was escape-proof, that did the job of incapacitation. Evidence for this statement abounds. Almost without exception, prison wardens were qualified only to administer a custodial program. Recruitment ran from police work to prison work. So, too, employment in other prison posts, from the assistant warden to the rank and file guards, followed this identical pattern. Practically no training programs existed for any prison staff, but what few efforts were made involved exclusively the use of firearms and the maintenance of discipline. Further, the rules and regulations of prison life looked exclusively to custody, to preventing riots and escape, to holding prisoners securely. However staunchly Progressives might urge making a prison like the community, when it came to internal discipline there was no room for justice—security was the first and last concern. Not only were the rule-books absurd in the scope of behavior that they regulated ("Banish from your mind all evil thoughts," well represents their tenor), but they never allowed for anything approximating due process procedures before punishment was inflicted—such stipulations might, after all, undermine prison security. In a similar spirit, prison rules did not allow guards to do anything except guard the inmates. Fearful that guards might conspire with convicts, officials preferred to enlarge the distance between them. As one national survey of prison conditions in the 1930s concluded: "Either guards are not trusted to understand the prisoners with whom they deal or are not expected to do so. In any case, the highest hope expressed, that the prison 'intends their reformation, if possible' seems rather remote."[10]

It is also apparent that through the first half of the twentieth century, prisons were places of pervasive brutality. Wardens used the new privileges introduced into the routine to the end of discipline. They would deprive a disobedient inmate of freedom of the yard, or the use of the commissary; and they, like their predecessors, would deprive inmates of "good time." But punishments did not stop here; physical punishments were pervasive, even in disregard of the many public statutes that outlawed corporal punishment for inmates. It is true that twentieth century prisons frequently substituted solitary confinement for physical punishment. It is not at all clear, however, that solitary, as actually administered in these decades (with a total deprivation of all comforts, most sanitary facilities, and food) was less brutal than the whip. Even more important, solitary did not serve to outlaw the whip but rather, for the difficult case, solitary came first and then the whip.

Surviving documents do not allow historians to produce quantitative measurement of punishment. Prisons, like southern plantations, either did not keep records or kept untrustworthy records of the exercise of punishment. More than one investigatory body was frustrated by the fact that "the method of discipline is the most difficult thing to cover because the prison officials are sensitive about it and the prisoners are intimidated from testifying." Nevertheless, it is not difficult to come to the conclusion that punishment not only undercut a rehabilitative effort but also was altogether cruel.

It is useful to review one incident in detail, not because it offers a clue to the extent of punishment, but because it clarifies the dynamics at work in prison punishment.[11] In the spring of 1939, 41 inmates in San Quentin went on a hunger strike in order to protest the institution's food; they refused to enter the mess hall or to go to work. The principal keeper immediately confined them to solitary, and what happened to them there became the subject of an investigation. First, the San Quentin Prison Board conducted closed hearings on the incident and found no one guard guilty of brutality; the state prison director, however, reopened the case, and in the fall of that year the governor took his own testimony. No one actually disagreed on the facts of the case. A number of the strikers were removed from their cells, forced to stand in a circle 22 inches wide, and those who refused to follow this order were beaten. And no one denied that California's constitution prohibited corporal punishment for inmates. But then how had such a violation occurred and why had the board not taken corrective action?

The defense that the guard and board members offered is significant as a presentation of a line of argument that they believed to be creditable and legitimate. Without such harsh action, the Board insisted, San Quentin would have become a "circus prison." To dismiss any of the guards who beat the inmates would "not only shatter the morale of every reformatory in California, but will undermine the discipline of every prison in the United States." And the guard responsible for the beatings was equally adamant in making this point. Had the troublemakers not been beaten, "it would have encouraged others to have done the same thing until there would have been a general disregard of the rules." For him the issue was simple: "Was the prison to be run by the warden or by the prisoners?"

Indeed, the attorney for the board and the guard protested the fact that the governor was holding the meeting. The board and its officials "had complete jurisdiction" over prison affairs and no one had the right to second-guess them. "There is no authority by which you can limit the amount or the severity of the punishment, provided the circumstances in the original instance required it or justified it." Such a notion as cruel or unusual punishment had no meaning within a prison. Everything depended upon the amount of provocation and the force needed to maintain control.

To substantiate these views, the guard in charge of solitary, one Lewis, explained why the punishment escalated. A back-up sanction was always required within a prison. If one penalty did not work, a tougher one had to come next—and this was always the case. When Lewis had arrived at San Quentin, solitary was too lax. "It had been a failure . . . the men had no further fear of solitary. . . . The men would lay back in there; they would talk and laugh and raise all the trouble that they cared to . . . solitary to them was a joke." As Lewis took charge, the warden's only instructions were "to keep order in solitary." So first he instituted a rule of silence; then he took away reading materials, and next, the right to smoke; still "they didn't mind solitary" so he "pinched down a little harder." He prohibited the men from sitting on their beds during the day. "But I still found that some men would stay in there week after week." So he came up with something new: drawing a 22-inch circle on the floor and having the inmates stand in it for five hours a day, without moving—"They were made to stand all in one [way]—facing in one direction."

These procedures, adequate for the ordinary circumstances, were insufficient for the extraordinary one. When the San Quentin strikers sent to solitary refused to enter the circle, the only option left was to whip them. In other words, the circle, too, required a back-up sanction, that is, corporal punishment. Accordingly, Lewis beat them until they would stand on the spots. "If I had failed for one minute down there, we would have had rioting and bloodshed in San Quentin." The board completely concurred. As one member declared: "I think that any restraint that the guards administered to the prisoners to the point of compelling them to obey the rules is justified, in that no prison can be conducted otherwise."

Other investigations of prison discipline in the 1920s and 1930s confirmed the typicality of this experience. The Kentucky penitentiary cuffed troublesome inmates to cell doors; in Rhode Island, unruly convicts were cuffed by one arm to a ring in the wall. Jackson, Michigan, put men in cages so constructed that the victim had to stand upright, unable so much as to turn around.[12] The critical point, however, is not to multiply illustrations of cruel and unusual punishments, but to understand the dynamic that led to their invention and use. Discipline had to be maintained and so if milder forms of correction did not work, harsher ones had to be employed, and the process of escalation had an inevitability about it. If solitary was not sufficient to compel obedience, then corporal punishment had to follow, or else the prison would become a circus. Without embarrassment, prison officials were prepared to act upon and defend publicly the notion that "there is no authority by which you can limit the amount or the severity of the punishment, provided the circumstances in the original instance required it or justified it." And with this pronouncement we come to the essence of prison administration: to the need, first and last, to keep order, a need which simply did not allow a system, even had the technology been available, to implement a rehabilitative program.

Rather than offer further examples to confirm this point, let us here explore a rather intriguing sort of confirmatory evidence. The 1930s was a period in which prison movies enjoyed unprecedented popularity. In fact, Americans took their image of the prison life from these films and the image was, on the whole, accurate. (For example, one favorite film technique was to spin a newspaper around and then rest on its headline, "Parolee commits. . . ." The scene would then move to a very dour looking parole board meeting, an image which conveyed just how much the parole board became the point of criticism for coddling the criminal.) Nevertheless, prison movies presented their directors with a very special problem. It was essential that the movie have a hero, and since wardens and guards were not generally considered to be fit characters for heroes, it was a prisoner that had to have the part. Getting the hero into prison was not very difficult—he could either be set up and unfairly take the blame for others or he could have wandered off the true path, made one fatal misstep, and thus ended up inside. The difficulty was that since the movies were accurate, it was obvious to all who watched it that prison life was anything but rehabilitative; indeed, whatever the public might hear from reformers, clearly prison life was miserable. Just how grim conditions were became all the more apparent to the movie watchers because they were, perforce, observing the prison through the eyes of the hero-inmate.

The movie makers obviously had not intended to produce films which were distinctly antiinstitutional, and, therefore, they somehow had to correct this impression, in other words, to justify the grim conditions of the prison. They reached a common formula to accomplish this feat: in the middle of the movie, without any preparation or warning, they staged a prison break; the escape was carried out by desperate, animallike men who would stop at nothing. This scene served the movie makers well in two distinct ways. First, it allowed them to have their hero foil the escape, show his true colors, and be rewarded with release. The escape, in other words, gave them a way to get their hero out of prison. But it also served a second function. With the escape foiled, the hero and the warden would engage in a brief dialogue to the effect that the prison was filled with desperate men who would stop at nothing to escape. In fact, when the plot to escape was foiled, its leader would, like a savage beast, bring about his own death by leaping from the wall or choosing to run for it although gunfire was all around him. And so the hero and the warden would acknowledge that although prisons were terrible places, there really was no element of choice here—given the needs of custody, the institution could organize itself in no other way. The inmates had to be incapacitated at all costs—and the prison routine had to satisfy this need. In sum, in the film as in real life, the need of custody took first place. Everything had to be forgiven in the name of security.

This statement brings us to the second and much more difficult problem: On the basis of this historical record, what conclusions may be drawn for present-day policy analysts? To frame the issue more specifically, on the basis of an understanding of this dynamic, is it appropriate to conclude that all programs in criminal justice that simultaneously attempt to confine and to help are doomed to fail? Indeed, is it right to insist that policies which suppose that a humane system of incarceration is possible may well be mistaken?

At the very least, the historical record does reallocate the burden of justification. Anyone who would propose that he is capable of administering a system that is at once corrective and rehabilitative, or anyone who would suggest that he is capable of administering a humane prison system, does have the obligation to answer a series of queries. It is for him to defend his position—he must bear the burden of proof. Not only must he explain how he will recruit a trained staff to his program but also he must tell us how will his system handle questions of boundary maintenance. What will prevent his design from degenerating as it moves from sanction to back-up sanction?

It is entirely possible for innovators to insist that they will choose their inmates carefully, and if they are wrong in any one given instance, they

will simply dispatch the intractable sort to a more secure, less rehabilitative setting. But then several observations become in order. First, this
degree of honesty would be refreshing, for then we would know that any
successes that the new program enjoyed had at least as much to do with
the selectivity of the inmates as with the techniques employed. We would
be well aware from the outset that the program only worked with a group
of already cooperative prisoners and, thus, we would understand that the
system had only limited, not general, applicability. Second, we would also
recognize that although it might be possible to administer one decent
institution, that institution would depend, necessarily, upon the presence
of a less desirable back-up. Yes, prison A might be able to reduce its
custodial needs, but only by relying upon the security of prison B. One
can tamper with a single and distinct element in the system, not with the
system as a whole.

It may be appropriate (and the tentative language is purposeful) to
move even beyond this position in order to suggest that not only is the
burden of proof shifted onto the innovator but also that he has an
extraordinary difficult presumption to overcome: without a most compelling justification, we remain suspect not only about the ability to deliver
rehabilitation but also the ability to maintain a humane level of custody.
This point is particularly relevant at this moment because it has become
popular to argue that strictly custodial prisons, which do not depend upon
the rationale of rehabilitation, can serve incapacitative purposes, and serve
them decently.[13] While a rationale of incapacitation may be more honest
than a rehabilitative one, it does lend the impression that one can hold the
inmate and not do harm, that confinement and decency throughout *all*
sectors of an incarcerative system can be achieved. To those who would
hold to such a position, who would promote incapacitation as a legitimate
purpose and justify incarceration through it, the issue of responding to the
difficult case, the escalation of sanctions, is no less pressing. They, too, are
duty bound to explain how they can administer a system of incarceration
that is not cruel. Otherwise, we will have to make a calculation that they
do not suggest: Is so much incarceration worth so much brutality?

SOME POLICY IMPLICATIONS

To the degree that one is persuaded of the validity of the dynamic
described here, then a series of policy statements become appropriate.

Since the historical record does not suggest alternatives to incarceration, and since to date there is a marked scarcity of suggestions as to how punishment of serious offenders can be carried out without incarceration, this analysis does not lead to an abolitionist position, to breaking down the prison walls once and for all. But it does point to other less dramatic but no less important conclusions. First, given the intrinsic character of the system, it would seem not only fair but also wise to begin to dispense sentence time in spoonfuls (more like Holland and Denmark), than in bucketfuls, which has characterized American sentencing practices from the nineteenth century to the present. Second, the doubtful cases should be excluded from an incarcerative sanction. Wherever possible, offenders should be spared incapacitation because of its uncontrollable excesses. Third, this approach would place a new premium on imaginative solutions to the problems of crime, so that we would be far more prepared than we are now to experiment with alternatives. At the moment such experimentation seems incidental to the system, the work of a reformer here or there. The effort should be mainstream, one of the first obligations of criminal justice administrators.

It may not be possible in this society to abolish altogether a system of incarceration. However, it may be possible to resort to it less frequently, to use it for fewer people, and for shorter times. If the historical record moved twentieth century punishment in that direction, it would have made a major contribution to promoting decency in criminal justice.

NOTES

1. Howard Gill quoted in the Norfolk Diary, Bureau of Social Hygiene Collection, Rockefeller Foundation Archives, entry of November 21, 1933, p. 587.

2. National Probation Association, *Annual Report for 1926,* p. 31.

3. *Survey* 22 (1910), p. 607.

4. *Commonwealth v. Ames,* 213 Penna., 48 (1905).

5. See chapter two of David J. Rothman, *Conscience and Convenience* (Boston: Little, Brown, 1980) for an elaboration of this argument.

6. Thomas Osborne, *Society and Prisons* (New Haven, CT: Yale University Press, 1916) and Julia Jaffrey, ed., *The Prison and Prisoners* (Boston, 1917), *passim.*

7. U.S. Attorney General, *Survey of Release Procedures: Prisons,* pp. 156-157.

8. Warren Spaulding, "The Treatment of Crime," *Journal of Criminal Law and Criminology* 3 (1912-1913), p. 378-381; Charlton Lewis, "The Indeterminate Sentence," National Prison Association, *Proceedings . . . 1900,* p. 175.

9. National Commission on Law Observance and Enforcement, *Penal Institutions* . . . (Washington, DC: Government Printing Office, 1931), p. 61.

10. *Ibid.,* pp. 43-47; Attorney General, *Survey,* pp. 69-70.

11. See "Hearings, Proceedings, Charges," by John G. Clark, Director of Penology, against the California State Board of Prisons Director, before Culbert L. Olson, Governor, November 3-9, 1939, in the California State Archives, Sacramento.

12. National Commission, *Penal Institutions,* pp. 29-30; Attorney General, *Survey,* pp. 122-123, 126-127.

13. See, for example, Andrew Von Hirsch, *Doing Justice* (New York, 1976) and Norval Morris, *The Fugure of Imprisonment* (Chicago, 1974).

ABOUT THE AUTHORS

THOMAS J. DUESTERBERG taught most recently in the Department of History at Stanford University. His dissertation treated the subject of "Criminology and the Social Order in Nineteenth-Century France," and he has published an article on "The Origins of Criminology in France" in a recent volume sponsored by the Academy of Criminal Justice Sciences. He has also presented papers to the annual meetings of the Academy for the past two years.

CHARLES E. FAUPEL is a research associate in the Division of Criminal Justice, University of Delaware. Mr. Faupel is a candidate for the Ph.D. degree at the University of Delaware. His current research is in the area of drug abuse, with particular focus on the relationship between heroin use and street crime. Prior to his current activity in drug research, he has researched and published in the area of disaster and disaster response.

THEODORE N. FERDINAND is Professor of Sociology at Northeastern University. He has received LEAA grants to study the Illinois Youth Center-Geneva (an institution for delinquent girls) and to study the Boston courts between 1814 and 1850. His extensive publications on juvenile delinquency include *Typologies of Delinquency* (New York: Random House, 1966), *Juvenile Delinquency* (Philadelphia: Lippincott, 1975), *Juvenile Delinquency: Little Brother Grows Up* (Beverly Hills, CA: Sage, 1978). He had also written widely on historical criminology.

MARY GIBSON is an Assistant Professor of History at Grinnell College, Grinnell, Iowa. She did her doctoral work in modern European history at Indiana University and received her Ph.D. in 1979. Her dissertation analyzed the history of urban prostitution in Italy from its period of unification up to World War I. She has published an article on feminism and prostitution in nineteenth century Italy and has given several papers on women and crime. She received a grant from the National Endowment for the Humanities to continue her research at Brown University during the year 1979-1980.

TED ROBERT GURR is Payson S. Wild Professor of political science at Northwestern University and began a three-year term as chairperson of the department in 1977. His research has focused on political conflict, authority, and institutional change. His 1970 book, *Why Men Rebel* (Princeton University Press), received the American Political Science Association's Woodrow Wilson Prize as the year's best book in political science. He is author or editor of a dozen other books and monographs, among them *Politimetrics* (Prentice-Hall, 1972); *Patterns of Authority,* coauthored with Harry Eckstein (Wiley-Interscience, 1975); *Rogues, Rebels, and Reformers* (Sage Publications, 1976); and *The Politics of Crime Conflict,* coauthored with Peter N. Grabosky and Richard C. Hula (Sage Publications, 1977). With Hugh Davis Graham he coauthored the Task Force report, *Violence in America: Historical and Comparative Perspectives* (1969; revised edition 1979).

NICOLAS FISCHER HAHN teaches criminology at the College of Criminal Justice, Northeastern University. As Director of Northeastern's Center for the Study of Women's Prisons, she is engaged in a national study of the origins and development of the women's prison system (funded by the National Institute of Law Enforcement and Criminal Justice). She is the editor of *Sociobiology of Deviance: Eugenics in the Late Nineteenth and Early Twentieth Centuries,* a 20-volume series of reprints, (Kraus-Thomson, 1980) and has had articles in *Atlantic Monthly, Criminal Law Bulletin, Criminology* (forthcoming), and the *New York Times,* among other places.

MARK H. HALLER is Professor of History at Temple University. His specialty is American urban history and his field of research is the history of American urban crime and criminal justice. He is the author of numerous articles of the history of the police, gambling, bootlegging, loansharking, and other aspects of urban vice and crime. He has been a consultant to the National Commission on the Causes and Prevention of Violence and the Commission on Review of National Policy toward Gambling.

JAMES A. INCIARDI is Professor and Director, Division of Criminal Justice, University of Delaware. He has extensive teaching, research, field, and clinical experiences in the areas of substance abuse and criminal justice. Dr. Inciardi was the director of the National Center for the Study of Acute Drug Reactions at the University of Miami School of Medicine, Vice President of Resource Planning Corporation, and Associate Director of Research at the New York State Narcotic Addiction Control Commission. He is currently editor of *Criminology: An Interdisciplinary Journal* and has published more than 70 books and articles in the areas of substance abuse, medicine, criminology, and criminal justice.

CARL B. KLOCKARS is Associate Professor of Criminal Justice at the University of Delaware. He is the author of *The Professional Fence,* a life history of a large-scale dealer in stolen property; editor of *Deviance and Decency,* a collection of essays on the ethics of research with deviant subjects; and is currently working on an ethnographic study of detective-level policing for the Twentieth Century Fund. His other publications include scholarly works on probation and parole, research ethics, and criminological theory. Dr. Klockars has served as a consultant to Law Enforcement Assistance Administration projects on trade in stolen property, white collar crime, and the management of criminal investigations.

ROGER LANE is Professor of History at Haverford College, Haverford, Pennsylvania. He is the author of a number of studies of urban police, crime, and violence, including *Policing the City: Boston 1822-1885; Riot, Rout, and Tumult: Readings in American Political and Social Violence;* and most recently *Violent Death in the City: Suicide, Accident, and Murder in Nineteenth Century Philadelphia,* a book which traces the impact of the Industrial Revolution on violent behavior. His articles have appeared in the *Annals of the American Academy of Political and Social Science, Crime and Justice: An Annual Review of Research, The Journal of Social History,* and the *New England Quarterly.*

DAVID MIERS is Senior Lecturer in law at University College, Cardiff, Wales. He is coauthor (with W. L. Twining) of *How To Do Things with Rules* (Weidenfeld & Nicolson, 1976) and author of *Responses to Victimization* (Professional Books, 1978). He has written extensively on the topics of criminal injuries compensation and criminal law and legislation, both of which are subjects he teaches, and more recently on gambling legislation.

ERIC MONKKONEN teaches urban history in the History Department at the University of California at Los Angeles and is the coordinator of the

Criminal Justice Network of the Social Science History Association. He is the author of *The Dangerous Class* (Harvard University Press). His second book, scheduled for publication in 1980 by Cambridge University Press, is titled, *Hands Up: Police in Urban America, 1860-1920.* This book analyzes the growth and behavior of urban police in the 20 largest American cities.

JAMES F. RICHARDSON is Professor of History and Urban Studies at the University of Akron. His publications include *The New York Police: Colonial Times to 1901* and *Urban Police in the United States.* He is currently working on a history of politics and public policy in Cleveland, Ohio, from 1900 to 1930, and he plans a book on the recent history of opera in the United States.

DAVID J. ROTHMAN is Professor of History at Columbia University and Senior Research Associate at the Center for Policy Research. His scholarly interests have focused on American social history. He is the author of *Politics and Power* (1966), *The Discovery of the Asylum* (1972), and *Conscience and Convenience.* He is also the organizer and co-author of *Doing Good* (1978). He currently serves on the Board of Directors of the New York Civil Liberties Union and of the Mental Health Law Project. Presently, he is also Codirector of the Project on Community Alternatives for the mentally disabled, a project investigating the process of deinstitutionalization.

MARGARET A. ZAHN is an Associate Professor of Sociology at Temple University, specializing in the fields of criminology and deviant behavior. She is writing a book on homicide in the United States and is also doing a study of homicide in Europe. In addition to doing research and teaching on violence, Dr. Zahn is studying the Italian women's movement. She has served as a consultant to a number of projects in the area of prisons and, as a teacher, has been responsible for developing a wide array of courses in the United States and abroad.